Conversations with
Karl Ove Knausgaard

Literary Conversations Series
Monika Gehlawat
General Editor

Conversations with
Karl Ove Knausgaard

Edited by Bob Blaisdell

University Press of Mississippi / Jackson

The University Press of Mississippi is the scholarly publishing agency of the Mississippi Institutions of Higher Learning: Alcorn State University, Delta State University, Jackson State University, Mississippi State University, Mississippi University for Women, Mississippi Valley State University, University of Mississippi, and University of Southern Mississippi.

www.upress.state.ms.us

The University Press of Mississippi is a member of the Association of University Presses.

Copyright © 2023 by University Press of Mississippi
All rights reserved

∞

Library of Congress Cataloging-in-Publication Data

Names: Blaisdell, Robert, editor.
Title: Conversations with Karl Ove Knausgaard / Bob Blaisdell.
Other titles: Literary conversations series.
Description: Jackson : University Press of Mississippi, 2023. | Series: Literary conversations series | Includes bibliographical references and index.
Identifiers: LCCN 2023025645 (print) | LCCN 2023025646 (ebook) |
  ISBN 9781496847690 (hardback) | ISBN 9781496847706 (trade paperback) |
  ISBN 9781496847713 (epub) | ISBN 9781496847720 (epub) |
  ISBN 9781496847737 (pdf) | ISBN 9781496847744 (pdf)
Subjects: LCSH: Knausgård, Karl Ove, 1968—Interviews. | Novelists, Norwegian—Interviews.
Classification: LCC PT8951.21.N38 Z46 2023 (print) | LCC PT8951.21.N38 (ebook) |
  DDC 839.823/74—dc23/eng/20230719
LC record available at https://lccn.loc.gov/2023025645
LC ebook record available at https://lccn.loc.gov/2023025646

British Library Cataloging-in-Publication Data available

Karl Ove Knausgaard: Books and Writings in English

Each book's publication date reflects its year of publication in English. The original Norwegian publication date of each book is earlier.[1] The essays in periodicals are, for the most part, originally published in English, though written in Norwegian. Book *excerpts* in periodicals are not listed.

A Time to Every Purpose under Heaven (entitled *A Time for Everything* in the 2009 American edition) (Novel) (2004)
"Karl O Knausgaard's Top Ten Angel Books" (Essay) *The Guardian* (December 11, 2008)
My Struggle: Book One (British title, *A Death in the Family*) (Novel) (2012)
"First the Nightmare, Then the News" (Essay) *New York Times* (April 22, 2012)
My Struggle: Book Two (British title, *A Man in Love*) (Novel) (2013)
"The Magical Realism of Norwegian Nights" (Essay) *New York Times* (February 28, 2013)
"Knausgaard on Angel Di Maria: Looks Like Kafka, Plays Like a Dream" (Essay) *New Republic* (June 20, 2014)
My Struggle: Book Three (British title, *Boyhood Island*) (Novel) (2014)
"I Am Someone, Look at Me" (Essay) *New York Times* (June 10, 2014)
"The View from My Window Is a Constant Reminder" (Essay) *The Millions* (11 November 2014)
My Struggle: Book Four (British title, *Dancing in the Dark*) (Novel) (2015)
"My Saga, Part 1" (Travel essay) *New York Times* (February 25, 2015)
"My Saga, Part 2" (Travel essay) *New York Times* (March 11, 2015)
Necks By Thomas Wagstrom (Introductory essay by Knausgård to a book of photographs) (2015)
"Michel Houellebecq's *Submission*" (Book review) *New York Times* (November 2, 2015)
"Vanishing Point" (Essay) *New Yorker* (November 17, 2015)
"The Terrible Beauty of Brain Surgery" (Essay) *New York Times* (December 30, 2015)
My Struggle: Book Five (British title, *Some Rain Must Fall*) (Novel) (2016)
"On the Value of Literature" (Essay) *Esopus* 23 (Spring 2016)
"The Shame of Writing about Myself" (Essay) *The Guardian* (February 26, 2016)
"On Reading *Portrait of the Artist* as a Young Man" (Essay) *New York Times* (May 25, 2016)
Home and Away: Writing the Beautiful Game by Karl Ove Knausgaard and Fredrik Ekelund (Letters between the authors about the 2014 World Cup) (2017)

Towards the Forest: Knausgård on Munch (Art book essay) (2017)
Autumn (Essays) (2017)
"Gum" (Essay) *New York Times* (August 10, 2017)
Winter (Essays) (2017)
"The Hidden Drama of Speedskating" (Essay) *New York Times* (January 30, 2018)
"A Literary Road Trip into the Heart of Russia" (Travel essay) *New York Times* (February 14, 2018)
Anselm Kiefer: Transition from Cool to Warm (Art book introductory essay) (2018)
My Struggle: Book Six (British title, *The End*) (Novel) (2018)
Spring (Novel) (2018)
Summer (Essays, diary, fiction) (2018)
Inadvertent (Why I Write) (Essay-lecture) (2018)
So Much Longing in So Little Space: The Art of Edvard Munch (Biography) (2019)
"To Be a Bird" (Essay) *New Yorker* (May 2, 2019)
"On the Writing of Jon Fosse" (Essay) *Literary Hub* (September 30, 2019)
"The Slowness of Literature and the Shadow of Knowledge" (Essay) *New Yorker* (November 6, 2019)
"Into the Black Forest with the Greatest Living Artist" (Essay on Anselm Kiefer) *New York Times* (February 12, 2020)
In the Land of the Cyclops: Essays (Art, culture, and literary introductions and essay commentary) (2021)
The Morning Star (Novel) (2021)
Mamma Andersson: The Lost Paradise by Mamma Andersson (Art book essay by Knausgaard) (2021)
"Why the Novel Matters: Against the 'Imperialism of the Absolute'—A Personal Manifesto on the Art of Fiction" *New Statesman* (October 26, 2022)

Note

1. See also Henrik Keyser Pedersen's *Karl Ove Knausgård bibliografi*: http://www.bibliografi.no.

Contents

Introduction   xi

Chronology   xxi

Book Case TV #207: Memories Can't Wait   3
   Frederic Colier / 2012

Karl Ove Knausgård at Passa Porta Festival 2013, Brussels   10
   Anna Luyten / 2013

The Light behind the Bookshelves   25
   Daniel Fraser / 2013

"Completely without Dignity": An Interview with
Karl Ove Knausgaard   32
   Jesse Barron / 2013

Karl Ove Knausgaard in Conversation with Stephen Grosz   44
   Stephen Grosz / 2014

In Search of Karl Ove Knausgaard   55
   Jared Levy / 2015

"Opening a World": An Interview with Karl Ove Knausgaard   60
   Steve Paulson / 2015

Karl Ove Knausgaard on Lars von Trier's *The Idiots*   67
   Dennis Lim / 2015

Why Karl Ove Knausgaard Can't Stop Writing   78
    Liesl Schillinger / 2015

"Babel": Karl Ove Knausgård   88
    Maria Scrivani / 2016

In Which Karl Ove Knausgaard Hangs Out in His Car, Talking on Life, Children, and Not Really Caring What America Thinks   91
    Paul Holdengraber / 2016

"Literature Should Be Ruthless"   100
    Kasper Bech Dyg / 2016

"My Munch"   107
    Alf Marius Opsahl / 2017

"The Innocence of Things": A Conversation with Karl Ove Knausgaard   117
    Srikanth Reddy / 2017

"You're Not a Real Writer until You Have Enemies": *The Millions* Interviews Karl Ove Knausgaard   126
    Alexander Bisley / 2018

Karl Ove Knausgaard Looks Back on *My Struggle*   129
    Joshua Rothman / 2018

"Rejoicing to Heaven, Grieving to Death": An Interview with Karl Ove Knausgård   142
    Anders Beyer / 2019

Conversations with Tyler: Karl Ove Knausgård on Literary Freedom   154
    Tyler Cowen / 2019

An Interview with Karl Ove Knausgård: The Sixth Author for Future Library   176
    Katie Paterson / 2020

"Writing Isn't a Sacred Activity, It Is an Ordinary Activity":
A Conversation with Karl Ove Knausgaard   181
   Bob Blaisdell / 2020

Karl Ove Knausgaard on Exploring a "World Out of Joint"
in His New Book   196
   Leila Fadel / 2021

On Interviews and Interviewing: A Conversation
with Karl Ove Knausgaard   200
   Bob Blaisdell / 2022

Index   209

Introduction

ALF MARIUS OPSAHL: But when you sit and talk about Karl Ove Knausgård in these interviews everywhere, is it like talking about a character, almost?
KARL OVE KNAUSGAARD: No. It's like *being* a character. It's like going into a character.[1]

The fame of and regard for Karl Ove Knausgaard surprises, I think, even those of us who admire him as one of the greatest authors of the twenty-first century.

His subject is *what*? *His* struggle? *What* struggle? The avalanche of his fame started rolling in 2012 when the English translation of the first of six volumes of *My Struggle* was published. *My Struggle* (titled *Min Kamp* in its original Norwegian, 2009–2011) has brought him notice and notoriety everywhere from his native Norway to Argentina. The series has been translated into at least twenty-five languages.[2] As Jesse Barron writes: "Before, there was no *My Struggle*; now there is, and things are different. [. . .] A man has written a book in which a man stays at home with his kids, and his home life isn't trivialized or diminished but studied and appreciated, resisted and embraced. An almost Christian feeling of spiritual urgency makes even the slowest pages about squeezing lemon on a lobster into a hymn about trying to be good."[3] In these novels, totaling thirty-six hundred pages and written in less than three years, he shows us that the human personality is so vast it can never be fully surveyed. *My Struggle* is about oneself as a literary subject, discovering the peculiar depths of a human personality. But there is no getting to the bottom of that literary character Karl Ove or, the author has led us to believe, to any of us. It's not that his character is endlessly fascinating to Knausgaard but that the author in fictionalizing his own daily life makes it seem endlessly suspenseful and fascinating.

The series was, however, so popular that its buzz was resented or despised. "I think people almost vomit when they hear my name because I'm so often in the news," he told Liesl Schillinger in 2015. "It's true. Oh, God. I try to keep a low profile in Norway, but it's hard. It's terrible."[4] (I confess

I was overwhelmed with irritation at his alternately rugged and vulnerable photographic images' ubiquity and that it took me several years before my curiosity, piqued by one tiny essay of his, got me to seek out his books, which instantly became my new literary passion.)

Knausgaard's varied and mostly excellent other works, including what are for me just as marvelous and surprising, his post–*My Struggle* Seasons quartet of short essays and literary experiments, have achieved some international regard but significantly less attention. As of October 2022, he is in the midst of the fourth volume of an annual, pointedly eventful, purposefully unautobiographical fictional series, which begins with *The Morning Star* (2021) and will continue (always published first in Norwegian) for at least four volumes. His first two novels, *Out of the World* (1998, not yet published in English) and *A Time for Everything*, were award winners in Norway, published when Knausgaard, born December 6, 1968, was twenty-nine and thirty-five. The last novel Knausgaard will ever publish, *Blindenboken* (*The Blind Book*), was written in 2019 for the artist Katie Paterson's Future Library project; Knausgaard's novel and those by several other novelists will be printed on paper made from trees that were specially planted for this project in a forest outside of Oslo. They will be published, Gaia willing, in 2114.[5]

Some of us love reading interviews with authors whether or not we know or enjoy their work, and some of us have had the experience of sympathizing with (though bored by) the cagey or careful or reluctant interview responses of our literary heroes. But it is remarkable that the person who wrote *My Struggle* is the same as the author and character of those autobiographical novels. That is, as an interviewee trusting his spontaneous responses, he continually discovers fascinating and fresh musings about everyday life and art. Though life is routine, he rarely repeats himself. The interviews extend our sense of the vastness of Knausgaard's personality and experiences. In these interviews he discusses, besides writing and his own work, painting and painters, movies, directors, and screenwriting, translation, Borges, Flaubert, and the Bible, and popular music.

Thousands of book lovers in Europe and North America have had the pleasure of seeing in-person a nervous Knausgaard shake a leg or sway as he reads from his work or in videos slowly weigh his interviewer's words and then remark simply "Yeah" or "No." But, as if duty-bound to his interviewer and audience, he spurs himself into his writing mode, relaxing into natural and usually brilliant thought, freshly reflecting in a way that his readers will immediately recognize as purely Knausgaardian. The Norwegian journalist Alf Marius Opsahl notes in his feature article: "Friendly, but also uncomfortable. From time to time he spoke in long tirades, as if his thoughts were flying in all directions. But he then would also suddenly become introverted and silent, as if what he wanted most of all was just to disappear back to where he'd come from: the balcony, chain smoking in solitude."[6] There in these conversations on stage or sitting opposite an interviewer is the same artist who wrote *those* books. Whether over Zoom, over the phone, or smoking in his writing cabin with a patient and attentive journalist, he is unusually consistent in tone and manner and persistently free in the expression of his thoughts: "A lot of people ask if [writing] is therapy for me, but it is not, not whatsoever, but it still is kind of a healing thing to do. You are creating something which is not yourself, it's something outside of yourself, which is great, and it leads you to places where you haven't been or even thought you should go to, and you don't know why. What is this kind of dynamic between you and literature basically? I mean, I'm writing it, but it doesn't feel like it because it feels like I'm throwing myself out to something objective, to language or to literature, and something else is coming back, which directs me another place and another place and another place. It's a way of getting free from yourself in a way. It's the only place I know of where I am free of myself."[7]

I have a theory that the hyperfocused zone he enters when writing and being interviewed is so strong that it almost doesn't matter who is sitting beside him or across from him. He told me the interviewer *does* matter ("That's the thing with events and interviews [. . .] it is never just about questions and answers, but also about the dynamic between the two persons"[8]), but it is not apparent in the many dozens of interviews that I have watched or read or the two I've participated in that the dynamic much matters. We interviewers are not his chums; no matter how careful, off-base, knowledgeable, routine, or confused our questions are, he's strictly professional: cool but polite. Speaking is work for him, like writing, serious and focused, and he is ever striving only not to lie. He is deferential but not deflected: "I want to write how I really think things are, instead of how I think you should think I think things are. For me, saying how I really think things are turns everything into banality and stupid things, almost all the time, and that's the risk of the project for me. But then it's a realistic depiction of a man, forty, from Norway."[9]

If you, this book's reader, are a writer, his statements on writing are as practical as they are inspiring: "I start every day thinking I have nothing to say. I don't know anything. And I don't think much. But then if I just start to say, no, I'll write a page about one thing, something just turns up. And *that* is writing for me. That's why I'm writing. Because it opens up the world. It isn't my thoughts, because if I just look at something and should try to say something about it, I wouldn't be able to say anything at all. But if I write about it, it's different."[10]

Despite his professed shyness and claims of indifference in the published interviews with him and feature articles about him, he has been, in his fame, a most accommodating literary star, accessible to a myriad of us, whether we are professionals or fans (many are both). I had reviewed three of his Seasons quartet, *Winter*, *Spring*, and *Summer*, and had read almost every page of his that had been translated into English (I admit that I lost steam in *A Time for Everything*, his second novel, and though there *is* a time for everything, I never mustered the time or interest to finish that one). It occurred to me when I received an advance copy of a collection of his writings on art, artists, and writers, *In the Land of the Cyclops*, that in *My Struggle* he recounts that when he was a young budding writer, he interviewed Norwegian authors (as well as European rock musicians) and that, in the midst of the fame and blowback of *My Struggle*, he was continually participating in interviews about the ongoing series. I realized another way of writing about Knausgaard would be to talk to him. I imagined we would have a jolly good time chatting. I should have reflected on Liesl Schillinger's words: "I had been unnerved by the prospect of interviewing a man whose every secret had already been printed, published, discussed and dissected. I confessed these fears to him. 'I have secrets, some things I haven't told anyone,' he reassured me."[11] As these interviews show, there are thoughts and reflections (and probably secrets) that he has never otherwise written or spoken about elsewhere.

His unusual candor in the midst of an interview surprised even the veteran journalist Anna Luyten. On the stage with her in Brussels, Belgium, Knausgaard remarks: "It's really important to be free and independent in the writing, and that has to do with some sort of—for me at least—some sort of lack of empathy that makes it possible for me to write."

She asks: "It makes it also possible to be honest?"

"Yes, that's right. It's impossible for me to be honest in personal private space with friends."

"Are you honest *now*?"

"Yes, but this is like—*almost* like writing in a way, because I don't know you, I don't know you. I can talk relatively openly now, but if we meet afterwards I will not. If you maybe say something political, I would say, 'I agree, I think you're right.'"

In the interviews, Knausgaard usually creates a space for himself, as he does when writing, to overwhelm his social guardedness; this then manifests as the familiar vulnerability and guilelessness of so much of *My Struggle*.

Archipelago Books, the wonderful Brooklyn-based publisher of many of Knausgaard's books, helped to arrange my first interview with him, and in the midst of the pandemic and a few days after America had elected Joe Biden and deposed the orange monster, Knausgaard and I talked on Zoom; he in lockdown with his family in London and I at home in New York. The interview was difficult and satisfying. We did not become chatty or friendly; I was excited and amazed to be talking to him and afterward to be exchanging drafts of the hour-long interview by email. Though he had declared elsewhere that he didn't read his own interviews, he was willing and perhaps happy to clarify a few spots where I either couldn't understand or hear what he had said. He added several hundred words to the transcript, and I was pleased to think that he had written more in English in the revision than he had written in English for publication before.

Hearing him speak in English, it was clear that he could compose a book in that language. In the volume's "exit interview," to which he considerately consented, he denies, however, that he could do so. I respect his opinion but, as a language teacher, don't agree on this point. Besides which, in all but three of these conversations, he has spoken (he may as well have dictated) all of his fully engaging and lucid words in English. Read, for example, his delivery of this reflection: "I taught creative writing and that kind of minimalism was the *best* thing you could do. I mean, that was the best prose. The Hemingway technique: Show it, don't tell it. . . . And I never do that. [*Audience laughs*] I tried to do that for ten years, and I realized, if you do the opposite, if you just put things in and see what happens . . . that's good. Even if it's bad, what you put in it, it became more complicated and things start to happen that you don't control. And that control thing is very important. It's very important *not* to have control when you are writing."

Despite the input and egos of his interviewers, Knausgaard is never suppressed or bent out of shape but always his ever-examining self. As Alexander Bisley notes: "Scandinavia's leading literary figure of the last decade has things to say, seasoned with gesture and glance. He can be minimalist with his responses, though: Some questions and observations elicit 'Yeah' or 'Yeah. That's true,' accompanied by a nod, a raised eyebrow, or—most tellingly—an affirming smile or laugh. Knausgaard is a fine exemplar of Scandinavia's dry, deadpan humor." Knausgaard seems pleased when, for example, before an audience with psychoanalyst Stephen Grosz in a London bookstore, he provokes repeated laughter—not at jokes, exactly, but at the absurdity of truth! For example: "I realized it's very, very easy to write a novel. You could write a novel in eight weeks. It's not a problem. It's easy. [*Loud laughter from audience and from Grosz*] It is: *just to do it*. Yes. But to get there, where it's easy, that's five or six or seven years with struggle with the text, you know?"[12]

An audience member in Chicago poses a situation and a question:

> **QUESTION:** I picture the painting *The Fall of Icarus* when I read your work sometimes. Because it's all regular life happening, and then this little tragedy in the corner. Do you think about innocence when you write it?
>
> **KNAUSGAARD:** Yeah, that's a very good question. No, I don't. [*Laughter*] Because I see it almost as a personal weakness, the naïveté, that I don't understand things that are going on around me.[13]

Knausgaard's surprising assertion of naivete means, I believe, that he only realizes life when he is working—that life continuously happened and happens—but that he doesn't comprehend it in its own time. Perhaps the evidence is in *My Struggle*, where everyday life seems to be happening for the author and for us, his readers, only as he writes it.

Having reread *My Struggle* and the Seasons quartet before writing this introduction, I still wanted to read a biography of Knausgaard. There is no biography of Knausgaard. In this volume, however, the best and most personal introduction to him is in Liesl Schillinger's feature article "Why Karl Ove Knausgaard Can't Stop Writing" (see pages 78–87). At that time in 2015, he was still living with his second wife and their four children in Sweden, which is where he wrote his most renowned books. He has written so much about himself and in hundreds of interviews has said so much about himself, that it's fair to wonder, as we might about our long-time partners, what *don't* we know about them? What *don't* Knausgaard's readers know? What future biography will ever be able to contain him after the seemingly unlimited *My Struggle*?

Reading Tolstoy's *Anna Karenina* when I was young made me believe that life is a literary experience, and then in my late middle age, Knausgaard has shown me that I still believe it. No matter where you are, sitting on a toilet, staring into a mirror, crying with shame, that is life, and, if at an artistic distance you can write about it, that just might be literature. Knausgaard observes that "the thing about literature is that it's collective after all, it's for everyone, relational. That's what makes literature so special, for the moment you begin to write literature, it's no longer about yourself or about your own problems, it's about something else."[14]

Hearing Knausgaard speak Norwegian is like hearing a close friend switch into his, her, or their native tongue. *Oh! That's* his real fifth-gear voice. It has an energy and play that doesn't seem obvious in English. (For a *listen*, see "Literature Should Be Ruthless" on Denmark's Louisiana Channel or on YouTube.)

But how to *pronounce* Karl Ove Knausgaard? Like so, according to Jay Deshpande: *Karl Oov-uh K'NOUSE-gourd*.[15] But when *I* listen to Knausgaard say his name, it sounds to me more like this: *Kahl Oo-va Knaus-god*. In any case, hit the *K* in Knausgaard! In Middle English, Chaucer's English, we used to pronounce the *k* in *kn* words, don't you *k*-now? The Norwegians never lost that kick in the k. His last name in Norwegian *looks* like this: Knausgård. All of his books in English transliterate that *å* into *aa*. If the interviews in this volume were published with his name as *Knausgård*, that is how we present it. Otherwise, we default to *Knausgaard*.

Almost all of the interviews included here were conducted in English, even when the interviewers were not native-English speakers. For better or worse, English is twenty-first-century literature's lingua franca. In the interviews transcribed from radio or video, I have tried to resist correcting Knausgaard's or his nonnative speaking English interviewers' very occasional grammatical errors and misapplication of prepositions. I have silently corrected some subject-verb agreement issues or have realigned or evened out plural-plural or singular-singular correspondences. (For nonnative speakers of English, the demonstrative pronouns *this, that, those, these* can be tricky.) I have silently deleted from the video and recorded interview transcriptions many but not all of the hesitating instances of "you know." Pauses are presented as unadorned ellipses. Deletions and indecipherable phrases are rendered as ellipses in brackets [. . .]. I have silently corrected minor errors in the transcriptions of other interviewers' work and have, except in quotations from his books, corrected British spellings (e.g., colour, theatre) to American spellings.

There is a twenty-six-thousand-word bibliography of works by and about Knausgaard in various languages compiled by Henrik Keyser Pedersen at the University Library in Oslo.[16] It is, like all projects trying to map the world, incomplete. I am grateful, nonetheless, to Mr. Pedersen for sharing it and for considering my queries. For more details of Knausgaard's life and writings, see the chronology in this book.

Working on this collection of conversations, I continually thought I was reaching the end of the published and posted interviews in English or the articles translated into English about him, but I never did. Every time I looked, there were more—and there is almost not a single dud in all the interviews. There could certainly be another book of this length of conversations in English or in translations to English as compelling and revealing as this one. Some excellent interviews I have read I have not included simply due to limitations in the size of the books in this series or because permissions by the rights holders were not forthcoming or prohibitively expensive. To my regret, my lack of Norwegian or Swedish (Knausgaard lived in Sweden for fifteen years) has prevented my access to hundreds of Scandinavian interviews and articles, particularly those in the 1990s and in the early 2000s.

I am extremely grateful to all of the rights holders who have granted me permission to include their interviews and to the permissions administrators at the *New Yorker*, the *Wall Street Journal*, and National Public Radio. I thank Charles Buchan, of the Wylie Agency, for helping to schedule the final interview with Knausgaard and for being the go-between on my follow-up questions to the author. Knausgaard has not read but has seen the list of interviews in this volume. Jill Schoolman, as the publisher of Archipelago Books, brought Knausgaard to America's attention and also helped set up interviews with him for me, for which I am grateful. Editor Mary Heath at University Press of Mississippi has been wonderful and diligent at all stages of this project. My son Max Blaisdell, a journalist, helped me with transcription software and with his comments and corrections on various interviews. Lisa Teasley, the fiction editor at *Los Angeles Review of Books*, helped guide my first interview with Knausgaard to publication; I am also grateful to the former editor-in-chief of *LARB*, the poet Boris Dralyuk, for giving that initial proposal his enthusiastic encouragement. I thank the contributors Frederic Colier and Liesl Schillinger for their sharing further impressions of the time they spent in person with Knausgaard. And finally, I thank Karl Ove himself for his participation in all of these interviews, an activity that, as he says, gives him *nothing*: "I don't get anything out of it really [*laughs*]. Since it's only talk, and since it's centered on my situation, it just disappears."[17] But in conversation after conversation, he has certainly enlightened and delighted us, his readers.

BB

Notes

1. See "My Munch," by Alf Marius Opsahl, p. 113.
2. I derived this figure from Henrik Keyser Pedersen's *Karl Ove Knausgård bibliografi* at www.bibliografi.no.
3. See "'Completely without Dignity': An Interview with Karl Ove Knausgaard," by Jesse Barron, p. 32.
4. See "Why Karl Ove Knausgaard Can't Stop Writing," by Liesl Schillinger, p. 81.
5. See "An Interview with Karl Ove Knausgård: The Sixth Author for Future Library," by Katie Paterson, below, pp. 176–80.
6. See "My Munch," by Alf Marius Opsahl, p. 108.
7. From an unpublished interview in English by the Italian journalist Riccardo Stagliano for an article in Italian, "Scrivere. Tutto il resto e noia" in *Il Venerdì di Repubblica*, November 14, 2014. I appreciate Mr. Stagliano's permission allowing me to quote from it.
8. From "'Writing Isn't a Sacred Activity, It Is an Ordinary Activity': A Conversation with Karl Ove Knausgaard," p. 181.
9. See "'Completely without Dignity': An Interview with Karl Ove Knausgaard," by Jesse Barron, p. 39.
10. From "The Innocence of Things: A Conversation with Karl Ove Knausgaard," by Srikanth Reddy, p. 120.
11. See "Why Karl Ove Knausgaard Can't Stop Writing," by Liesl Schillinger, p. 82.
12. From "Karl Ove Knausgaard and Stephen Grosz in Conversation," by Stephen Grosz, p. 48.
13. From "'The Innocence of Things': A Conversation with Karl Ove Knausgaard," by Srikanth Reddy, p. 125.
14. From "Rejoicing to Heaven, Grieving to Death," by Anders Beyer, p. 143.
15. Or read and listen here, "How Do You Pronounce Karl Ove Knausgaard?": https://slate.com/culture/2015/03/karl-ove-knausgaard-how-do-you-say-his-name.html.
16. See Henrik Keyser Pedersen's *Karl Ove Knausgård bibliografi*: http://www.bibliografi.no.
17. See "On Interviews and Interviewing: A Conversation with Karl Ove Knausgaard," p. 202.

Chronology

1968	Born December 6, the second son of Sissel Norunn Hatløy and Kai-Aage Knausgaard, in Oslo, Norway.
1969–1982	Grows up in Tromøya, an island in southern Norway. Starts school at age six in 1975.
1982–1987	Adolescence in Tveit, a suburb of Kristiansand.
1985–1993	Publishes music and album reviews in local newspapers.
1987–1988	In his gap year after high school, works as a schoolteacher in northern Norway.
1988–1989	Studies at Bergen's prestigious Writer's Academy; at nineteen, writes his first novel (unpublished).
1988–2002	Lives in Bergen, Norway.
1989–1990	Studies art and literature at the University of Bergen.
1989–1992[?]	Works as part of his Norwegian national service at a campus radio station; works on an oil platform.
1992	Publishes his first fiction, "Déjà vu," in *Vinduet*.
1993–1996	Publishes various journalism, including interviews with writers and musicians, and criticism in national periodicals and literary journals.
1995	Marries Tonje Aursland.
1997	Returns to Kristiansand to write *Out of This World*, a novel.
1998	In July, sees a dead body for the first time, his father's. Publishes *Out of This World* (unpublished as of 2023 in English), which wins the Norwegian Critics Prize for Literature.
1999	Meets Linda Boström.
1999–2002	Coedits the Norwegian literary magazine *Vagrant*.
2002	Leaves Bergen and Tonje Aursland in the spring. Moves to Stockholm, Sweden.
2004	First child, a daughter, born to him and Linda Boström in January. Publishes his second novel (titled *A Time for Everything* when published in America), which is nominated for various Norwegian and European literary awards.

2005	Second child, a daughter, born to him and Linda Boström.
2006	The family moves to Malmo, Sweden.
2007	Marries Linda Boström. Third child, a son, born to him and Linda Boström Knausgaard.
2008	Starts writing *My Struggle* on February 27.
2009	The first three volumes of *My Struggle* are published in Norway.
2010	The next two volumes of *My Struggle* are published in Norway. Starts Pelikanen, a publishing company, with his brother Yngve Knausgaard and Asbjorn Jensen.
2011	Serves as a consultant on a new Norwegian translation of the Bible. Finishes *My Struggle: Book Six* on September 2. Publishes the final volume of *My Struggle* in Norway. The family moves to Glemmingebro, a village in southern Sweden on the outskirts of Ystad.
2013	Gives the closing speech for the 150th anniversary celebration of Edvard Munch's birth.
2014	Fourth child, a daughter, born to him and Linda Boström Knausgaard.
2015	Wins the annual World Literature Prize awarded by the German newspaper *Die Welt*.
2015–2016	Publishes his Seasons quartet (*Autumn, Winter, Spring, Summer*) in Norwegian.
2016	Separates from Linda Boström Knausgaard in November.
2017	Divorces Linda Boström Knausgaard. Wins the Jerusalem Prize for his work encouraging the "freedom of the individual in society." Publishes his biography of Edvard Munch in Norwegian; curates Munch exhibition in Oslo. Publishes *Home and Away: Writing the Beautiful Game*.
2018	Publishes a collection of art and literary essays, *In the Land of the Cyclops*, in Norwegian. Has a son with his third wife, Michal Shavit; they live in London with all seven of their children.
2018–2019	Writes a libretto-novella, "Waiting," for Calixto Bieito's stage version of Grieg's *Peer Gynt* suites for orchestra.
2019	Writes *Blindenboken* (*The Blind Book*) for Katie Paterson's Future Library.
2020	Publishes the first novel of at least four volumes of a new series, *Morgenstjernen* (*The Morning Star* is published in English in 2021).

2021   Publishes *Ulvene fra evighetens skog* (not published as of 2022 in English, *The Wolves from the Eternal Forest*) as the second of *The Morning Star* series; publishes a book about Anselm Kiefer in Norwegian (*Skogen og Elva: Om Anselm Kiefer og kunsten hans*).
2022   Publishes *Det tredje riket* (*The Third Kingdom*) as the third of *The Morning Star* series.
2114   The Future Library will publish his novel *Blindenboken* (*The Blind Book*).

Sources

Cross, Ted. "A Complete Visual Map of Karl Ove Knausgaard's 'My Struggle.'" https://themillions.com/2018/11/a-complete-visual-map-of-karl-ove-knausgaards-my-struggle.html.

Pedersen, Henrik Keyser. *Karl Ove Knausgård-bibliografi*. www.bibliografi.no.

Vøllo, Ida Hummel. "The Functions of Autoreception: Karl Ove Knausgård as Author-Critic and Rewriter." Submitted for the degree Doctor of Philosophy in Comparative Literature at the University of Edinburgh, 2019. https://era.ed.ac.uk/bitstream/handle/1842/36160/Vøllo2019.pdf?sequence=1&isAllowed=y.

Conversations with
Karl Ove Knausgaard

Book Case TV #207: Memories Can't Wait

Frederic Colier / 2012

Frederic Colier's "*Book Case TV* #207: Memories Can't Wait," Sept. 21, 2012. (This longer version of the interview, "Books du Jour Specials: Karl Ove Knausgaard," was posted on YouTube on April 15, 2015.) Reprinted by permission.

[Editor's note: For this volume, Frederic Colier recalls the circumstances around his television interview of Knausgaard in New York City.]

My meeting with Karl Ove Knausgaard was completely impromptu. We met during the Brooklyn Book Festival in September 2012. He was sitting behind a table, by himself, in the Borough Hall main lobby, waiting to sign his books, in which no one appeared interested. He looked disheveled, definitely coming across as someone from a Nordic brood, self-absorbed, but also as a patient observer. There is panoptic quality about him once he locks eyes on you. I knew nothing of him beyond what his American publisher, Jill Schoolman at Archipelago, had shared. She was just releasing the first volume of *My Struggle*, which had been released in Norway to high acclaim. In the States, no one knew of his writing, and this included me. This was, to my knowledge, his very first TV interview in America.

I had secured a TV series, *Book Case TV*, which then morphed into the high production *Books du Jour*. At first, the program was not a large operation, a three-person team working with little planning. The team would show up at festivals or conferences and interview authors on the fly. This is how the interview with Knausgaard took place. I invited him to our set, and he accepted without asking questions, who we were, where would we broadcast, what was our viewership, and so on. Unlike American authors who tend to take on a performative affect when on camera, Knausgaard never compromised. He looked tense, avoiding eye contact, his focus fixed into the distance. I could not quite reach or find him. He remained on his perch, never meeting me halfway. I had to climb up to reach him. He was very precise with his words, making sure he conveyed his thoughts as clearly as possible. There were a couple of awkward moments on my part; I was not sure how to steer the conversation. I had a hard time guessing what his book was about besides being a memoir, a long reflection on the stages of his life, and what made it so extraordinary. Perhaps he felt it . . . and was trying to help me. But despite the blazing intensity of his answers, he exuded a generosity buttressed by a vulnerability that he did not try to conceal. He offered himself as is, an authorial "full frontal."

Frederic Colier: So the panel you attended, what panel was that?

Karl Ove Knausgaard: It was a panel about writing about yourself. It was Sheila Heti and myself discussing the difference between autobiographies or memoirs and novels.[1]

Colier: The Norwegian school and the big existential school of philosophy from Kierkegaard and others, there seems to be a strong interest with the self—

Knausgaard: Yes, that's right.

Colier: And why such concern with oneself? Why is it so important about oneself that you have to write about it?

Knausgaard: Because it's really a question of identity for me, and it's so much going on in that area at the moment. You've got national identity, the pressure of national identity; you've got the pressure on male identity. These things have changed a lot during my generation. It's different to be a man in Norway and Sweden now than it was one generation ago. All those changes are really important for me to explore in a way to find out, and that was why I started this project—and I have written three thousand six hundred pages about myself. My life.

Colier: Are you that interesting?

Knausgaard: People keep asking me that: "Why are you so sure you're an interesting person?" But it's not about that. It's not about me telling stories about my life. It's just kind of an exploration into . . . I'm using myself as a kind of a raw material then—and it sounds really terrible [writing] that long about [myself]. But it's really not like that in the end. I mean it's the same thing being sixteen in France, being sixteen here, being sixteen there.

Colier: So we're talking about *My Struggle*. The first volume has been translated into English?

Knausgaard: Yeah, correct.

Colier: And it's written in Danish or in Swedish?

Knausgaard: It's written in Norwegian.

Colier: In Norwegian, okay. It's six volumes. When are they going to come out in the States?

Knausgaard: The next one is coming out in April, and then I think they will be coming out [every] six months.

Colier: So the first volume covers which period of your life?

Knausgaard: That's the starting point for me, it was the fact that I had become a father. I turned forty, and my father—when he was forty, he left the family and started to drink, died as an alcoholic, and it was kind of a total, total disgrace.

Colier: How old were you? He was forty; how old were you?

Knausgaard: When he left, I was sixteen. I wanted to write about his story and my relation to him, so this first book is about his death, and I think I could do that when I understood that he was a human being, not only a father or an icon or something static, but as a matter of fact felt the same way I did; because there's a mystery for me. Why should a man want to fail? Because I think he did it on purpose. I think it was kind of slow, slow suicide in a way.

Colier: So he was lacking a will to live? Or self-sabotaging?

Knausgaard: He was trying to get away. I think he had an inauthentic life raising two children. He was a politician; he was a teacher, you know, but he was also filled with rage. He was very hard on me, very tough on me. I was afraid of him, and I think he just was longing for freedom; that's why he started to drink and left everything behind, and then he was caught in alcoholism, and then at one point I think he just—

Colier: Gave up.

Knausgaard: Yeah, so he moved back to his mother's house, and there he was living, drinking with her for maybe a year, and me and my brother went down there the minute he died, and it was like a catastrophe zone. It was bottles everywhere. It was excrement, it was blood, it was terrible, so what we did, we cleaned up the house and cried. And this book, the second part of this [*My Struggle*, Book One] book is about cleaning the house and crying. That's all it is.

Colier: So you feel when you write about your personal story, like you say, memoir or recollection, whatever you call it, there's a cathartic effect to help you try to find answers, or if not, you get some clarity on the past.

Knausgaard: No, it's not catharsis. It's not about catharsis, it's about writing a good novel, you know?

Colier: Okay.

Knausgaard: But I think for me the catharsis is in the process, is in the fact sitting there writing. The moment I stop writing I am back in my old misery, but the act of writing is good.

Colier: But what would have been lost if you had not written the book?

Knausgaard: For me?

Colier: Yes, because it was a commitment on your part at some time: "I have to do this."

Knausgaard: I think my life was—I felt like my life was kind of meaningless, like in the Talking Heads song, "I have a beautiful house, a beautiful wife, how did I get there?" I feel kind of inauthentic too, I have to say. So writing is a way of giving meaning to life.

Colier: Towards your life, yes.

Knausgaard: Then I read a lot, and it's the same thing: Why do I read? There's a hunger for meaning. Why do I want to look at art? A hunger for meaning. And this book is basically about trivialities, everyday life, so where is the meaning in that?

Colier: It's a great question.

Knausgaard: I think the only way we can really find out is through writing or is through filmmaking or the arts.

Colier: Acceptance.

Knausgaard: Yeah, but that's the difficult part. This is a question of you can heighten it when you write about it. I mean if you see a picture, a painting from seventeenth-century Holland, it could be a still life—like a glass and maybe an apple or something, and when you look at it, it feels like almost divine. I mean, it's really something, that—but then, it's just a glass. Why do I feel so strongly towards that? Maybe it's because I can see it, how it is.

Colier: You feel that when you look at something outside, like a book, it's outside of yourself; you find comfort from something outside. When you do the everyday life thing, you are living it, and the hard part is to be okay.

Knausgaard: Accept it.

Colier: Acceptance, without looking for something external.

Knausgaard: That's the paradox of this writing. You turn away from society to do it, but I think something has gone—has been destroyed in me from when I was a kid. I think: *I need this.* I've always read a lot, and I've always written a lot, and I need it; this is just a way of living to me. My wife keeps saying to me, "You don't recognize anything, you don't understand anything, you don't feel anything, unless you write about it. Then you come back, and you understand everything." If you are quarreling or if something's going really bad, I just keep it at that distance. When I write about it, I can break down in tears.

Colier: Is it safer?

Knausgaard: No, I think it has to do with a social situation. You kind of—you maneuver around, but when you're writing you are open; that's the whole point with writing.

Colier: The writing for you, maybe it's like a safe world that turns external—

Knausgaard: No, no, not a safe world, because you have to take risks when you're writing, so if it's safe when you're writing, then it's that—it's nothing to do with safety, but it maybe has something to do with that, calming myself in a way, but then again . . . writing, what is it about? It's about selflessness, to get out of yourself, so that's the state of mind I'm always looking for.

Colier: Early on you mentioned what it's like to be a male these days in Sweden. So in Sweden and compared to twenty years ago, you feel like as a male, as an individual, the society, all this pressure on the inside sort of invisibilizes you—

Knausgaard: —as a man.

Colier: As a man. Who are you, being swallowed up in those big maelstroms of events? And then, "Where are you?"

Knausgaard: Yeah, in a way. It's like this: there's a lot of things you are supposed to do when you're a man and becoming a father in Scandinavia. For instance, you're just supposed to stop working. Taking care of the kid yourself, you know? Being home with it and do all those things that women previously did, all by themselves, and I felt when I had my first child like I was—I didn't really want to do that; I was bored with it, and I feel kind of sometimes like getting in very shameful situations, where I feel like I lose my masculinity completely, sitting with a little baby singing with other mothers, you know, doing this, and I was losing everything—I felt—and I was filled with a kind of rage. Why do I have to do it? Because it's totally socially unacceptable *not* to do it. And if you say no, I don't want to do this, then you are—almost—you're a conservative or a reactionary. I've been called names in Swedish, because of this attitude, and I don't say it's wrong to be with your kids—the other way around—but it's . . . This book is about kind of adapting to *that* situation and really—how was it for my father? Why is it that my father's generation was so different, and so on, and so on? And I just found these things interesting. I'm not kind of propagandizing for something, I'm just writing to find out why and how. And so basically, it's about identity, and identity is the feeling of yourself and a confrontation with social surroundings, right? That's the main conflict.

Colier: Identity is very fluid. You become on your knees with your baby. You are still the same person, but your identity flows in and out, and you want to retain one persona, like, "I'm a writer." That's very difficult.

Knausgaard: Yeah.

Colier: Because it's all of it. So, Volume Two takes us where?

Knausgaard: This book is about death, so the second book is about love. It's the exact same structure; it's everyday life, trivialities. Death—which is a mesmerizing thing—everything becomes meaningful around death. It's the same with the second. It's trivialities, banalities—love, which makes everything magic. Then it's the struggle for . . . You know, when you fall in love, everything is kind of heightened and fantastic and then *chik*! It goes down. And me and my wife, it was very dark circumstances in our relationship, and I wanted to write about that. It was like hell sometimes, and is that possible to describe? It was, but very many people got hurt, of course, but I just wanted to. That's how love is for me. The troubled side is as important as the good side.

Colier: How long did the six volumes take you to write? How long have you been working on it?

Knausgaard: I published—I used one year on the first two, which came to eleven hundred pages, and then the plan was to publish all the books in a year, so I had to write four novels that year, which I did. I did, but the fourth wasn't good enough, so I had another year. So it's three years altogether on those books.

Colier: That's very quick because that's a big piece of work.

Knausgaard: Yeah, there was a concept for me: I have to write as quickly as I can. So five pages a day, then ten pages, then twenty pages every day. I have to do it, which is a good thing.

Colier: So basically, it was recollections and no revision or very little revision?

Knausgaard: Yeah, just keep moving.

Colier: Moving forwards. Well, I can't wait to read the book. And what do you do in Sweden?

Knausgaard: I live in the countryside with my family.

Colier: How many children do you have?

Knausgaard: Three.

Colier: Okay, are you still on the floor on your knees?

Knausgaard: Yeah, sometimes I am, and then I run a small publishing house by myself, translate some books, and then I'm writing most of the time now.

Colier: Do you teach?

Knausgaard: Sometimes. It's creative writing, but very little, very little.

Colier: Well, Karl Ove Knausgaard, thank you for being on *Book Case*. I wish you all the best in New York and then the tour. You are off to where, next?

Knausgaard: I'm heading back home. This is the last stop.

Note

1. "Ice or Salt: The Personal in Fiction" at the Brooklyn Book Festival. As the advertising had it: "W. B. Yeats once wrote, 'All that is personal soon rots; it must be packed in ice or salt.' Authors Siri Hustvedt, Norwegian author Karl Ove Knausgård and Sheila Heti will consider how writing technique—'ice or salt'—transforms the personal into art that connects to a broad audience. Moderated by Phillip Lopate."

Karl Ove Knausgård at Passa Porta Festival 2013, Brussels

Anna Luyten / 2013

Passa Porta, March 24, 2014, https://www.youtube.com/watch?v=JiFGMq6Ots4.
Reprinted by permission of Passa Porta, International House of Literature,
Brussels © 2013 and Anna Luyten.

Anna Luyten: With me is Karl Ove Knausgård. He is the greatest literary sensation of the moment, and we welcome him here in Brussels at the brand-new Dutch translation of his novel *Zoon* [*Son*]. *Zoon* is the third volume of the six volumes of the biographical *My Struggle* series, following *Father* and *Love*, and it is one great ambitious autobiographical project.[1] Let's talk about ambition. Let's talk about autobiography, and let's talk about Karl Ove Knausgård. In your book *Zoon*, you asked a question: "Who is this Karl Ove Knausgård?" Is he different when he's ten? Is he someone else when he's twenty? Is he somebody else when he's thirty? Who is this Karl Ove Knausgård of *Zoon*?

Karl Ove Knausgård: Before I started to write, I had a quite clear idea who he or I was. So I think if I should write *that* down, it would be maybe ten pages, but the major thing in this project is to explore identity, what identity is, you know? And I found out during this thirty-six-hundred-page run that it is kind of immensely complicated, and it's impossible to decide what shapes an identity. So what I do—I am looking for the relations.

The major relation in this book is the father, between the father and son, and I think I knew him—knew who he was—when I was ten. I didn't ask about why he did behave like he did or anything like that; I just accepted him. Then there was a kind of rebellion when I was seventeen, eighteen. I didn't want to have anything to do with him, and I thought I hated him. And then he died under kind of the most bizarre circumstances really. He drank himself to death. So he fell, and I thought I hated him, I thought I wanted him dead, but when I came to the house where he died I was crying, and I didn't know why I was crying. And this is the starting point of the novel: *Why did I cry?* And then I became a father myself, and that changed everything. Then all of a sudden, he wasn't no longer a kind of—this Godlike icon, statue, unmovable. I realized he was like me. He had his own feelings, his own desire. When he was forty, he wanted to leave the family. Because he got kids when he was twenty, and he had to take care of us, and I think he had a life he didn't want to live actually. It wasn't his life, he wanted something new. He ran away; he started to drink. It was kind of a freedom project.

When I was thirty-eight, having my own kids, I too wanted to escape. I, too: "This is not my life; I can't stand this; I have to do something else." So the difference between the two of us is that he started to drink, and I started to write. [*Audience laughter*]

Luyten: So these books are escaping methods?

Knausgård: In a way it is, but it is also to try to understand. And having children myself, I didn't know what it was to be a father; I really didn't know. I thought, "This is going to be easy," and to just be kind to them, and everything will be all right, you know? [*Audience laughter*]

Luyten: But there is always a practical side?

Knausgård: Yes. And then I find myself shouting at my daughter—*she's two years old*. I think she's behaving the way she should not behave, and I mean she's two years old, and I'm screaming to her. And if I look back, well, that's my father screaming to me, and there's his father screaming to him. I mean, I started to understand—not to forgive him, my father, but understand him a little bit more, and then I started to write this book.

And to answer your question, it's an almost different thing being ten, being twenty, being thirty. You are yourself, but you are also the role. I mean, you're a man—that means something. You're a father—that means something. You're Norwegian—that means something. And it's very complex material, but what I found out is: "Who's Karl Ove?" That's maybe 2 percent or 1 percent who is exclusively me. Maybe not one person, maybe even less that is exclusively me. The rest is culture; the rest is my father; the rest is all the other things.

Luyten: In this book *Zoon*, you also describe how the zeitgeist is escaping and sculpting and doing everything with someone's identity. What influence had the zeitgeist of the seventies in Norway on you?

Knausgård: I think it's very important—I think we tend to praise individuality and think we are unique. Of course, we are unique, but I think it's so strange because if we go to the sixties, everybody seems to look the same. They have the same kind of opinions, and then there is a youth movement in '68; everybody's left wing . . . and Marxists, Maoists. Now no one is Maoist; no one is Marxist. These things change. We think it's kind of individual, but it's not. It's a collective movement; it's "we." One strange thing that has happened in Scandinavia—I don't know how it is here—but it's the role of the father has changed radically from my father's generation to my generation. So now it's you basically have to be spending much more time with your children, you have to quit the job, stay home with them alone, because you should be—it should be equal. And everybody does this, and *everybody* is a father in a different way than their own father was.

And I got a letter the other day from a Swedish writer, and he said, "I've been reading four of your books, and I have to say even though your father behaved very badly to you, hurt you, I can't help having sympathy for him." I have sympathy for him. "And I think you are more like him than you would like to admit." And he said, "I *guess* you are a good father, and obviously your father was not, but if your father had been a father today he would have been behaving exactly like you." There is a perspective there I like. It's kind of you give away—what was the word?—*responsibility* in a way to this "we," this feeling of here and now, and we are in this together. But at the same time, I think it's true. I think individuality is overestimated wildly.

Luyten: You were, as an individual, a very anxious young boy. Did this change?

Knausgård: Yes, it did. I was very—I was crying a lot when I was a kid.

Luyten: You were always crying.

Knausgård: And I try to describe this in the book, because it's crying without any real consequences. It just came, it's just a feeling, a way of expressing a feeling. You have laughter, and you have crying, and it was kind of a good thing, I think. When you're a kid, you're very close to your feelings. That *could* be difficult because you can't sort them out; it could be a mess for you, but then it's also a good thing to be close to your feelings. And to *write*, this kind of a way of going back to this state of mind, I think I try to do that in the book. Because this is a book about youth, and it's *really* a book about joy. In my first novel, I wrote a sentence that said that nostalgia is shameless.

Luyten: "Nostalgia is shameless."

Knausgård: Yes, because even if you had a horrible childhood, you can get a kind of really strong feeling—of very good feelings—if you smell something you smelled then, of something very very good. And I wanted to explore what that good is, and that's just being a kid, I think. Everything you see, you see for the first time. Every sensation is very strong, and I can see that in my own kids now. It seems like their lives are a lot more rich than my own life at the moment. So I think maybe childhood is the goal of humanity. We are here to take care of them. But that's the thing being a child, because you're so close to your feelings, and you're so close to the world. And this book is about joy, but it's also about fear, because I was very afraid of my father, and this is kind of a dynamic that I wanted to explore to find out. So it starts out I'm very afraid in the house, and I'm very happy outside of the house. In the end of the book the fear inside has kind of changed the world outside, but I don't—I'm not afraid of these things anymore. But what happened to me in my later life was that I laid a lot of restrictions on my social life. I didn't dare to have friends, for instance, because they could say no to me, you know? So I have been sort of solitary in my life, and I think that has to do with the relation to the father in a way.

Luyten: This was a very complicated relation—you already told us about that—but this relation and the way he behaved, sometimes you couldn't guess what his behavior would be the next day or the next hour. He could be very happy or very angry. That trait also you—so you became a little bit, let's say it very polite, *manipulative*?

Knausgård: Yeah. Yes, and I'm basically still that. I want to please people.

Luyten: Mm-hmm.

Knausgård: I want everybody to be pleased, and you should think this is empathy, that you care for people, but that's not the case when people—when I'm not with the people, I don't really care. But if it's present, I want them to be happy, but that just has to do with me. I would just want to please them as I wanted to please my father, and this "not-empathy" thing, it's very important for writing.

Luyten: Why?

Knausgård: I think if you care a lot for the reader, if you want to please the reader, for instance, then it becomes kind of a show of something not true. You could write clever sentences; you can so on and so on. So it's very important *not* to try to please the reader. It's really important to be free and independent in the writing, and that has to do with some sort of—for me at least—some sort of lack of empathy that makes it possible for me to write.

Luyten: It makes it also possible to be honest?

Knausgård: Yes, that's right. It's impossible for me to be honest in personal private space with friends.

Luyten: Are you honest *now*?

Knausgård: Yes, but this is like—*almost* like writing in a way because I don't know you, I don't know you. I can talk relatively openly now, but if we meet afterwards I will not. If you maybe say something political, I would say, "I agree, I think you're right."

Luyten: You don't have to be afraid of me.

Knausgård: I'm afraid of conflicts.

Luyten: You're afraid of conflict?

Knausgård: Yeah, very much so.

Luyten: Although your books were a source of a lot of conflict.

Knausgård: Yes, so this was the *worst* thing that could happen to me—it happened with these books. But then again, sitting alone by myself, there's no conflict. I'm just writing. And people said to me, "Oh, you're so brave because you went through all this." But I wasn't brave. I was just—it was like hell the things that happened, and I just had to wait, and I know it would go over in a year or two. People were very angry at me, and so on, and so on. So this has nothing to do with bravery. It has to do with an urge for freedom in writing and then just wait till the consequences are gone.

Luyten: But how honest can literature be?

Knausgård: Literature, I think, is the place where the possibility for honesty is the greatest, and I think it's so because it's such an intimate [*indecipherable*]. You don't have anyone present when you're writing, and you have someone present in your head. There's always a "we" in the head.

Luyten: It's a "we" which is in your head.

Knausgård: That's morality or the ethics of the world. And it's very strong, and if you cross that line, you feel ashamed. So shame is a kind of a mechanism to regulate the self in society. So what I needed to do when I was writing is to get rid of that "we" in my head, to get rid of that "No, you can't do this" or "What would they think if you wrote this?" And so there is a conflict between self and society, in literature in general, I think, and specifically in this project. So I had to get rid of it, and I'm doing that just by—I think speed is very important for me, just to write very very quickly, almost escape from the thoughts, escape from the "we," but every time I got into some controversial things, I could feel it in my body. It would start to hurt in my body, and so that was kind of what regulated the writing for me. If it hurts, okay, then it's dangerous, then I have to be careful. And it has nothing to do with me, but I can give away everything from my life, no problem, but it has to do with other people.

Luyten: You're called "the literary sensation." Can you understand this? Why your life is so important for us, for all of us as readers?

Knausgård: No. [*Audience laughter*] That is impossible for me to understand. And it still is. When I did this, I didn't think of—I thought this is kind of an experimental thing. How far is it possible to go into trivialities or banalities or everyday life. And I thought this would be almost impossible to read, because in the second book there are, for instance, like five pages of describing how to change a diaper or doing all those kind of things you try to escape from in real life. Now we have to *read* about it as well.

Luyten: I learned a lot about baby gymnastics in your second part.

Knausgård: Yeah, that kind of thing. So I never thought that this would be for *other* people. Maybe someone who was interested in a kind of realism, or something like that, but then these books got a lot of attention, and something happens that never happened in my writing life before. I started to get letters, and very personal letters, very intense letters, dealing with subjects that my books are dealing with, but very personal.

Luyten: Like confessions?

Knausgård: Yes. I got for instance a letter from someone sitting in jail, I think thirty pages of his writing about his life. Because I think he felt a kind of connection to me in the books, and then he wanted to tell his story back, and I got a lot of things like that coming, and it has nothing to do with gender, because a lot of these are women. Nothing to do with generation, a lot of letters—from a ninety-five-year-old woman.

Luyten: Ninety-five.

Knausgård: Yeah. Writing, saying to me that "life is long. So relax, life is long. You have plenty of time." [*Anna Luyten and many in the audience laugh*]

Luyten: Still ten volumes to come?

Knausgård: But these things—it's a dream for a writer. This is what you really want to come to the point, where people don't think this is literature, but it's something else. It has to do with life, and that's—I can't understand it—I can't. It's hard for me to relate to it, but I think it's a dream. This is it—to get there—and I think this has nothing to do with quality either because I started to read this on the plane here, and I thought, "Oh, no, this is not really good," but I think that doesn't really matter and there's something else going on there. I hope.

Luyten: You say there is something else going on there. Some people call this a coming-of-age novel. I think it's much more. It's also a meditation or sometimes you have little essays about things like memory, for instance.

Can you remember childhood, or can you recall childhood very well in literature? I mean you use a lot of conversations between you and your mother, for instance.

Knausgård: Yeah.

Luyten: Do you really recall them in your head?

Knausgård: No, they are made up. All the—you can't, you can't remember conversation *exactly*, even the conversation we had just before we came in here. You can't recall it in detail; it's impossible. And if you did, you wouldn't hardly understand it, because we talked differently than we think. So now all those kinds are made up, all those conversations are made up. What I did is try to—I have maybe ten memories clearly from my childhood.

Luyten: What are the ten clearest memories?

Knausgård: I've written about some of them. They are kind of the central point in the novel. All those memories, writing them down evokes something else around them, and there is something else around *them* again, and so on, and so on. So I think we have very much of our lives still present, but we don't use it, it's just there somewhere, and it's possible to find them again—if you really want to do that.

One of the most clear memories is a scene about me being in a swimming pool with my friends, and I loved to swim, and everything was magic. It was winter, taking the bus there, going up to the swimming pool. It's dark. Everything is magic—as it could be for a child—and then when I'm going back home, getting dressed in the dressing room, I can't find my sock. Losing one sock. And I know this is a catastrophe; this is a disaster because if my father found out, all hell will break loose because this is—I'm not supposed to lose anything, you know? Looking for the sock, I can't find the sock, and I'm more and more in despair. Then I take the bus home. "Okay, I have one chance: sneak in, find another sock. Maybe he won't notice." But he always noticed these things, like he was kind of detecting. . . . *Oh, he's coming*. And he was there in the door watching me taking off my boots. "Where's the sock?" And he was very angry, and I was very afraid of him. His anger was the worst. This episode is there in the book.

Luyten: There is another episode when it's your first school day, and your mother is bringing you to school, but she doesn't find the way, and you don't remember the way either.

Knausgård: No.

Luyten: So you're too late.

Knausgård: Yeah.

Luyten: Is this typical of your mother?

Knausgård: Yes, she can still—if she is going to a place—I think she can drive three hours the wrong direction without noticing. [*Laughs*] She's kind of absent-minded in these things. But the interesting thing here is, I remember this so good. The first day of school we are coming there too late. It's kind of a—I remembered and it's a little disaster and—but *now* when you have kids yourself, you're five minutes late? It's okay, it's not a problem. And it's—I see my kids—we are spending day after day after day after day together, nothing specific is going on, I mean, and then there is maybe some small thing you're doing wrong. Maybe *this* is the thing they will remember from their childhood. So vast a time around you, but for a kid you just take *this*: I remember *this* and *that*. And then you make your own theory of how it was to grow up there, and I think maybe you start to understand your parents when you are forty or forty-five or something like that.

Luyten: But due to this scene, I understand the difficult relationship also better between you and your father. This was a very strange relationship.

Knausgård: Yeah.

Luyten: They divorced also after a while. And once you said that before you started these novels you were trying to write about the relationship between your father and mother, but it didn't work out very well.

Knausgård: No.

Luyten: But you did it very well in the different novels of *My Struggle*. What did you learn about the relationship between them, writing all those books?

Knausgård: What I did learn about the relationship to my father?

Luyten: Between your mother and your father?

Knausgård: Oh! . . .

Luyten: That they love each other. Because in one of your books she said, "I really loved him."

Knausgård: Yeah, and you know, that's something she said when I was *writing* this book because I was talking to her about *him*. They were together for twenty-four years, and then they divorced, and I never asked her really why she was with him all this time. Then I started to write about it, to talk to her about it, and she said—and she never uses that word—we don't use that word *love*, you know, my family. No. I never said to my mother that I love her—*never*. And I never will. We don't do that. But she said—and that was a sensation for me—she said, "But, Karl Ove, I loved him." And *that's* the explanation. And she told me about the first time they met and who he was then, and he was a very troubled man, but he was still a man of . . . *formidable*, she said to me. There was something to him, and he was troubled, but also, I think . . . There was a mutual thing going on with them, which *I* couldn't see when I was a kid. For me, it all had to do with loyalty.

My mother was loyal to my father, and she was loved also, but there was always a problem. If I confess something to her about my father, maybe she will tell him. And of course, I can see that if my children said something to me about my wife, I will tell her. If you are a kid, you could feel like a betrayal, and there were some episodes where I felt betrayed by my mother. That was only because she was a parent with him. So, yes, I think my father needed my mother. She's a very ethical woman. She never does anything wrong. She doesn't drink, she's very Protestant, and I was also a Protestant. It was almost in my bones, and he was a man with chaos inside of him, so he needed this. Then when he went away, that grip also went away, and a kind of chaos came back, and he committed a kind of suicide in the end, I think.

Luyten: You're talking about religion in your novels. Also, sometimes the theme of religion comes up. You also worked on the translation of the Bible.

Knausgård: Yeah.

Luyten: What function has religion for you? Not only in literature but in your life?

Knausgård: For me, I'm not a religious man, but I'm very curious, and I'm always kind of seeking something. I think I'm seeking meaning, looking for meaning, and normally that's in literature where I find it. For me, literature and religion are related in a way. I mean, for me the thing with literature and art is if you read a novel or a poem, there is a certain thing of selflessness in there. You lose yourself; you lose track of yourself. You are someone else. And it could be almost ecstasy if you read Dostoevsky, for instance. You could read two hundred pages and nothing is going on. Three hundred pages, nothing is happening. And all of a sudden it is like a light, it's like something is a cold light there. You don't know what it is, but you would want to read and read and read. You are in the center of something, and I think that is—it has to do something with religion in a way. That's why my second novel was about angels, and that was the first time I was writing about the subject of religion, and what fascinated me was that the angels were half between the divine immaterial and the real material world, and I wanted to look upon that difference. And the main thing with Christianity is that God came and was flesh and blood. He was here among us in historic time. That's a sensational concept, and it changed really everything and shaped Europe and the history of the world so dramatically. So just okay, this is *interesting*. I want to write about it.

Luyten: In one of your books, your friend is saying to you, "You want to be a saint."

Knausgård: Yeah.

Luyten: You have this *Confessions* of Augustine? Your books are also confessions?

Knausgård: For him to be a saint, it's not a compliment. For him being a saint, it is something very bad, something you should not be. But he had a saint complex, but I am so *ashamed* of things I do, and I also restrict myself so much. So for me my only places where I can be free and not restricted are in writing and in drinking. That's the two places where I can be not a saint, and if I do that, if I drink, I am destroyed for the next week, even though if I didn't do anything wrong, because just the idea of having no control of myself is very, very frightening and scary.

Luyten: It's frightening and scary, but you are trying to find—you are trying to find a way *not* to control something.

Knausgård: In writing, that's the most important thing, to get loose of control, no control whatsoever, and that's very difficult to obtain, I think. But that's what writing is about. That's about to be free in writing, be free in your mind, free in your thinking. That's a good thing.

Luyten: You were talking about childhood in this book also. In *Zoon* you describe the landscapes of your youth. You also already said, when you're young—when you're a child—everything is fresh, everything is new, so these impressions during your youth are very important. What importance had the landscapes of Norway for you as a person, the man who you became, the writer who you became?

Knausgård: [*Laughs*] That's a very difficult question to answer really because what shapes you is you, and you can't see it. To see it, you need a point outside of yourself, and you don't have that, so that's a very difficult question to answer. But I thought there should be more differences between Belgium or the Netherlands and Norway. Maybe this book will be very *difficult* to read here because the culture is different.

Luyten: We also had the Formica tables, very late in the seventies, in the kitchen.

Knausgård: Yeah, and it's much more alike than we like to think. But I met the translator of this book, Paula Stevens, in Oslo, and she had a lecture about how to translate mountains, hills, into a *flat* landscape, which is very difficult because there's so many words that have to do with this thing, which I guess don't exist in this area. I hope she succeeded. It was a challenge for her. But in the book of angels, I wanted—in the end—I wanted to retell the stories of the Bible, and I tried to do that in the desert or in the landscape of the Middle East—but I don't know it—so I wrote about maybe camels, tents, sandals—what else is there? I don't know. No freedom for me, and I couldn't really retell it. So then I asked myself what if I put the Bible into Norway?

Luyten: In Norway?

Knausgård: What will happen? I'm free! I know Norway, I can just write about the sky and out in the woods, and that thing I think was very interesting with the Bible because it's so old, and it's so very, very different from us. I mean, a different way of thinking, different way of living. It's very strange. And if you read it, it looks like—the letters look like for me like small bushes or small trees, so I don't understand it. And then if you get a Royal translation of it, that's also almost meaningless. Almost you can't understand it. But then that's the distance. But then, for my grandparents, this was the world for them. I mean, they were really dominated by this book. It was very close. And I just wanted to go in this closeness, distance, closeness, distance, and try to open it up in a way. Those stories are *fantastic*. Cain and Abel, it's just eight lines in the Bible, eight lines, and it's *the* story about brothers, but it's eight lines. I try to—okay, everything in those eight lines has to be present in my book, but then I go in between them and make a kind of a novel. So a hundred pages about Cain and Abel, which are very similar to me and my brother.

Luyten: So in this book you are talking about your brother?

Knausgård: Yeah.

Luyten: Your brother was very important for you as an example in this book. In your first book, he is also there, but in a different way.

Knausgård: Yeah.

Luyten: What's the difference of the brother in your youth when you are very young and your brother when he was older?

Knausgård: When I grew up, he was my older brother—four years older—and when you're a kid, that's a lot. So he was my hero. I think he was the best thing in my life, and I admired him, and he always did things before me, always knew how to do it. He introduced me to music, for instance, and football, and all those things. And it remained like that when I was sixteen. He was still like that, but when I got in my twenties, then I went to his place—he was studying in Bergen. I started to study in Bergen. And everything became very complicated between us. I fell in love, for instance, with a girl, and he took her, and they were together, and we started a kind of competition, and I was kind of getting more and more close to him intellectually, and things became very difficult then. I think the most easy thing would be if I'm his little brother, and he's my older brother, and that's it, but then it gets a kind of equal thing. I think it's not that problematic for him, but for *me* it was very problematic to see: "Okay, I'm as good as him." I don't like that. I want him to be better. Then it's fixed. It's like it should be. I think that's the moment in everybody's life—if you have a father or mother, then you kind of . . . These things change, and you realize they don't really know what they're doing after all. I'm maybe no better, and that could be difficult to cope with, I guess.

Luyten: And you always stayed his little brother?

Knausgård: That thing, with him having this girlfriend—who I loved—for a year, ended with me very dramatically. I was drunk, I took a glass and threw it in his face. So a very aggressive act, and I thought, "Okay, this is I'm unrepairable. We have to split, and he will never want to see me again." But he forgave me the next day and—

Luyten: The next day already?

Knausgård: Yeah, but then he was back there, you know? And I still am dependent upon him. I still want him to deal with the difficult things in life for me—so it's complicated, but it's also good material for novels. [*Audience laughter*] You know, Cain and Abel—but this is a kind of a basic story. It is two brothers. It is an archetypical story, so you have mother-daughter, mother-son. These are archetypes, so it's—even my father dying with his mother, drinking, it's an archetype. If you know *The Ghost* by Henrik Ibsen, *that's* the story. Everything in life is like this. It's very specific, it's very *my* story, but at the same time it is common. These patterns, you see them everywhere.

Luyten: But there is also a pattern of forgiveness in all your books. It may be strange to mention. You mention it in *My Struggle*, but there is a lot of forgiveness in it.

Knausgård: Yeah, that's just by accident. [*Laughs*] I think if you do—and I've been thinking a lot about this—because if you do try to understand something, I think then you forgive. I mean, understanding and forgiving are very similar to each other. And I've been thinking a lot of this because in the end of this project I wrote about Adolf Hitler, and I wrote about his youth and his upbringing, and the more I wrote about him the more I could understand him. This is also a bit dangerous because you don't want to forgive *him*, you know, but there *is* a human.

And having done that, the thing in Norway, the massacre happened, so I wrote about *that* in the same way because if you go and look at Anders Breivik's youth, you see this boy really didn't have a chance.[2] Something must have happened in his life. You can understand that, and it's difficult, because you don't want to forgive him. *I don't forgive him*, but I can understand it. But these things are related. That's a good thing about novels is that you can do that. Nazism, Hitler, these kinds of emblematic things, even Auschwitz, which is an emblematic thing. We don't really understand it. It is just something out there. If you go in there and kind of explore it and try to go deep in it, then you have an understanding of it. And you can't understand everything. You can only understand—you need only to understand one thing, one fate, one destiny, then you will get it. Auschwitz—it's just a name. You *have* to go in there. This is one person, this totally rich life—all these relatives, then you maybe can get a little glimpse of the catastrophe, and in a novel, you can do that. Hardly no other media can do that, I think.

Luyten: So can I say that all these novels where you describe yourself in your own life are the best weapon against narcissism?

Knausgård: No. [*Laughs*] It is of course an element of it, but it is also the *opposite*. There is also kind of a self-hatred in it or a destructive thing, but I honestly don't want to tell my stories. That's not what I'm doing there. It's a search for meaning, and it's such a meaning in my life, of course, but it's still—it is possible to generalize it and see—look at it as a search for meaning, in general, I think.

Luyten: So the description of banality of real life can also bring us to—what you said—*forgiveness* or to a new standard or a new ethical standard?

Knausgård: I think we all the time have to remind ourselves about the world around us because it so easily just disappears into routines. We don't see it; we don't, and it's—

Luyten: Give it attention.

Knausgård: Yeah, the same relationship. Go in there, you're in love, I mean everything is magical, and then you just take the other for granted, and then it disappears. So in my life I use literature and art and film as a way to remind me of the reality around me. And that's also why I write like I do. And my wife, she's a writer, and it's very strange, but when I read her novels or short stories, *then* I can see her because that's her inner life. But that's possible to see her, okay. This is a rich and—but in the daily life, yeah, it's just sometimes before I know what she's doing, and I just—and it's the same for her with me.

Luyten: Literature for love.

Knausgård: Yeah, but the strange thing here is that it's—to do that, you turn away from life, because it's you have to turn away from other people to do this writing. It's a paradox.

Luyten: You finished the six novels. You finished *My Struggle*. At the end, you write that you're happy because you—I'll [quote] the full sentence: "I am happy because I am no longer an author."

Knausgård: It's even, "I'm *so* happy that I'm no longer an author."

Luyten: "So happy." But you told a colleague of mine, while writing the sentence you were crying.

Knausgård: I was crying when I was writing the end of the novel because it's about my wife. She was hospitalized during the writing because partly of the writing, and that's a good example. When this happened, I really didn't see it that good. Okay, I had to deal with taking care of the kids and taking care of the situation. But when I started to write about it, I really understood what it was, and this is a catastrophe for everybody. That was possibly why I was crying. Then I sent it to my editor, and he said, "Oh, you haven't written *any*thing." Everything was *inside*. I thought I had written it, but I hadn't, and I had to go new round the same thing. You have to go further and further, and I was crying all the time because it's so . . . *then* I can see it, you know.

Luyten: The tragedy of being an author.

Knausgård: No, that was a really joyful sentence to write, and this was the *only* sentence I had in mind the whole project. I knew that it should end there.

Luyten: That was the perspective.

Knausgård: This is a book about life and literature, and it's a book about turning away from society, turning away from friends, living more or less isolated in literature, escaping from everything. And I wanted not to look away from the world and into literature, but the other way around. Look from literature into life and try to live—start living—and I wanted it to end there, and I wanted to mean it, and I did that for a while—I meant it. But then, you know, then I came back.

Luyten: Back to the demon.

Knausgård: Because it's so—yeah, it's a big part of me, this turning away from everything. But I'm trying, and also this book is about ambition. And it's a book about how many things—that ambition can destroy you. And I wanted it just to end in a good place.

Luyten: And now you're writing a new book. You started up a small publishing house, too?

Knausgård: Yes, I have. So we are translating books and publishing them in Norwegian. Very small, it's four titles—*eight* titles—a year, but it's very fun, and it's a social thing. We are four or five people doing this, and I've been writing a collection of essays, and I'm writing a film manuscript, so I'm doing a lot of things, but I do not write fictional novels, at the moment at least.

Luyten: Okay, thank you, Karl Ove Knausgård.

Knausgård: Thank you very much for being so patient.

Notes

1. The Dutch edition of *My Struggle* is entitled *Mijn Strijd*. In Belgium, Holland, Spain, and Great Britain, among other countries, each volume of *My Struggle* has its own title.

2. Anders Breivik murdered sixty-nine children at a Norwegian summer camp in 2011.

The Light behind the Bookshelves

Daniel Fraser / 2013

3:AM Magazine, April 29, 2013, https://www.3ammagazine.com/3am/the-light-behind-the-bookshelves/. Reprinted by permission of Daniel Fraser.

Daniel Fraser: I'd like to start by asking about the book's title. The working title was *Argentina*. However, you changed it to *My Struggle*. How do these two titles relate to the book, and what makes *My Struggle* more appropriate?

Karl Ove Knausgaard: This book is really about being at a place in life and wanting to be somewhere else, and Argentina has always been a sort of a dream country for me. I had always wanted to go there and had never been. The first time I was aware of it was in the football World Cup Final in 1978, but then it became a kind of a mythical country for me. Borges is from there, and for me, he is an incarnation of literature, and Gombrowicz, he wrote his diaries there, so it was the place of literature and myth, the place all my longing was directed towards. However, it's a bad title because nobody would understand that. But *My Struggle*, *Min Kamp*, is different. Well, first of all it says, "Fuck you. I don't care about you. I'm just doing this." But then there is also something basic in that title. It's *my* struggle, and the book is a description of a struggle. It's a small struggle, a real struggle which is also the book itself.

Another good thing was that it meant I had to read Hitler's *Mein Kampf*, and in the end, it meant I also had to write about it too. I wrote about four hundred pages in the last volume about Adolf Hitler, mostly about his path to *Mein Kampf*, because there are a lot of similarities in there, a lot of parallels in the descriptions of my life and the young Hitler's because we are both sixteen and in love and wanting to be artists and so on and so on.

But most of all, that difference and relation between: overall construction, life, the world, the biggest concepts, and the smallest ideas is something which is perfectly captured in the title.

Fraser: I wanted to ask you now about the mechanical aspects of writing *My Struggle*, in particular, the length of the book and the speed with which it was composed. How important were they and what did these mechanisms allow you to do?

Knausgaard: The speed is the most important thing. Both challenge the concept of form, but the speed has a practical element as well for me because I am a perfectionist in my writing, in my way of thinking, and I want to be clever, and I want to make it into real art, real literature. But I had to fight against that thing in me because I became so critical of my own writing, and I needed to get over that, and the only way I could do it was by speeding up because then you don't have time to be critical at all.

It also allowed me to escape the notion of knowing what to write. If you know what you're going to write, then that's death for me, then nothing is happening. If I plan something, it's just dead. And almost everything I write is dead in that sense really, but if I speed up, then something, all of a sudden, is happening because I can no longer control it.

There's also something else in there too. When I was nineteen, I went to a creative writing course, and we were basically taught that if something is bad, then you should just take it away, essentially a very minimalistic approach to writing. It took me ten years to overcome that and to understand it's possible to do the opposite—that if it's bad, you can just add more in because then something else is happening.

It's the same thing with the length. If you write a hundred pages, then it's all about concentration; it's all about sentences or language. But if you write thirty-six hundred pages, the sentences are no longer the important thing. It is something else that is going on that's difficult to explain.

Writing about life, I just love the thought of being able to write a hundred pages, two hundred pages, three hundred pages about one day, and then just spend maybe ten sentences on ten years and try to make a dynamic. But I am really sorry for doing this because now I cannot do it again. I'd love to do something like Marcel Proust because for me that's the perfect novel, but I have wasted it away. It's too late. It was this; this is the result.

Fraser: There's a point in the first volume where you write about a "calibration of the senses . . . the point where all necessary distances have been set." Was the form an attempt at breaking free from what you describe?

Knausgaard: Yes, that's absolutely so. That has to do with concepts and ideas. The way we think of ourselves is static; it's unmoving and fixed, and I just wanted to crush all that up, to move in those directions where I don't know what things really are. I mean I wrote a lot of pages about taking care of children, doing all these things which don't have any meaning, but I just go in there amongst the everyday and describe it and hope that something will show itself.

Another thing is that when I turned forty, it was kind of like I was dead. I thought, "This is it, and it's going to be like this for the rest of my life." And the only way for me to deal with that was through literature. It's difficult to explain, but I had to attempt to get closer to life, which is a stupid thing to do, but that's what I was trying to do, to avoid all the structures and forms of the novel.

A Man in Love [*My Struggle*, Volume Two] really has no dramatic plot. It's a really horizontal book in a way, whereas the third book is a very ordinary classic childhood description, almost like a cliché. That's the danger with writing fast. You write quickly to get away from something, but that means you also do it mechanically, and you can end up with a cliché.

Fraser: That's one of the things I like most about the book, unlike so much of the overcrafted, sentence-obsessed literature of today, *My Struggle* has a complete lack of fear of cliché.

Knausgaard: That's the risk in this book; to bathe in banalities is a dangerous thing for a writer to do. But then you need to ask yourself what quality is. What is quality in literature?

Fraser: You wrote in Volume Two that literature's sole obligation is the search for something different. What difference is it that you are searching for in *My Struggle*?

Knausgaard: Literature when I was a kid was always a place I could escape, and when I grew up and became a writer myself, it was still a place where I could get away and get outside of everything and use it as a kind of perspective for everything. But this time, I am deciding not to move away, not to go away, but just try to describe this here as it is. The only thing I was looking for really was meaning, because I started off with such a desperate feeling of meaninglessness and knowing that that feeling isn't like things should be. To consider everything meaningless is one of the deadly sins, so I just try and make things alive, and the only way I can do that is in writing.

Fraser: Does it have any relation to the notion of difference Foucault describes?

Knausgaard: Definitely. His book *The Order of Things* is one of the two or three most important books in my life as a writer; reading it was a revelation for me, so he has to be in there somewhere.

Fraser: Death, of course, has a commanding presence in your work. How did your father's death change how you thought about death in general?

Knausgaard: His death or seeing him dead confirmed something for me which is very important: the physical material element of death is something I have been very occupied with. When I was twenty, I worked at a hospital for the mentally ill. The patients didn't have much of a life, and their strange forms made me see the body for the first time in that biological, materialist sense.

At the same time, my grandmother was very ill, and I saw her too and had never seen the body in that sense because we tend to hide these things away. When I saw my father dead, it was the same thing, I saw how individuality, psychology, culture—all those things—just disappear. In this book, I have tried to write about all things in a strictly physical sense, and I also view death from this perspective because so much of our lives are made up of other things, images, abstractions and concepts, so that's the real subject in *My Struggle*, that there is a difference between the way we think of ourselves and the way we really are.

We can say something about who we are, but that doesn't really mean anything. And in the end, it ends with a poem by Paul Celan. He is someone trying to move in those directions where there is no language at all, no world of material things. This is the exploration which is going on all the time in the book but only among the most banal events. Like the end of *The Order of Things*, where Foucault describes man disappearing like a face written in sand at the edge of the sea.

Fraser: Heidegger features a number of times in *My Struggle*. What effect do you think his thought has had on your work?

Knausgaard: I have never finished *Sein und Zeit*, and I don't know if I get more than 5 or 10 percent of it, but I just love to be in his language and the way he forces you to follow his path. There is also something attractive in his ideas about our automatic lives, and of course his reading of Hölderlin is very important to me and my work. My thoughts about Heidegger also reached a conclusion in the sixth book writing about the Nazis because he was of course a Nazi for a while, and it's very interesting how he got to that point. I feel the same longing and the same affection for him when I read Adorno's *The Jargon of Authenticity*. I am completely on Heidegger's side. I am not a philosopher at all, but I love to read his works, and they relate to my writing in ways I don't even know, but then I feel his ideas are sophisticated and difficult, and writing is not. But still he deals with life, and I deal with life.

Fraser: One quote in the book which really stuck with me was "The difference between nineteenth century nihilism and ours is the difference between emptiness and equality." I wondered if you might talk about what you meant by this.

Knausgaard: I cannot really talk about this at the moment, but if you wait, it will come in the sixth book, where there is a long discussion on the idea of equality.

Fraser: Poetry features quite heavily in the books too. I was wondering what influence poets and poetry have had on you as a writer?

Knausgaard: If you are a writer, you will recognize what you think the best is, the pinnacle of writing, the place where you think, "This is really the point of everything"; and for me, this is almost exclusively poets because of what they can evoke.

I never really talked about poetry or painting or art at all before because it is something totally different to writing, but in this book, I tried to. I read Paul Celan. I had never talked about him or even really understood the work, but I just read and was struck thinking, "Wow, this is really something else," the ultimate place of words. I read Celan's poems slowly, one word at a time, trying to see what's going on, but it was a strange experience, as unlike most poets the words are not the important thing. There is something else there in between.

And it is the same with art. It is a mystery for me as I find I am often moved by it and think it is very meaningful and very important, but I can't integrate it into my own life and make it relevant there. It's something outside of what's going on here, now.

Poetry is also the source of a lot of longing for me. If I read Hölderlin, I feel almost only longing and sorrow; it has to do with the feeling of being alive, I think.

Fraser: I wanted to ask about the religious themes in the book and how they relate to your materialism.

Knausgaard: My last book before this was about angels and the fall of angels and my fascination there was of the double character of angels, both divine and human. They have bodies and are wandering on Earth.

The idea for this book [*A Time for Everything*] was that the angels were tempted by life on Earth, they came closer and closer and eventually became Darwinists. They evolve until they eventually become like seagulls. Afterwards I was invited to do a retranslation of the Bible into Norwegian, and then I was writing with theologians and of course Hebraic experts, and when I was working on the first four books of Moses, I was amazed by the fact that there are no abstract motives, no abstract thoughts. It's all read through the body, all related to movement, which is the opposite of what my image of the Bible was. And it is that which I saw and have been using ever since really.

I am not a religious person, so for me religious ecstasy has the same meaning as it does in literature, as ecstasy in Holderlin and whatever is strongly connected to me. I am interested in those kinds of experiences.

In the research for *A Time for Every Purpose under Heaven*, I read a lot of theological texts and found some amazing things. One of the most important things was that the story of Cain and Abel, the story of one brother murdering another, is only eight lines long. It's a really short story, and yet it has been constantly reinterpreted for thousands of years, and when I was writing about Hitler, the incident with the mass murderer Breivik happened, and I ended up writing about Hitler, Breivik, and Cain and Abel because there was something there in the story of Cain and Abel which was connected to these figures.

Fraser: You wrote that you are "never one for receiving" and that you desire distance/turning away, and quite clearly you have transmitted much of yourself in the book, and many who read it will feel that they know you intimately. How has that outpouring or act of transmission allowed you to distance yourself, and are these two things reconcilable?

Knausgaard: That is the paradox of this whole situation really. I turned away from everybody, even my family, to do this and to hide really. Then the reverse of this is that I am recognized everywhere, and people send me letters and speak to me as if we have known each other forever. But that has to do with what I was searching for: to be free in literature, and to be free in literature you really cannot allow any other to be present.

If you have a voice in your head saying, "I can't do that" or "I should do that," then it's no good. And in social situations, that voice is constant, and I really am no good at dealing with it because I'm so occupied with it, but in literature, I can be free from that and just be, with no other there at all. And it's interesting because in the other, there is the moral or ethical component of everything, and if you want to do what I did, you have to overcome the ethical, you have to overcome the moral, which is impossible in a social situation—but is possible in the novel.

I never thought that this was going to be read, and I honestly thought that people would hate it, but I still did it, so there is obviously something I want to say. It's strange turning away from life, which is necessary to write or do anything really, and at the same time doing it in order to make life more rich or more meaningful or more intense.

At the same time as I was writing *My Struggle*, Anders Breivik wrote his manifesto, and we are pretty much the same generation, and he did the same; he turned away. There is no other there in his work, and there's no moral component there, no ethics. The strange thing is he transgressed the literature to act on it in real life, but it is the same mechanisms in action. The only thing I learned from this project is to do with this: with the social and the self and relations and with freedom and what freedom is.

Fraser: The book is also about the inadequacy of writing. At one wonderful moment, you write: "And writing, what else was it but death?" How can the ultimate impossibility of writing, the fragmentary nature of memory, reconcile itself in this work, in literature?

Knausgaard: That's a very good question and to the point, but it's impossible for me to answer. It's impossible for me to reduce it.

Fraser: Finally, I just wanted to ask, seeing as you end the book with the line "I am so happy I am no longer an author," if this is the end of writing then?

Knausgaard: Not the end of writing, the end of being an author. Since then, I have been writing essays, which is a completely different form. I wanted this book just to end in life and to turn away from literature into life. And I wanted it to end there and the sentence to be true. I really must be filled with desire to live. And it was like that; it was a relief to write that sentence. Now I want to write again, but really there is nothing. I have some strong fascinations I want to write about but not the urge. I don't know.

"Completely without Dignity": An Interview with Karl Ove Knausgaard

Jesse Barron / 2013

Paris Review, Dec. 26, 2013, https://www.theparisreview.org/blog/2013/12/26. Reprinted by permission of Jesse Barron.

Of the two people who have written books called *My Struggle*, Karl Ove Knausgaard is the less notorious. In Scandinavia, where the tradition of memoiristic writing is less prevalent and self-exposing than it is in America, he wrote, for three years, twenty pages a day about himself, his friends, his wife, and his kids. When the first of the six books was published, reporters called everyone he'd ever met. It sold half a million copies.

But unlike most literary controversies, this one's less interesting than the work that provoked it. Knausgaard has written one of those books so aesthetically forceful as to be revolutionary. Before, there was no *My Struggle*; now there is, and things are different. The digressiveness of Sebald or Proust is transposed into direct, unmetaphorical language, pushing the novel almost to the edge of unreadability, where it turns out to be addictive and hypnotic. A man has written a book in which a man stays at home with his kids, and his home life isn't trivialized or diminished but studied and appreciated, resisted and embraced. An almost Christian feeling of spiritual urgency makes even the slowest pages about squeezing lemon on a lobster into a hymn about trying to be good.

Book One ends with that impossible thing: an original metaphor for death. The last sentence of this interview may do the same for writing.

On the line here are both a man's soul and his ass. The work has pissed off his fellow Norwegians, including the one he married. But the biggest risk is, in a single work, expending all the unconscious material of forty years of life. He calls *My Struggle* his authorial suicide, and after talking to him last weekend, I believe him, but I don't think it means he won't write another book.

Mr. Knausgaard lives in Sweden and doesn't know how to use Skype. We tried to get the video to work, but in the end, we spoke to each other through black rectangles. Occasionally, I could hear his kids in the background, and the tap of a pen or his fingers on the desk, which made me terrified that I was boring him. His accent in English sounds Austrian— Sacha Baron Cohen doing Bruno—and he's plain-spoken and self-doubting. "So," he would conclude after talking for a few minutes, "I'm afraid that's another stupid answer." It was the only time he really got something wrong.

Jesse Barron: Did you keep diaries when you were young?

Karl Ove Knausgaard: Yes, I did, but I burned them when I was twenty-five or twenty-six.

Barron: Why?

Knausgaard: I was so embarrassed, I couldn't stand it. It's the same with *Min Kamp*, I can't stand it. If I could I would burn that, too, but there are too many prints, so it's impossible.

Life develops, changes, is in motion. The forms of literature are not. So if you want the writing to be as close to life as possible—I do not mean this in any way as an apology for realism—but if you want to write close to life, you have to break the forms you've used, which means that you constantly have the feeling of writing the first novel, for the first time, which means that you do not know how to write. All good writers have that in common, they do not know how to write.

Barron: But isn't burning a novel different from burning a diary? Burning a diary is repudiating a former version of yourself.

Knausgaard: It's one thing to be banal, stupid, and idiotic on the inside. It's another to have it captured in writing. When I started to write more systematically, I just couldn't stand that bastard diarist-self, and I had to get rid of it. So I did, alone in my student apartment, page after page.

But as anyone with the least knowledge of literature and writing—maybe art in general—will know, concealing what is shameful to you will never lead to anything of value. This is something I discovered later, when I was writing my first novel, when the parts that I was ashamed like a dog to have written were the same parts that my editor always pointed out, saying, "This, this is really good!" In a way, it was my shame-o-meter, the belief that the feeling of shame or guilt signified relevance, that finally made me write about myself, the most shameful act of all, trying to reach the innocence of the now burned diarist-self.

Barron: Scandinavia doesn't have a tradition of tell-all memoirs, but it does have diarists. Olav H. Hauge, the Norwegian poet, wrote a three-thousand-page diary which was published after his death, when you were about twenty-six. Did you have a strong reaction to it?

Knausgaard: Yes, I did. I read it very intensely over a short period of time, during a kind of crisis in my life. I was obsessed with it. And it was very strange because he wrote his diaries from 1916, or something, until 1990, so it covers his whole life. And he was basically only on his farm. Nothing happens in his life at all. And he really writes about nothing. Nothing is going on there except for him thinking and harvesting apples.

It's a kind of hypnotic writing, which really should be boring. I mean, there are a lot of examples of it. Lars Norén, the Swedish playwright, published a diary just recently, which I read during the writing of *Min Kamp*, and it was the same thing. Fifty pages about gardening, and it should be really awful, really boring. But there's something magic in it, something hypnotic, and it's the same with Hauge. He's repeating himself all the time. It's not good if you consider it as an essay, it's not good if you consider it as storytelling, but it is still hypnotic. And I think that has to do with you feeling that you are very close to a self.

Barron: The crisis you experienced while reading Hauge—was it artistic or personal?

Knausgaard: I had been unfaithful to my then wife and for a year succeeded in not telling her. Then, one day, someone called and said he wanted to talk to "the rapist Karl Ove Knausgaard." My wife handed the receiver over to me and looked like a ghost. The caller said if I didn't admit that I was a rapist, he would come over with some friends and beat me unconscious. That marked the beginning of the crisis.

A few days later, I went out to an island, where I had been before to write, and lived there for two months, again trying to write. It was a small island, miles out in the open sea, with only three other inhabitants. One of them actually died when I was there. I saw the ambulance boat coming, and the medics carrying him, covered, onto the boat in the snow. I thought of suicide every day, and read Hauge's diaries, which was such a comfort, such a good thing. It was me and him, and the wide open sky over the sea, and the stars at night.

Barron: It reminds me of something in your book—"What is a work of art if not the gaze of another person?" But you hadn't really written about yourself until *Min Kamp*. Your second book is about a fictive angelologist from the sixteenth century.

Knausgaard: When I started out on *Min Kamp*, I was so extremely frustrated over my life and my writing. I wanted to write something majestic and grand, something like *Hamlet* or *Moby-Dick*, but found myself with this small life—looking after kids, changing diapers, quarreling with my wife, unable to write anything, really. So I started to write about that. During that process, I realized that this was material. I didn't like it, but still, it was something, not nothing. If you read Hölderlin or Celan, and admire their writing, it's very shameful, writing about diapers; it's completely without dignity. But then, that became the point. That was the whole point. Not to try to go somewhere else than this. This is how it is.

Barron: It's not like writing in a diary, though. A novel opens space between a writer and his or her material, the space of literature. There's less distance between writer and diary than between writer and novel.

Knausgaard: It's all the difference in the world. I had tried to write from the age of eighteen but didn't succeed at all. Then, when I was about twenty-seven, I changed my language. This is difficult to explain. You can write a radical Norwegian or a conservative Norwegian. And when I changed to a conservative Norwegian, I gained this distance or objectivity in the language. The gap released something in me, and in the writing, which made it possible for the protagonist to think thoughts I had never myself thought.

But it isn't only about language. There's a kind of objectivity in the form itself. It is not you; it is not even yours. When you use the form of a novel, and you say "I," you are also saying "I" for someone else. When you say "you," you are simultaneously in your room writing and in the outside world—you are seeing and being seen seeing, and this creates something slightly strange and foreign in the self. When you see that, or recognize that, you are in a different place, which is the place of the novel or the poem.

In *Min Kamp*, I wanted to see how far it was possible to take realism before it would be impossible to read. My first book had a strong story, strong narration. Then I would see how far I could take a digression out before I needed to go back to the narration, and I discovered I could go for thirty or forty pages, and then the digressions took over. So in *Min Kamp* I'm doing nothing but digressions, no story lines. Language itself takes care of it. The form gives something back.

Barron: Can you talk about how you remember the past when you're writing?

Knausgaard: Writing is recalling. In this matter I am a classic Proustian. You're playing football for the first time in twenty years, for example, doing all those movements again, and it makes the body remember not only the strangely familiar movements, but also everything connected to playing football, and for some seconds, a whole world is brought back to you. Where did it come from? I think that all our ages, all our experiences are kept in us. All we need is a reminder of something, and then something else is released.

When I started the novel, I imagined our house, myself walking towards it. It was snowing; it was dark; inside was my father and my mother, and I remembered the feeling of snow, and the smell of it, and the feelings I had toward my father at that time, and toward my mother, and there was the cat crossing the road, and on the other side of the river, the lights from a car. The silence in the woods. My friend, Jan Vidar, he was there somewhere, and the girl I was mad about, and the way I thought of him and her, and the light from the window kind of glowed, and I remembered an episode from the ski slope, and opened the door, and there, on the floor, the shoes from that time, the smell, the atmosphere.

My memory is basically visual, that's what I remember, rooms and landscapes. What I do not remember is what the people in these rooms were telling me. I never see letters or sentences when I write or read, but only the images they produce. The interesting thing is that the process of writing fiction is exactly the same for me. The only difference is that these landscapes are imaginary. These images are related to the way you think of a place you never have been, where you imagine everything, the houses, the mountains, the marketplaces. Then, the second you are there and see how the place really is, the weight of its reality crushes your imagined version. But where did that version come from in the first place?

Barron: Your father and Jan Vidar are characters in *Min Kamp*. Do you feel that a memoir or realistic essay has ethical obligations to its subjects?

Knausgaard: Yes.

Barron: What about writers more generally? Do you agree with Faulkner, who told this magazine that "'Ode on a Grecian Urn' is worth any number of old ladies"?

Knausgaard: A great Norwegian poet, Georg Johannesen, one of the leading intellectuals in the sixties and seventies, got a similar question once. If the house is burning, and you can only save one thing, what will you take with you, the Rembrandt or the cat? He would have taken the cat. I would do that too. Literature is about people, not books, as paintings are about people, not canvases or colors.

The notion of humanity can be dangerous and is easy to misunderstand because all works of art that we praise and think of as a part of humanity, the culture, the great collective, were created by individuals who had to fight for their individuality, to go against the very same culture.

You can't put the we, the "Ode on a Grecian Urn," before the self, the old lady. This was what the Nazis did, thinking that the best of the we made it reasonable to kill some individuals on their way. But then again, becoming independent and free, which is a premise for all art, means to go against the social, the we, and since it is in the social that morality is located, writing often is, and has to be, immoral. That's your different moral obligation, I guess.

Barron: Is there any point in thinking of *Min Kamp* as a kind of confession in the Augustinian sense, like a spiritual autobiography?

Knausgaard: There certainly is a longing in the book for that dimension. But it's never something I thought of stylistically.

Barron: So maybe I'm wrong about Augustine, but you've studied the Bible, right? You translated some of it. Your second novel concerns a pretty traditional theological question: Can the nature of the divine change? I can't help feeling that you have a deep relationship to religious writing, something beyond the typical modern longing for a "spiritual" dimension of life.

Knausgaard: This really is difficult to talk about, I have to say.

For two years, I worked as a kind of adviser on a team that translated the Bible to Norwegian. It was there I learned to read. The gap between the two languages was a shock and made it possible to experience, not only to recognize, the gap between language and the world. The arbitrariness everybody talked about in the eighties was all of a sudden visible for me.

Another lesson was that in the Old Testament, everything is concrete; nothing is abstract. God is concrete, the angels are concrete, and everything else has to do with bodies in motion, what they say, what they do, but never what they think. No speculations, no reflections. Even the metaphors are connected to bodies. I became especially interested in the story of Cain and Abel, when Cain's countenance falls, and God says, "Why is your countenance fallen? Lift up!" Cain doesn't look anyone in the eyes, and no one looks in his. This is to hide from the world and from the other. And that is dangerous.

In the sixth book of *Min Kamp*, I wrote four hundred pages on Adolf Hitler's *Mein Kampf*. Hitler was a man who lived a year without seeing anyone, just sitting in his room reading, and when he left that room, never let anyone close, and stayed that way, intransigent, through the rest of his life, and one characteristic thing with his book is that there is an "I," and a "we," but no "you." And while I was writing about Hitler, a young Norwegian who had stayed some two years all by himself and written a manifesto with a strong "I" and a "we," also without a "you," massacred sixty-nine youths on an island. In other words, his countenance fell.

The gap between the language and the world, the emphasis on the material aspects of the world, and Hitler writing *Mein Kampf* led me to Paul Celan, because the language he wrote in was destroyed by the Nazis. He couldn't write *blood*, which circulated in his veins, or *soil*, which he walked on. Suddenly neither word represented something general, which implicated a we, for the we in this language was not his we.

So his final poem about the Holocaust is a poem where every word seems to be created for the first time, all singular, for the we is lost, from an abyss, a nothingness, and in this, something other than history is visible, namely, the outside of language, which really is unthinkable, because thoughts are language, but it's still present, still there. It's the world, out of reach for us, and it is death.

Barron: What do you see as the difference between yourself and a writer like Celan?

Knausgaard: My book is very much about what experiences *are* and what they're *good for*, but it isn't one of those experiences in itself. It's a secondary thing. It's a secondary book, a book about experiences that doesn't produce those experiences, if you understand the difference. That's why I'm writing about Celan instead of trying to write like Celan. It really is second best. I know this, and not a thousand good reviews can make me forget. In the end, I want to write a book that is the thing itself. That is the ambition, of course.

Barron: Can you envision what that would be?

Knausgaard: No. That's impossible. I just have to start to write and hope that something will happen during the first thousand pages.

Barron: Mood is a big part of your work, the little shifts in how it feels to be yourself from one moment to the next. Feeling fine one minute, and the next thinking, What a pile of shit this was. Is that your experience of life, or is it just something the form gives back?

Knausgaard: It's a result of following situations very closely. But that doesn't mean there aren't existential consequences! In a novel, as in real life, moods and atmospheres, these small changes in the mind, are a part of thinking and reflection.

We have an idea that pure thought exists. It doesn't. In my world, all I see are hidden agendas, more often than not hidden even from ourselves. People know nothing of themselves, why they do the things they do. They think they know, but oh no, they don't. For example, Adorno defends reason in *The Jargon of Authenticity* and attacks the phenomenologists. This is only a few years after the war, and his arguments are full of rage, but he doesn't recognize it himself. Unreason, feelings—these belong to Heidegger and his followers. But Heidegger, for his part, did discuss mood and found it central to the way we relate to the world because we are always in a mood, like there is always weather.

Mood affects thinking. It makes it much more complex. And because I have over three thousand pages, I can use the essayistic digressions in a narrative sense. I have essays representing myself at twenty-five, which are really, really stupid and say a lot of things that are purely infantile and idiotic. Then, five years later, I'll have another essayistic part that relates to that but is a bit more sophisticated. Something has happened. There is a kind of narration in the essayistic things which you don't do as a straight essayist. As an essayist, you just write. You don't use yourself in that sense. You don't provide the stupid essay to show how age changes your thinking, for example.

I was in Germany—I was talking to my German editor—and we were talking about this because in the last book there is that long essay on Hitler, treating Hitler as a human being, and this is a very delicate and sensitive matter in Germany, of course. So what shall we do with it? Shall we have some historian read it and modify it, treat it as an essay? Or shall we just treat it as a madman from Norway writing whatever he thinks?

Barron: What did you decide?

Knausgaard: To keep it as it is.

Barron: Do you care what people think of you?

Knausgaard: I want to write how I really think things are, instead of how I think you should think I think things are. For me, saying how I really think things are turns everything into banality and stupid things, almost all the time, and that's the risk of the project for me. But then it's a realistic depiction of a man, forty, from Norway. If you read the book, you can see how these opinions—about Hitler, for example—came about. What produced them.

Barron: When you say "a realistic depiction of a man, forty, from Norway," are you comfortable with the narrative that goes, "Karl Knausgaard's book is the greatest account of our generation?" That's what the culture minister said of you.

Knausgaard: I am really embarrassed about it. I find it hard to deal with, really, so I've decided not to think about it, not to go there, not to read those things. I can't read about this project.

Barron: Are your children old enough to have read it or read about it?

Knausgaard: They aren't old enough to have read the books, but they have searched their own names on the Internet, and they come running into me, "Daddy, why are we on the Internet?" I say, "Because you're in this book," but I've never explained what it is. Very soon, I'm going to read something to them, to make it sort of undramatic.

Barron: Are you worried it will hurt them?

Knausgaard: Maybe they'll be troubled by it when they're teenagers. But I haven't only taken things away from them; there's something given to them as well. My life would certainly have looked different if I had gotten something like that from *my* father.

Barron: It seems very normal for your kids to be Googling themselves. Do you?

Knausgaard: It fucks my mind completely up if I go in there. The first two years, when I wrote it and published it at the same time, I avoided everything, because it was so intensely massive in Norway, I had to just avoid it. But now I see where something's written, so I just have a picture of where I'm coming up. Okay, that's from Australia, I'm being mentioned there, but I don't read it.

It's like following the stock market or something, going on Amazon and seeing where the books are. It's a technical, mechanical thing, but I can't go in and read even a very good review. I can't stand the thought of being this figure and having done this thing. And every time I talk about it or give interviews about it, it eats my soul, and it's getting worse and worse every time I go out there, and I have to stop. I'm going to stop. But it's such a temptation to do it because it's a confirmation of something, and something is happening, and all that, but it's really poison. I have to stop. I'm going to stop.

Barron: When we were emailing to get ready for this interview, you said you'd never used Skype before. Can I ask what you think of it?

Knausgaard: I really hate it, I have to say. I dislike the fact that we are letting go of our local places, in the sense of what surrounds us, not just restaurants or shops. What has happened in the last thirty or forty years, I deeply despise. The physical world is gone.

Barron: It reminds me of how you write about Lucretius, loving him for his awareness of the world's physical presence. It's interesting because your books address that problem theoretically, but at the same time their texture is very physical. You run your hands over every object—toast, bottles, cigarettes, tablecloths.

Knausgaard: That was something I was thinking about all the time during the writing. It's central to me. But as you said, it's a paradox. It's writing; it's not a real thing.

The sixth book really does end in Norway, with Anders Breivik killing sixty-nine children on Utøya Island. This happened while I was writing. And it really is this situation where he has these images of the world. And then he goes in there, and he kills those people. And that's a physical act. One of the things he said in court was, "It was so strange, shooting maybe seven teenagers; they were standing at the wall, and they were not moving. Why weren't they moving? I would expect them to be moving, trying to get away, but they were just standing there while I was shooting them." It didn't correspond to the images he had in his mind.

And the novel ends there, in that place, in that collision of the abstract heaven we have above us and our own physical earth. Which is what Breivik's killings were. This is the same thing that happened in the Nazi era, when Hitler imposed an abstract image upon the physical reality of the world. That's what interests me about daily life, when this happens.

Barron: While Breivik was shooting all of those people, he was listening on headphones to *The Lord of the Rings* soundtrack. He played *Call of Duty* obsessively. He inhabited virtual worlds.

Knausgaard: Breivik did play a lot of computer games. He played professionally for years. This is the interesting part of what happened, the boundaries between what's imaginary and what's real. It's totally blurred in him. That was the thing that makes it possible for him to kill. Because normally it's impossible to kill, or at least impossible to kill more than one or two.

If you're in the US Marines, you're trained in this dehumanizing process. You're trained as a professional, and you do it with your friends, you do it for them, and even *then* it's difficult. But Breivik did it all by himself, so it shouldn't be possible, but it is possible, and that's one of the things I reflect upon in the last book.

Barron: Marines, Nazis—these things seem so much larger and more ideological than the small, everyday events in Books One and Two.

Knausgaard: My book is completely anti-ideology, in all senses. It is about the opposite of ideology. It's about the little and the small, where in life we are. But it ends with the collision of that world with ideology, which is why I wrote about Nazism and those kinds of things. That's why it ends there.

Barron: Did you ever play video games?

Knausgaard: Yes. This was in 1992, '93. I played *Doom* and those kinds of games, where you just shoot people. I could play twenty-four hours, no problem. I was completely addicted.

Barron: Do you still smoke?

Knausgaard: Yeah, I do.

Barron: Because you're addicted, or do you enjoy it?

Knausgaard: I do enjoy it, unfortunately. There is a writer in Sweden called Stig Larsson, not the crime writer but another one, a modernist, a fantastic writer, and he was a drug addict for the last twenty or thirty years, and he had a heart attack, so he had to stop. It was speed he took. But he said, "If smoking helps me, it's my duty as a writer to smoke. And if speed helps me, it's my duty as a writer to take speed." In a way it's true. But I have to stop it one day—I mean, I have kids.

Barron: What about alcohol?

Knausgaard: I'm so restricted as a person, and not very good socially, so drinking is a kind of a freedom for me. But the consequences are big for me. I can't stop. I get extremely drunk.

We had some friends over three weeks ago, and I was the only one who drank, and I get so extreme I can't remember anything, really. This was a disaster, you know, a dinner party and the host is the only one who's drunk! One half bottle of spirits. I was just—I can't stop. I don't fall over; I don't go to sleep; I can just drink and drink and drink and drink; and you can't really see it on me, but inside I am just totally messed and fucked up. And as I have kids, I have to have a certain kind of dignity in my behavior, and that's not what I do when I'm drunk. So I try to be very careful, that's what I'm saying.

Barron: Can I ask how the novel has affected your marriage? It's so extreme, what you've done. It's like you invented a new kind of marriage, where half the couple is transparent and has no secrets.

Knausgaard: I didn't think of that when I was doing it. I didn't think of the implication at all, in that sense. I was so frustrated that I didn't foresee the consequences. I thought, If the consequences are that she's leaving me, then okay, she can go. That was how it was. There was a certain desperation that made it possible. I couldn't do it now.

But still, there is much more to a relationship than what you can say. You just take one more step back into yourself. I've never understood psychoanalysis. Mentioning things doesn't change anything, doesn't help anything, it's just words. There is something much more deep and profound to a relationship than that. Revealing stories and quarrels—that's just words. Love, that's something else.

Barron: Did the writing of *Min Kamp* give you what you were hoping for?

Knausgaard: I can't speak for other writers, but I write to create something that is better than myself, I think that's the deepest motivation, and it is so because I'm full of self-loathing and shame. Writing doesn't make me a better person, nor a wiser and happier one, but the writing, the text, the novel, is a creation of something outside of the self, an object, kind of neutralized by the objectivity of literature and form. The temper, the voice, the style. All in it is carefully constructed and controlled. This is writing for me—a cold hand on a warm forehead.

Karl Ove Knausgaard in Conversation with Stephen Grosz

Stephen Grosz / 2014

stephengrosz.com, May 21, 2014, https://www.stephengrosz.com/2017/02/in-conversation-with-karl-ove-knausgaard/. Reprinted by permission of Stephen Grosz.

Stephen Grosz: It's a great pleasure to be here this evening. *My Struggle* is a long and complex project, and I thought the first thing I wanted to talk about was fathers. Because I thought there's so much in the first three volumes that we have in English, and there's so much in that which is poignant to me in the first volume, the death of your father. And in the second volume, you becoming a father yourself and the ideas of masculinity and growing up. In the most recent volume, I think one of the things which moved me the most, I mean, there's so much about fatherhood, but I thought one of the most heartbreaking and moving things in the first volume was your reaching out to your father at various points, and his refusal of intimacy. [. . .] not coming to football games or shaming you, teasing you at times and talking about the divorce. And it's also, I think, related to his drinking and the drinking that happens. And there's someone I know, an alcoholic, once said that the opposite of alcohol isn't abstinence, it's intimacy. And I felt that what was so painful and poignant, what you write about so incredibly well, is that movement in the family, being a boy, trying to be in touch with his father, and the father not accepting that. And I wondered to what extent the writing itself was trying to work through how to be intimate with your own children, how to be different from your father, to what degree the writing was a process of change for you?

Karl Ove Knausgaard: These things—I never thought about these things when I wrote it. I mean, I never thought about my father, that he had a problem with intimacy. It wasn't like that. I just tried to, you know, to capture who he was. And I never thought of the writing process as an aim to something else, but the writing in itself. But for me, I have a problem with intimacy myself in my own life. But not when I write. I mean, there is something I gain from writing, which has to do with intimacy in my life, which I think is the most important thing in this project for me. It would be impossible for me to reach out to anyone and talk about my life and talk about my problems or in person—that would be impossible—but there is something with literature that makes it possible because it is an intimate situation. It's only the reader and the writer, and it's like . . . you could be free, without restriction in literature in a totally different way than you can in your social life, you know, and that's the opposition for me, the restriction in the social life, restriction in the family, and the freedom in literature, that's kind of the—*there's* where the energy comes from, you know? Right where it opens up.

But to answer your question about . . . I guess I'm . . . One of the things that makes it possible for me to see my own father and to write about him was the fact that there I was, a father myself—that changed very much in me because all of a sudden, I could identify with him. Because being a father is a kind of an unmovable, iconic position in a family, at least it was in my family, you know? And I think I didn't think that my father was human even. I mean, I didn't think he had feelings. I didn't think he was longing for something. He was just my father. And then I became a father myself, and then I started to long [to be] out of the family: "I didn't want this, I want somewhere else." And then I could, when I started to write about him, to connect with him, and understand: Okay, *this* was how he felt. He was like me, but with a twist. But it was like me in a way.

Grosz: It's really interesting what you're saying because I had a question as you were speaking. I thought, "So the energy for writing came from *becoming* a father, not—I thought at first—because of the death of your [father]." Though sometimes a death propels us to try and resolve something, but it's more the becoming the father yourself?

Knausgaard: Yeah. And death is death. I mean, death doesn't produce anything. And the first thing I wanted to do was to describe my father's death because it was so intense for me. And it was kind of the story of my life. And I wanted to get a grip of him, just out of personal reasons. And I knew this is also material for a novel, right? If I can, you know, get a grip on this—but death is abstract. It's a huge concept. It's impossible to—it was very difficult for me to write about. *How do you write about it?* And the solution was to write about the opposite—about really the finality of being sixteen. Nothing is going on. But this still is full of life, but it's no story, nothing big, nothing important going on. So the novel starts there, a hundred pages of that. And *then* I could write about my father's death.

Grosz: Right.

Knausgaard: And see through that finality in a way, and not in a conceptual way at all because that was the frightening thing when my father died, and I see him dead—that's death. It isn't a concept. It's very biological and physical and very, very strange to understand.

Grosz: Another thing which came as I read the book and which I'm thinking about now, as you're speaking, is there's a passage in Freud where he says something like that—each of us needs to make a friend of the necessity of our own dying. In other words, that we have to tame our dying and accept it in some way. And I thought that the project—another thing about it—was you coming to terms with one day, of course, that you and I will both be like your father is at the end of Volume One.

Knausgaard: Yeah.

Grosz: We're going to both die. And so that the project too is about accepting that and about seeing life, but also accepting that truth, so one can live well.

Knausgaard: Yeah, but I think one scary thing for my life when I was starting this project was that I—not actively—but I had a kind of a death wish, you know? There was always a solution, always a way out; there was always in there that kind of solution. And I think the same thing was with my father. I think he started to drink when he was forty, and I think in the end he wanted to die, so it was kind of a slow suicide, and that is *extremely* shameful and difficult, if you have kids, and you have everything, and still you feel like that. And that's the starting point for this book. I wondered, "How did I get there, to this point in my life? How, why, why is the world, you know, *gray*? Why isn't—I'm not happy. And why is there no meaning in my life?" So this book is a way to try to find meaning in this life, in a way. And the only way I can find it is through writing and through art, and *that* helps seeing life. So I'm very distanced to life, and I can only see it when I write about it . . . People think since there's much detail in my book that I'm very observant and very present, *but I'm not!* I don't see anything at all, but when I write about it, then it comes to me, you know? So I'm present at a distance.

Grosz: Right.

Knausgaard: I think that's a way of me to live. I think it's a very good thing—reading, writing, art in general. This book is also about that.

Grosz: Actually, with what you said, I'm going to look at something in the book because I think that's right. One of those moments where I felt—

because there is all that detail and the living through the detail. But one of the moments that really struck me—I found very difficult as a reader—are the pages just in the first volume when your father tells you that he and your mother are going to divorce. And, I mean, I can read it, it's very short, and we can look at it together, but it's *so brief* at the very moment one expects *lots*.

Knausgaard: Yeah.

Grosz: It is the tiniest exchange in the whole book. It's so brief, and it has—he basically says, "*We're going to divorce*," and you say, "Okay."[1] Then there's this other thing which happens, which is you cry, but you believe that they're tears of happiness, and then a little bit later on, your mother and you discuss it too. And again, it's very brief, and I felt—I was so curious, just the *reading* of that. What was going on as a writer? Were you—are those moments you can't write full because they're painful or are they moments . . . ? What is it that you want the reader to think or feel because so many other things are given full? I felt at those moments you sort of . . . and it almost felt, *this is not digestible*. I can't—*this is what happened*.

Knausgaard: Mm-hmm. I don't think I, you know, planned an impression when I wrote it. And I don't really know why I did it like that, but I think it has to do with what's the major thing there is—communication between the family members and something traumatic is going on. There is no communication there—no one is talking about these things, and that's—I don't know if that's Norwegian or Protestant or what it is, or it's only our family, but that's what I wanted to capture there. And I've been thinking about that since you started with intimacy. And my mother and my father, they never said that they loved us, *never*. And even now they don't do it. And I don't do that to my kids either, because in a way I think, "We don't talk about these things." It's kind of, it's like, if you *say* it, it has no value. It has to be, you know, be shown in a way.

Grosz: Right.

Knausgaard: But from the outside that could be seen as something almost emotionally retarded in a way, *but it isn't*. And I think that section with my father telling about my mother, there was a kind of understanding between us in a way, and I felt it as a kind of a . . . He was talking to me about something important. And that was good, you know?

Grosz: Yes.

Knausgaard: There is another thing you could say about narration in that—about that—because, if you know the Bible, the most important episodes in the Bible are four lines, eight lines, and Cain and Abel is, I think, it's eight lines. And in your mind, these stories are huge and impressive, but then if there are minor things going on in the Bible, then it's just—it's words, words, words, words. All the important things are extremely concentrated. And very *potent*—it's the word in English?

Grosz: Yeah.

Knausgaard: Powerful. And I taught creative writing, and that kind of minimalism was the *best* thing you could do. I mean, that was the best prose. The Hemingway technique: Show it, don't tell it. . . . And I never do that. [*Audience laughs*] I tried to do that for ten years, and I realized, if you do the opposite, if you just put things in and see what happens . . . that's good. Even if it's bad, what you put in it, it became more complicated, and things start to happen that you don't control. And that control thing is very important. It's very important *not* to have control when you are writing.

Grosz: Right. That's interesting, because when I read the interviews with you and the descriptions, I always feel they're slightly . . . How can I put it? They're a very romantic notion of the writer, that you have this great burst of image, but that it's just unedited, pure. How true are these descriptions of twenty pages a day, fifty pages when you meet Linda, when you wanted to get it in a twenty-four-hour period? How true are these descriptions?

Knausgaard: That's true!

Grosz: It is.

Knausgaard: *Yes.* But the thing is, I realized it's very, very easy to write a novel. You could write a novel in eight weeks. It's not a problem. It's easy. [*Loud laughter from audience and from Grosz*] It is: *just to do it.* Yes. But to get there, where it's easy, that's five or six or seven years with struggle with the text, you know?

Grosz: Right.

Knausgaard: And then all of a sudden, you can do it. *That's* my experience of writing. And I try to find those places.

Grosz: But there are some parts which you must revise—the beginnings in some of these essays are so elegiac and elegant and beautiful, the last pages of the first volume or the first pages.

Knausgaard: No, the opening I used very, very much—spent a lot of time writing and I think two months or something—just the opening. But then it's all speed.

Grosz: What is the energy behind that—the drive?

Knausgaard: It is a kind of discovery I had when I was twenty-six or twenty-seven. That I was writing—and I couldn't—what I was writing, I couldn't have planned it. I couldn't have thought it out. It was just happening there. And I couldn't recognize it as mine. It was something different, and that was kind—that was a very—that was a *fantastic moment* in my writing, really fantastic. And then I knew, okay, this is possible. You don't have to think. I mean, you don't have to use your intellect at all. You can just, you could just write it, there is something else taking over, and that something else is not—I mean, it's not inspiration or something divine, it is a reading experience; it is a writing experience. It's like, I mean, all those kinds of processes are based upon *handicraft*—is that the word you have? To be experienced? I mean, a football player, if he starts to think, should I kick the ball left or right, then he's, you know, he's out of the game. You just have to do it. And a second discovery I had at that time was that what I experienced then was a kind of a selflessness. There's a moment where you are not present, you are present, but you have no notion of yourself, which also is a *reading* experience, I think. So the connection there is—

Grosz: That's interesting.

Knausgaard: —is what I try to reach when I write. I *don't* think of what I'm going to write about or anything like that. I just write, and then something happens, and if it's not happening, then I just throw it away.

Grosz: It's interesting because those moments, like that moment I mentioned about where your father tells you about the divorce—I feel writing always takes place retrospectively. It's always about something that *has happened*. So there's always that gap, and I felt that those moments, it's writing so smoothly, you're so in the—I almost felt like it was a diary at that moment, you're so in that moment, but there are things which I didn't understand. Like, do you then think, when you say it's "tears of happiness," do you believe that *now* as looking back or do you think—because the effect on the reader to me was, "That's what a sixteen-year-old boy feels."

Knausgaard: Yeah.

Grosz: He is crying—*obviously* he's crying because his parents are getting divorced—but he *thinks* it's because he's in love and this girl that he's met. But he's confused. But in the text, you're put into that confusion. I don't know if I'm being clear.

Knausgaard: Yeah, but I understand what you [mean]. I think when I wrote it, I was very much the sixteen-year-old boy believing he was [*laughs*] absolutely in love. But of course at the same time I knew then that the other thing was . . . because the intensity in the feelings are similar in a way, *connected*. But I never sorted it out when it happened and not when I wrote it.

Grosz: Right.

Knausgaard: I mean, it's like for me, the first book is about my father's death, and the second book is about me falling in love and my children, but it's the same time, same kind of intensity, same kind of meaningfulness, the same kind of concentration in death as in falling in love. It's very similar things, and in my life, these things have always come together, I feel. . . . I have never got the chance to sort anything out. It's just a mess. And I don't see the books as a tool to sort things out, but I see them as a way to explore and expand maybe and try to reach for the complexity, which isn't verbal and isn't in the reflection, but they are someplace else.

Grosz: And it does that. I mean, that's part of what makes the book so fantastic is that you—the feeling of being in a family, in the *feeling* of what it's like, and the tensions and the desires that aren't being met and the rebukes and the shaming, but it's also just present, and the kind of, almost like a tide coming and going within the family. I wanted to ask about—in almost every interview that I've read talks about your guilt about the project.

Knausgaard: Yeah.

Grosz: About feeling bad, about having written about real people.

Knausgaard: Yeah.

Grosz: And, again, this may be the thing you were saying—Protestant or Norwegian. Because I was just very curious about that because, I mean, there was something in the paper today, and you said at one point in one interview that it felt like killing someone and then afterwards saying you're sorry or that you've done a terrible thing and that you apologize. And I jotted down here in a public statement, your uncle—these things people said—"Put yourself in our position!" I thought it was—imagine how you would react for fourteen family members saying, "You know, you shouldn't have done this." And you saying that you were frightened of their reaction, and you felt it was dangerous. Can you say something about all that, about what you feel? Because frankly, if you were a friend of mine, and we were here, I would say to you, "It's your life. If you want to write about it, you should write about it. And if somebody thinks they're not being seen and written about in a nice way, they should have been nicer." [*Audience laughs*] And if someone doesn't feel like—want to be portrayed as an alcoholic, they should have drunk less. [*Laughter*] And when your uncle says these things, I feel maybe *he's guilty*. Maybe he should have done more for your father or your grandmother, these relatives, you know. It's *your* life. And, you know, you should write about it.

Knausgaard: Yeah [*shyly*]. I wish you were around at that time. [*Grosz and the audience laugh*]

Grosz: What are you frightened of? I mean, really? Because I feel it's a fantastic accomplishment. It's a great achievement. And it's something you should be very proud of, what you've achieved, and it feels sort of being attacked by, in that way, by guilt and shame.

Knausgaard: Yeah. I knew this wasn't—when I started out—that this was maybe in a way more or less suspect, but I didn't really care about it because I didn't think that I would publish it. And I thought, okay, my family, they won't like it, but it—I never expected anything. And then I sent it to them, and the reaction was "lawsuit and we're going to—". . . . Then they tried actively to stop the book. And that was the worst thing I've experienced my whole life.

Grosz: Right.

Knausgaard: That period, it was really like hell, and there are so many aspects there. One thing is that I was—you are a psychoanalyst, so maybe this is the place for me to talk about these things. [*Audience laughter*] But I was afraid of my father, and—he was, you know, I couldn't almost do anything without him being very angry at me, and he controlled me in a way, and then he died, and then my uncle was in his place.

Grosz: Right.

Knausgaard: Very much so. So when my uncle says something, I'm afraid, I mean, really, really afraid. And then there is a kind of a cultural heritage for me, which has to do with shame. And I'm extremely shame-ridden. I mean, crossing one little border is like hell for me. I remember when I got the driving license. I got that when I was thirty-eight. And when I was out driving, it was like, afterwards, I had a massive hangover two or three days. I was: "What have I done? I shouldn't have done it." And it's like that. So this thing was the worst thing imaginable for me to do, to hurt so many people and to write about them. It was the worst thing I could do. And *then* they get public with it, and I really . . . But I had someone saying the things that you said, "*This is your life. This is your story. Why don't you take it a bit more easy on it?*" But it isn't easy.

Grosz: I think it's a complicated thing because I do think writing has aggression in it. When we write, there is some aggression. We are taking stories—and I know this from case history—we're making them ours.

Knausgaard: Yeah.

Grosz: Your father isn't now "our" father—your brother's and yours. He's *my* father. He's just your—and you're putting into stone a story: It will be *the* story. And there *is* aggression in that. I know as an analyst, sometimes even making an interpretation, just one thing to a patient, they're telling you something and you're shaping it, and you have to be careful because you feel a responsibility. But it felt that there was something in this that you need to be seen as, you know, as a good guy and as a good person—that you wouldn't do something harmful, but it's *not* harmful to write something which you believe is true. It's not—I mean, it may upset somebody, it may bother them, but . . .

Knausgaard: Yeah, I know—I mean in principle—that you are right. But in practical life, it's not like that. [*Audience laughter*]

Grosz: The other thing which I thought about it was, which—I don't notice it—but the success that you've had that you've written this. And there can be guilt from being, in a way, a celebrity, of becoming famous and becoming well known for this work too. And I've certainly seen it and can empathize with sort of spoiling something or almost saying I'm preventing an attack by saying, "Look, I'm already a wreck. This is . . . I'm so awful having published this book, leave me alone. I mean, I can't take anymore. I don't want any more criticism." But as a way of trying to—almost feeling guilty—about achieving so much and having had such a fantastic success. I think, *well-deserved too.*

Knausgaard: No, that's something I can't handle at all. I don't. I try just to—I don't think of it. I do not read anything that's written about me and I moved to the countryside. Nobody reads there. And I think that's . . . I actually wrote a piece about this, an essay about becoming famous and fame, recently, where I've been thinking about these things.

Grosz: What did you write? Because I'm very curious.

Knausgaard: It's going to be published this summer in a newspaper.

Grosz: What are the ideas in it? What did you think about it or feel?

Knausgaard: There is one cultural thing, which is in Scandinavia, it's like you're not supposed to think you are better than anyone else. You're not supposed to think that you are any good. These are the laws about how you're not supposed to think you are worth anything. And I grew up under that. You couldn't have a hat or do anything different before you were mocked seriously, and you could never show ambition. Because then you thought you were someone, you know? That's the dark side of this. The good side of this is solidarity. It's *we*, it's you *are* one of us, stay to us, stick to us. And all those things have changed in Scandinavia, but it still is a sense of being famous is not good. Being a celebrity is not good, and being and joining that kind of life is not good. So all the celebrities in Norway are very keen on saying, "Look, I'm just like you. I have this little car and I'm ordinary, right?" So everybody is ordinary. Even the king, the most famous picture of the king was he on the tram paying the conductor. That's the iconic picture of him. So that's the culture. But of course, almost everybody who does things like this, writing music, a lot of them have a kind of a quite big element of self-loathing, and so if self-loathing is the motor, then fame is the gas you defuel.

Knausgaard: I remember I read an article in the *New Yorker* about Bruce Springsteen, and he talked about the self-loathing. And you can never have enough. You want people to say "I love you," but all people will not want to say "I love you." And it could never—that thirst could never be fulfilled.

Grosz: I think one of the things that you're talking about, and I know the Bruce Springsteen article, one of the things I thought when I read that was there can't be—again, going back to the first thing of intimacy—

Knausgaard: Yeah.

Grosz: Intimacy requires equality. And once someone becomes a celebrity, that funny thing of how all celebrities hang out together because they can get on, they know the risks and the temptations, and they can have a relation, but there's something odd that happens about—I thought what he was saying was that he has gone into a world of no intimacy because there are very few people that he feels equal to, you know, in terms of where he is. It's interesting. I think the going about the thing of writing—the other thing which I wanted to ask about was in this thing about privacy and writing, is that: Was there anything you felt you *couldn't* write about in the book—that *shouldn't* be written about? Because it feels so free at times. But did you stop yourself at points? Because also you said—I remember reading that you'd written some, and then the stuff came with your family—and did that stop you inside or inhibit you or—

Knausgaard: No, but there is one thing I do not write—I write very little about—and that's sex.

Grosz: Right.

Knausgaard: And this is, should be, you know, the full life of a person, but it isn't. I couldn't—I couldn't write about it. [*Audience laughter*] But there is Book Four. It is about sex, but that's, you know, that's about being sixteen, seventeen, eighteen. Yes. And that's all about shortcomings and very embarrassing things, but it has no consequences for others. But I couldn't—I couldn't write about those kinds of things because it will hurt. I mean, it will give away so much a part of—

Grosz: It's—what you write is acceptable, I think, because the way you write, you're harshest on yourself.

Knausgaard: Yeah.

Grosz: So what you write is acceptable. A writer that wrote harshly about other people—you're toughest, I often feel, on yourself in the books.

Knausgaard: Yeah, I think that was kind of a threshold in the beginning. That was very difficult to overcome over. But when I did, I realized *this isn't dangerous*. There is one thing in Book Four that I never told to no one person at all. I never told it because it was so shameful, and it has to do with sexual shortcomings. And it really is extremely embarrassing. [*Audience laughter*]

Grosz: Right.

Knausgaard: And I thought, what can I do? Can I write this? And I tried. And then I read it to my friend on the phone. And I didn't tell him something was coming, and I read it, and he was just, you know, laughing [*Grosz bursts into laughter*], and it wasn't dangerous. And I think that's my experience with all these. You could just write it. Who could it hurt? I mean, what's dangerous? I don't know.

Grosz: I think we're getting near time for questions. I think it would be wrong not to ask the thing about the ending of the book, about the last sentence, and this idea of where the six volumes end with this: "I'm happy because I'm no longer an author."

Knausgaard: Mm.

Grosz: And I want to ask you if you are writing, and it seemed unbelievable to me—one, the idea that you could say that because it feels that the writing is so important to you. And are you writing now? Are you working on something? I mean, you've written this essay on fame. But are you writing?

Knausgaard: I'm writing a lot of essays. That's what I'm doing. But that's just, you know, to keep it going in a way—that's not what I want to do. I really want to do something. I want to be there again where you lose yourself and where you—I want just to be there. So I'm going to write, but it takes a long time—it takes five years to get there, I guess. . . . And then it's eight weeks.

Note

1. In the Don Bartlett translation, Farrar, Straus and Giroux paperback edition, see p. 166.

In Search of Karl Ove Knausgaard

Jared Levy / 2015

Interview Magazine, April 29, 2015, https://www.interviewmagazine.com/culture/karl-ove-knausgaard. Reprinted by permission of Jared Levy.

It is a struggle to start Norwegian writer Karl Ove Knausgaard's six-volume autobiographical novel, *My Struggle* (*Min Kamp*). The length is one deterrent, but there is the added challenge of dedicating so much reading time to the author as subject. Then there is the title, a direct reference to Hitler's *Mein Kampf.*

Yesterday, the English translation of *My Struggle: Book Four* came out via Archipelago Books. We spoke with Knausgaard over the phone about the challenges of the writing life, his book on soccer, and ignoring Bob Dylan's lyrics.

Jared Levy: What's the experience of your day today?

Karl Ove Knausgaard: It's been a good day. My daughter's participating in a musical. I drove her to rehearsal. It was such an extremely beautiful day, with sunshine, spring, and green everywhere. I'm filled with life today.

I'm also working on a project at the moment where I'm writing one text each day. I'm supposed to do that through the year, so I have 365 texts in the end. Today I wrote two texts, which is a routine. I get up at 5 a.m. or 4:30 a.m., and I write one or two texts before the kids are awake. That's a very good thing, just to start the day with. It's only one page, and I choose a word to write about.

Levy: Each day you wake up, and you write about one word?

Knausgaard: Yes, that's right. I was asked by the *New Republic* to write four hundred words in each magazine for a year about something kind of funny that ends the magazine. I started that, and the editor quit and everything changed, but I just kept continuing writing those texts. Then we decided to publish four books. The first book is going to be published in

September and then one in November, one in February, and one in May, I think.

Today I wrote about plastic bags, which was [...] very good [...] to write about. And frames. I try to write about small, insignificant things. I try to find out if it's possible to say anything about them. And I almost always do if I sit down and write about something. There is something in that thing that I can write about. It's very much like a rehearsal. An exercise, in a way.

Levy: How do these assignments, the one you mentioned for the *New Republic* and your recent essay about the Viking origins of the Americas in the *New York Times Magazine*, impact your writing life?

Knausgaard: When I started to write *My Struggle* everything changed: my way of writing changed; the speed of my writing changed; and what I was writing about changed. What I've been doing ever since is continuing the same kind of writing. When I did the *New York Times* piece, I wrote seventy pages. They asked me to write ten. I couldn't write it in ten, so I just wrote and wrote. It's the same as the writing in *My Struggle*. It could have gone straight into one of the volumes. It's a kind of repetition. It's the same subject meeting new situations with the same tone, the same way of doing something a little essayistic, some description, and some failure. It's a form of myself. It's interesting to write something outside of the novel form.

This summer I did a football book with a friend. We wrote about the World Cup in Brazil. We exchanged letters through the summer, and we published it. It's five hundred pages. It's about football, but it's also about everything else. In one way it's a repetition of *My Struggle*, but in another sense, it's freedom. Just to sit down and write. I could never have done anything like that five or six years ago. That was completely impossible. Then, writing for me was something, not something sacred, but something you have. I couldn't just sit down and write something. I had to work hard to make it into literature. Now, it's much easier, but that works both ways. There's a risk that it can become voiceless in the end.

Those pieces aren't different for me. They're the same. The writing and the thinking are still the same as they were in *My Struggle*. The only difference is that they are outside the form of the novel.

Levy: Those describing *My Struggle* often talk about the novel's length, but it seems to me that it could be much longer. How do you reduce the plentitude of moments in a composition about your life to a finite expression in six volumes?

Knausgaard: That's a difficult question. I never thought about my life when I was writing *My Struggle*. In a way, of course I was, but I was always thinking about the novel. What I realized, when I was writing this football book in the summer, is that that part of my life was completely absent in the childhood book, for instance. It was not there. I got questioned why, and I think it's because there are some premises that are made in the beginning of the novel that you follow. It's not like I tried to make anything complete in any way. I just want to tell that single story. It's got its own logic from the very beginning, from the first sentence. I never know where I'm going in the novel, and that's the only thing that can make it exciting enough to write about your own life.

Levy: The novelistic sense constrains you, in a way, to tell a story that is finite within a life that continues. I'm sure there are ways in which you think about what you've written that change and seem subject to revision.

Knausgaard: Yeah. And I could easily imagine another novel set in the same time period of my life, which would be completely different.

Levy: Something that jumped out to me in Volume Four, given my background and interests, is your relationship with music. In Volume Four, you wrote, "All I needed to know, all true knowledge, the only really essential knowledge, was to be found in the books I read and the music I listened to." You're writing there about your adolescent perspective, though I imagine, just as I feel, that there is truth that the only things worth knowing are in music and written in books. This relates to the anecdote of you listening to Dungen in the first volume. I love Dungen, but I have no idea what they're singing about because I don't understand Swedish. Is there anything on the lyrical level that speaks to you about Dungen's music?

Knausgaard: No, I actually seldom listen to lyrics when I'm listening to music. That's very secondary to me when I'm listening to music. No, I just loved Dungen when I was writing that book. I don't listen to them that much anymore, but I saw them live once a long time ago. They're a brilliant band. But I don't even listen to Bob Dylan's lyrics . . .

Levy: What other kind of reflections do you have on music's relationship to writing?

Knausgaard: I think there are a lot of similarities between writing and music. Music is much more direct and much more emotional, and that's the level I want to be at when I'm writing. Writing is much more intellectual and indirect and abstract, in a way. I'm not interested in those aspects of literature. I'm not interested in the words or the meaning of the words. I'm interested in disappearing in it completely, to not be aware of yourself at all. That's the way music works for me. It's purely emotional. It goes straight to the heart. There are no explanations. That's just it.

I have a desire for that in writing as well. There's a certain sense of rhythm in that. If you are disappearing from yourself, but you're still writing, then there is a kind of activity of thinking going on, which in my world is similar to what's going on in music. You don't think when you play music; you just try to play and be in it. It is the same for me when the writing is going really well. It's the same kind of feeling. I'm just in it. It's not the words; it's not the sentences; I'm not aware of it. Then it's good.

Levy: How do you go from the original sentiment, the original kind of "in it" in your native language, to having a work put out in the world in a different language, one that you speak and speak very well, but that is distant from the original being "in it?"

Knausgaard: I never read the translation before publication. I was contacted about it in the beginning, and I said I don't want to read it. I wanted Don Bartlett to be completely free in his translation. The most important thing for me is that the emotion is captured in such a way that the feelings that are in the original are there, much more than the details, if they are right or wrong. And it feels like that. When I'm reading aloud, it's like it is the same. That for me is a sign of a brilliant translation.

I've had parts translated of other things that I'm writing by other translators, which have been a completely different experience, which I can instantly say, "This is wrong." It isn't like the words are wrong, it's just the sense of it, it doesn't evoke the same things; it doesn't have the same tone, doesn't have the same voice, and that's pretty much in the details, I think. I think Bartlett has done a brilliant job. Those books had to be written very quickly and very fast, and I hope the translation should have the same kind of flow, where you're not afraid of mistakes, not afraid of banalities or things that are inadequate.

Levy: Is that difficult for you when you come in contact with your work translated in such a way that it doesn't feel in the spirit of what you have done?

Knausgaard: I think I've learned, because there have been many translations in many different languages, that the best I can do is have it how I want it in one place and that is in Norwegian. If it's like that there, then it is okay. That's the best I can hope for.

Levy: In closing, what is necessary for a healthy and successful writing life?

Knausgaard: For me, personally, it is very important that the days are exactly the same, so I have routines. I do the same thing every day. The strange thing about writing is that it's so easy to write a novel. It is really easy. But it's getting there to the point where it's easy that's hard. The hard part is to get there.

I had a little bit of success with my first novel. That kind of fucked up my sense of who I was as a writer. I started to try to fulfill other people's expectations and direct myself toward an image of myself, which made it impossible to write anything at all. I am in the same kind of a process now where I have to have a clean sheet to be able to write. And to do that you have to be able to do something where you risk yourself completely. There has to be a risk involved. The prospect of failing must be real. There needs to be something where the risk of failing is acute, in a way. It has to be for real. You can't pretend.

"Opening a World": An Interview with Karl Ove Knausgaard

Steve Paulson / 2015

To the Best of Our Knowledge and *Electric Literature*, May 28, 2015, http://electricliterature.com/opening-a-world-an-interview-with-karl-ove-knausgaard/. Reprinted by permission of Steve Paulson.

You might think international celebrity would help conquer his demons, but Karl Ove Knausgaard says he's still "full of self-loathing." This conversation—which aired on Public Radio International's *To the Best of Our Knowledge*—tackled the humiliations of youth, finding suspense in the everyday, imperfect memories, and Knausgaard's plans for his new project.

Steve Paulson: This book begins when you are eighteen, just out of high school and headed for your first job. You drink too much, and you're obsessed with losing your virginity. In some ways, the life you're describing isn't that unusual, but you seem to be full of angst. Did you feel tormented back then?

Karl Ove Knausgaard: Yeah, I think so, but I wasn't aware of many aspects of this because you are not that aware of yourself when you are eighteen. You're full of yourself, but you're not aware of yourself. So this book is basically about the conflict between the eighteen-year-old young man being full of himself, full of ambition, full of desire, full of longings and wanting, and the outer world and all the people he meets. He has no idea at all of who he is.

Paulson: Your project is so interesting because you are now extremely self-conscious, and yet you're trying to get inside the head of what you were like when you were eighteen.

Knausgaard: Yeah, that's really the interesting part of it. When I was writing, it felt like I was very close to that age. That age was the part of my life that I'm closest to, so it was really easy to write about. You know, in a way, I haven't improved much since I was eighteen. Of course, I have in other ways, but the core is the same as when I was eighteen.

Paulson: What are those core areas where you haven't changed?

Knausgaard: That has to do with emotions, feelings, desires, everything that you don't verbalize, everything that drives you. I've spent my life trying to understand those forces, not because I'm that interested in myself, but because I'm a writer and I'm interested in identity, and those forces are so powerful. And it's so raw when you are eighteen. We get much better at hiding it when we're in our forties or fifties.

Paulson: Was it still raw for you to go back and relive those adolescent years?

Knausgaard: Yeah, especially the relations that I had at that time, that I didn't see as clearly as I do now—for instance, my relationship to my father, which is a big part of this book.

Paulson: Which was very troubled. He was a difficult father. He drank too much and sometimes beat you.

Knausgaard: When I was growing up, he didn't drink, and he had kind of a normal life, but he was unpredictable, and that's always a problem for a child. But then when I was sixteen, he started to drink, and he left the family. He became an alcoholic and disappeared from my life. He got a new family and a new child, but something was still very wrong in his life. I saw some of that then, but I didn't see it all. You know, when you're that age, there is a very one-sided relationship with your parents, and you try to get away from them. You try to make your own life, and that also makes this period interesting to write about.

Paulson: Was it painful to remember the difficulty with your father, not to mention all the embarrassing episodes from your adolescence?

Knausgaard: The embarrassing episodes were a pleasure to write. It was just fun.

Paulson: Were you nostalgic for that period of your life?

Knausgaard: No, not at all. There is one bit in there, though, that's about my sexual shortcomings, and I have never said that to anyone in my life. I still don't talk about it to anyone, but I wrote it down. It's in the book, and when I think about how much I'm giving away, that's kind of hard. When I wrote it, I read it to a friend, and that was a terrible moment. He was the first person I was telling this to, but he just laughed. You know, he laughed and laughed, and that made it easier because it is funny. I think the recognition about sexuality when you are that age and the insecurity you have . . . you don't know, really. There's no manual.

Paulson: You also talk about how not much happens in life. You write, "How did we manage to be so patient? Because nothing ever happened! It's always the same, day in and day out." You go on to say, "The waiting—that was life." I remember feeling that way.

Knausgaard: Yeah. There is a strange element of hope. You think something will happen, and it could happen at any moment. I saw that when I wrote the first book in the series. When I am sixteen and going to a party, I have to hide beer in the snow. It takes a hundred pages just to get to the party. And we are rejected, so there is no party, and we just go back home. That should be a crucial blow to your self-confidence, but then you get up again and try something new. And that's just youth to go on and on, you know? There's so much energy in life.

Paulson: Well, what's astonishing is that you've written thousands of pages about a life where, frankly, not much happens. There are long stretches where there's not much drama, and yet it's often riveting. I don't know how you do that.

Knausgaard: This book came out of a great frustration in my life. When I started to write, I didn't have any reader in mind, and I thought to myself, "This is boring. This is of no interest to anyone." I was surprised when my editor wanted to publish it. And when the book became kind of a success, it was completely unexpected to me. But I think there is a certain feeling of real life in it, and as a result, lots of possibilities for identification.

And there is a certain narrative structure in ordinary life. You know, suspense could be when you go to the refrigerator and open it and wonder what's in it, and you go there, and there's nothing. What shall I do? Should I go down and buy something, or should I be hungry? Something like that has suspense in it, and it's the same structure as in any Hitchcock film, but just on a miniature scale. When I was a child and a teenager, I read a million books which had one thing in common—a very strong narrative. I mean, Wilbur Smith or Alistair MacLean or Ken Follett—all those thriller writers. The narrative is out of this world. It's so strong. I think some of this got into my blood, so I use it on very, very small things.

Paulson: It does feel like real life. Was it a conscious decision not to be too "literary" as you wrote these books?

Knausgaard: Yeah, very much so. That was the major idea in these books.

Paulson: How do you avoid being too literary?

Knausgaard: I try to write as fast as possible. You know, when I try to write something really good, I spend a lot of time writing and rewriting drafts. I polish the sentences and make them look good. But I didn't do that at all in this book. I did in the opening—maybe the first fifteen pages. I really worked through it again and again, and I think that's the best thing I've written. It is clever and beautiful. My editor suggested we take out the beginning because it's so different from the rest, and then you just dive into something much simpler and more direct. But I disagreed with him because I needed to have something in these books that was well written. So I had the opening only so you can see that I'm doing this on purpose. I know how to write, but it's not my ambition here to show you that I can write. My ambition is to get away from being clever. I try to connect to something else inside of me, which is much more unsophisticated, much more banal . . . sometimes idiotic, you know? Because that's a good representation of life—at least my life.

Paulson: So good writing can get in the way of representing real life?

Knausgaard: Yeah, maybe that's good writing. But I'm confused when it comes to a concept like quality. I don't really know what it is. What I'm trying to do is get away from all the concepts we have—the concept of identity, the concept of quality, of what a novel is, of what a day looks like, you know? Just try to write through all those conceptions. I don't succeed, but that's my aim.

Paulson: This sounds like stream-of-consciousness writing—following wherever your mind takes you.

Knausgaard: Yeah, but in a kind of narrative frame, so it's not completely loose. There's always a context. It's always in a room. It's always with other people or doing something by yourself. It's not like it's all stream of consciousness. Of course, all the things in these books are related to other books I've been reading. People talk about the amount of details in the book, but have you read *Ulysses* by Joyce? It's nothing but details. I'm not comparing it to Joyce, but everything comes from a place.

Paulson: The amount of detail you recount is astonishing. As you've said, you spent a hundred pages describing just getting to a party, and you have long stretches of dialogue with friends and relatives. Supposedly, this is all stuff that really happened to you. How accurate are these memories?

Knausgaard: They're accurate in the way that I capture the way I remember them. It's not accurate in the way they really happened because that's impossible. I mean, if you write about something that happened four minutes ago, someone will say, "No, it didn't happen like that." So it's a book about my memories and what's in my head. It's the memory I'm writing about, not the real events, and the dialogues are made up. I can't remember who said what twenty years ago. That's impossible.

Paulson: Did you ever check with friends or family members to see if you were getting the details right?

Knausgaard: I never did that. That was another thing with this project. I wouldn't do any research. It should be all about what's in my head when I started writing. I sent the manuscript to many people before it was published, and some of them said, "No, it didn't happen this way," but I still kept it that way because I wanted to be true to my memory more than to the real events.

Paulson: Do you have a really good memory?

Knausgaard: I thought I didn't before I started this project, but I think I do. But it's hidden. It's like a place you have to get access to—for instance, through reading or writing. Everything is there; it's just a matter of getting at it.

Paulson: So these memories come flooding back through the act of writing?

Knausgaard: Yeah, it's exactly like that. It is amazing, especially with Book Three, which deals with childhood, because it seemed like my childhood was inaccessible to me when I started. I had some memories but not enough to fill a book. But it was like something opened up when I started to focus on the physicality of being seven or eight—you know, running and climbing trees and all that stuff. There wasn't much thinking. It was a lot of doing. When I started to write about that, everything started to come back to me, like how things smelled and images of landscapes. Some of them are exact and true, and from there you go onto something completely different. A world opened up, and that was only because I was writing about it.

Paulson: This six-volume autobiographical series that you've written is called fiction, not memoir. Is that distinction important to you?

Knausgaard: I didn't really give it a thought when I was doing it. But it is a novel because I'm not interested in just retelling stories from my life. This is a search for identity. I use my life as raw material, and I use all the tools of a novel. There is a narrative structure. You could call it a nonfiction novel.

Paulson: Were these books fun to write?

Knausgaard: No, it was like a daily torture to write because I felt all the time that this is below my aesthetic standard. I have an idea of what it is to write well, and these books are not fulfilling that ambition. That's hard. I am also a person full of self-loathing. It's kind of a negative narcissism. I'm very occupied with myself but in a negative way. Everything I do is to try to get away from myself, but in this book, I'm writing about myself and trying to stay in that, and that was hard. Of course, knowing that this is going to hurt a lot of people is very hard, too.

Paulson: Because you're revealing so many personal details that make other people look bad.

Knausgaard: Yes, and what gave me the right to do that? Who do I think I am using other people, taking things from other people for my own purposes? So that's why I was reading it on the phone every day to my friend because I needed someone to support me, to say, "This is good. Keep going." And also my editor, who said the same thing. Without those people helping me, I wouldn't be able to do it.

Paulson: Do you still have that self-loathing?

Knausgaard: Yeah. But I also have these grand ideas of myself, you know? I mean, self-loving and self-hating. It's like I'm faking something, but it's hard to talk about. If I say what I really think about these books in public, then people come to me afterwards and say, "You can't say that! These books are so important for me." So I try not to talk about it. And this feeling of self-loathing, self-hatred—they are the core of the book, and I also want to find out why. I mean, I wake up in the morning, and I'm not happy, you know? It takes me three, four hours every day to get into a functional mood, and then it's okay. I don't know why it's like that, but something must have been broken. I think to be safe in yourself is the most important thing in childhood. And as a father, that's the one thing I try to give my children—that they can believe in themselves and be safe. I never felt like that, so there's a basic insecurity in me.

Paulson: Yet these books have been extraordinarily successful. You are a celebrated writer around the world. That hasn't made you happier?

Knausgaard: There's ambivalence. Yes, I'm extremely happy. I think this is a miracle. I never thought this would happen. I never thought I would do an interview in the US about my books. I was happy being a Norwegian writer and being able to publish books, so this is like a dream for a writer. And all the reaction from readers who really connect to it—that's why you write. So that's immensely pleasing, but it doesn't help, you know? It's a good thing, but it doesn't do anything, if you know what I mean.

Paulson: So where do you go from here? Do you have a new writing project?

Knausgaard: At the moment, I want to get out of everything about *My Struggle*. I want to get out of the psychology of it, the style of it, the tone of it. Now I'm just writing one text every day about one subject, so it's going to be 365 texts. There's a lot written about toilet seats, vomit, trees, the sun, cups, cars—all the things that I'm surrounded by, the materiality of the world. I'm going to publish them in Norway, like in four books. The first is out in September. It's a world view without people, without psychology.

So every morning, I pick a word. And the challenge is, is it possible to say anything meaningful about this object? And it is. Everything is meaningful if you start to do this. So it's just something I do almost before the day starts. It's a way of getting away from what I've been doing these last years.

Paulson: It sounds wonderful!

Knausgaard: Then I'm going to write a novel.

Karl Ove Knausgaard on Lars von Trier's *The Idiots*

Dennis Lim / 2015

Film at Lincoln Center, June 15, 2015, https://www.youtube.com/watch?v=ThCB9lFvzhY.
Printed by permission of Dennis Lim.

As part of the Film at Lincoln Center series Print Screen, Karl Ove Knausgaard was invited to New York City to present a movie that complemented and inspired his work. He presented Danish director Lars von Trier's *The Idiots*. After the screening, he joined Dennis Lim, the Film Society of Lincoln Center's director of programming, on stage to discuss its importance to him and his work.

Dennis Lim: Please welcome back Karl Ove Knausgaard. [*Applause*] Let me start by maybe just asking you to elaborate on a few points that you made in your introduction. You began by proclaiming Lars von Trier a genius.

Karl Ove Knausgaard: Yeah.

Lim: Do you want to maybe elaborate on the nature [*Knausgaard laughs*] of that genius?

Knausgaard: Well, you saw this movie. It's absolutely completely original anyway, and it touches me, and then it kind of works with things that normally literature does. I'm used to *novels* dealing with these things. It's like it is so outside of the frame of making films, it's doing something else. And when I saw this film, I realized what *I* was doing wasn't *real*, not good enough, and I think he—by using this frame for this film display, this pretending, it kind of hits the same place that Kafka does in *The Castle*—this kind of metaphor for something, and it's very difficult to say what it does. I mean, when you think about it—and I do a lot—it's hard to express it, but I find it just amazing. And it's like this: When I was writing *My Struggle*, *Antichrist* [2009] was released, and I couldn't see it—and I still haven't seen it because I know if I see one of his films I want to stop [writing], because it's—it hits something, *all* his films, where it *matters* in a very unusual way—a very technical way, I find it. And then still it's kind of overflowing with emotion. As I said, he is a manipulator. I don't know if you saw the film *Dancer in the Dark* [von Trier, 2000]. You know, it goes silent, it really goes silent in the end [*laughs*], and I was seeing that film, and it's the most spectacular film I've ever seen, and I saw it in a movie theater. It was full up. *Everybody* was crying. It was impossible to resist, and that's so weird and so strange—that combination of intellectual precision—you know, technical precision—doing this game thing, and then the emotions coming into it.

Lim: This film is also the first film that he made after issuing this manifesto, this Dogme 95 manifesto, with his vow of chastity and, like, calling for a back-to-basics approach to filmmaking. He described it as a purification to get rid of the artifice from cinema, and I think he worked very quickly on this film. He wrote it in a matter of days. I'm wondering if you identified with that aspect as well? I mean, in terms of the shift in your writing from the books you wrote before *My Struggle* to—

Knausgaard: Yeah, not *consciously*, and it's not like I was thinking, "I want to do Dogme in literature," but it is the effect of saying something like this, and the first Dogme film—or what is it called in English? *The Celebration*? It had the same kind of effect. It's not as good as this, but it's kind of the same thing he's achieving. So what that's about is really . . . it's like you're taking away all the special effects, all the things that makes film into something wonderful, something *imagined*. And he says you have to film a location; it has to be the real props; you can't fake anything, you know? And if you could transfer that to literature, what would *that* be? I mean, that would be like saying, "This is not a novel, it's just me writing, and I'm not making anything up. I don't want to make it beautiful; I don't try to—I just want to do it straight and simple." And *yeah*! There is a connection, but it's also a Protestant thing in that wish. And he's from Denmark, and I'm from Norway, and Bergman is from Sweden, and there is kind of a minimalistic working ethics involved somehow, but he broke several of the rules in that film, and I think this is the only Dogme film he made. Is that so?

Lim: Yeah, I think so, the only official one. Just moving beyond von Trier a bit maybe, I'd love to hear you say a little bit about your relationship with cinema? I think those of us who've read the books get a pretty good sense of how you feel about music or how you feel about painting—

Knausgaard: Yeah.

Lim: And then you were, in describing *The Idiots*, you were talking about how it does things that you associate with literature.

Knausgaard: Yeah.

Lim: I think in some ways your books do things that I associate with cinema or maybe with just the ways in which the sense of time in your books—they've been described as almost inducing a sense of real time, and then you know that ties into the durational aspect of cinema.

Knausgaard: Yeah.

Lim: The language is often used to describe your writing as "hyperreal," or sort of photorealistic. Can you say a little bit more about your sense? Do you have a sense that what you're doing has something—some affinities—with cinema, with a camera eye?

Knausgaard: I have never thought of that, but I am a very *visual* writer. It's not like— . . . I was trained when I was studying literature that realism was naïve, and it was naive to believe that there was something behind the letters—it was the letters that mattered, you know—the sentences, the letters, the materiality of the language, and so on. It was very much language when I was in my twenties, but when I'm *reading* and I'm seeing language, when I'm *writing*, language is completely unimportant. It is what the language evokes that matters, so I'm basically writing about images. That's what I'm doing. And that's right, I have been trying to write for film. I'm adapting my first novel into a film manuscript, and that's the hardest thing I've ever done. I realize there is a completely different language, a completely different way of thinking, and it's so easy with the novel, you know? You can just say, "It's like this, you are like that, and this was going on," and you can just write it. *There* you have to show it. So the director, he just laughed when I got the first draft because all the people are introducing themselves: "Hello, my name is . . . I'm working over there, and I'm . . ." I didn't realize that you can cut in and do all those kinds of things. It's a completely different way of thinking. So we are on the fifth draft, I think, and it's getting a little bit better, and then I see this and [*makes a sweeping motion with his arm*] I just want to throw it away . . .

I think one of the things with Lars von Trier is that he is so simple. He does it so quickly. I read an interview with him that he said when he wrote *Antichrist*, he just locked himself in a room with a bottle of liquor and was drunk and wrote it in a few days, and I understand *absolutely* completely why, because he's so clever and he knows everything about filmmaking, and that is really the death for an artist, to know too much or to be too clever, and he wanted to get away from that, and by that, he's being even more clever, making even better things.

Lim: The screenplay that you say you're writing, it's based on which book?

Knausgaard: My first novel, it's a fiction novel, it's called *Out of the World*.

Lim: So that's something you're working on now?

Knausgaard: Yeah, it is.

Lim: So who's the filmmaker?

Knausgaard: It's Fredrik Edfeldt. He's a Swedish filmmaker. He made two films before. We'll see. I like really well working with him, so I try to make it—give it to him. I want to know what *he* is interested in in this material, but it feels like something is lacking all the time, so what I did, I have a kind of a voiceover introduced, a voiceover which, I know, is kind of not—you know—but it solved *a lot*, to make it much more literary and at the same time pulls you in, in *his* mind, the main character.

Lim: I know you said also in your introduction that you have picked this—we did initially approach you because we do a series called *The Art of the Real*, which is a program on documentary, but that tries to expand the conception of documentary and has films that are sort of more hybrid, which is why we thought of you, knowing that you've described *My Struggle* as a nonfiction novel. Maybe could you say a little bit about the idea of the real as it relates to von Trier or *The Idiots*?

Knausgaard: I think [*laughs*] the concept of the real is at stake in so many places in this film. I think it's very complicated. I find it very interesting to compare with *The Idiot* by Dostoevsky, which is—the main character, there's no irony in him; he doesn't understand *any* play. There's no calculation; he's just there, and he says things as they are, and you see the circles around him collapsing, and then you can see it's a place; society is a play; it's a game, and von Trier is doing exactly opposite, you know? He's entering the same area from a play, and then he kind of enters into the real, which is this wonderful, wonderful scene, where the two idiots make love, and she said, "I love you." That's what I see in every movie: "*I love you*," and it doesn't mean a thing. But here it's kind of a one-and-a-half-hour building up until he can say it, and you understand what this is; you know? And it has to relate it to being an idiot, I mean, being a fool, being given over to your feelings, and then the second time it collapses is when you realize she's in deep sorrow, and her son is dead, and she just left everything, and you know that wanting to regress that you have where someone dies.

I mean, it's an immense longing for regression, and he deals with that in that film, but it takes—kind of you have to almost deserve to get there, and you have to see two, or more than two—hours to be there, so that's the real. That's where you meet. That's no play anymore. Love and death, no game—everything else is a game. Society is a game, everything is. Making film is a game. *There* is the reality, in a way. And I just love the way he enters those places. The first time I saw it, I found it very awkward and unsettling. I wanted them—"No, don't do this! Don't poke fun at those people! Please don't!" And now—I kind of was intrigued by the regression. I think I really wanted to regress in my own life, just to give up and sink and become some— an *idiot*, you know? There was lust in it for me, so I didn't laugh. The second time I saw it, I laughed. It is very funny, I think, in a way.

Lim: Have there been other films or other filmmakers that you think have been instructive to you in terms of your own work?

Knausgaard: Yeah, there is a moment in a Tarkovsky film. I think it is *Solaris* when they are on Earth in the beginning of the film, where there are some cups out in the rain, and it's green and it's raining, and it's raindrops coming on those cups, and it has nothing to do in the film. It's no relevance to anything. It's just a wonderful, wonderful image, and Tarkovsky is kind of—he has a story somewhere, but he kind of—it dissolves all the time into something else, so it's hard to see his films knowing what is his meaning. And I think that's "How far can you bend the film before it became meaningless?" It's only pictures, you know? And I think the same way with a novel. It's *those* moments, those raindrops on those cups—that's the novel! The other things—narrative—is a way to get there, but if you want something real, you have to go out of those frames, and then that becomes a cliché again, and you can't use it. That's why he left this project, because you can only use it once or twice, and then it's dead, really. It's dead.

Lim: I'm wondering if there are—if you see other affinities between your work and von Trier's? Have you seen the making—the documentary of *The Idiots*? There's a film about the making of *The Idiots*, which is called *The Humiliated*. And I think you get a sense of—this is a film that means to, I think, induce a certain discomfort. Von Trier plays a lot with embarrassment and mortification in his work, and I think . . . so do you, but in terms of shame and self-exposure. Is that a kinship you . . . ?

Knausgaard: Yeah, there is, yeah. There must be a reason why I relate so intensely to it, but I would never say that I am *doing* the same thing as he is. I have—I am too full of respect for it. I think it's Tarkovsky or by Kafka or something. I think it's—yeah—a modern classic.

Lim: Another connection that just occurred to me—I'm sure everybody here read the pieces you wrote for the *New York Times*—the magazine—your

American travelogue. Von Trier has made films about America without actually ever setting foot in America that have very strong ideas about America. What do you think of those films? *Dogville* and *Manderlay*.

Knausgaard: I've only seen *Dogville*, and I loved it, especially the ending because that's variable—it plays "Young Americans," isn't it?

Lim: Yeah.

Knausgaard: And the time when you see those pictures, it's brilliant [*laughs*]. I think he's . . . I don't know really what he thinks about America. Do you think he is—what is the word—prejudiced?

Lim: I'm not sure I could sum it up, but I think *Dogville* does have some strong ideas about America.

Knausgaard: Yeah.

Lim: So does the other one, *Manderlay*. We'll open it up to the audience for questions. [*Inaudible* . . .] The first part was about whether you needed to convince your publishers about *My Struggle*, given how different it was from your earlier, previous work, and the second part was about the writing process, yes?

Knausgaard: When it comes to my publisher, I think if I hadn't published those two novels before and been completely unknown to them, I am not sure if they would have published it. Because that's a difficult thing to know—if it's unlike something, if it's good or not good, what is this, you know? But having that kind of name I had was a kind of a guarantee that helped a lot, I think. Then I have to say my publisher is very literary, very, very good, and they do everything for their writers. So there's only novels and poems and short stories on the list, and they kind of made this happen, made it possible, made a space for it to be realized. So the second part of your question . . . if I edit much? . . . No, the first book was done like a normal book. I sat down with my editor, and we changed something and cut out something, but then we realized no, it *shouldn't* be edited, that the whole thing is that it is a process. It's writing while publishing, so it's hardly done anything with at all. So what I do, I just write, write, and if it's wrong, I just try to go in another direction, and that's the editing. And the whole point was to write very fast, so I started saying to myself—as a rule—"Five pages a day, no matter what." If I had been writing one page during the day, and it was one hour till I should pick up the children at nursery, I *had* to write four pages in an hour. And that's because—that's a very good rule—because you can't let your notion of quality rule you. So then it was ten pages, and in the end I wrote the last novel . . .

It's five hundred pages, and I wrote it in eight weeks. And it was just a matter of speed, and then you can also reach some places you don't do normally because you're so ashamed, but if you do it very quickly, it's kind of where you are ahead of your thoughts; you're ahead of your reflections. . . . That means it's a lot of bad writing, but that also means there is some intensity or something in there.

[*Audience question (inaudible)*]

Knausgaard: If I'm interested in documentary films? You know, I watch a lot of documentaries, but it's not like I'm specifically interested in them now.

Audience: Do you see your work as documentary?

Knausgaard: No, no, not at all. It's a novel; it is really fiction—even if it's nonfictional, if you understand what I mean? It's not like I'm trying to document *anything*, but I'm looking for something in that material.

[*Audience question (inaudible)*]

Knausgaard: You're asking about the comic aspects of *My Struggle*. And it is really both. I mean writing about being seventeen, that's obviously meant to be fun in a way. There is big irony between the character and the man who writes or the reader, but in for instance Book Two, I wrote that—that's about me and my wife and our children, and I wrote that as a *tragedy*. It was a tragic story, and then it was translated into Swedish, and I open it, and I start to read, and I realize, "Now it's a comedy!" You have just to take one step to the side, and you can see it, and it kind of becomes funny, but if you are in the middle of it, you don't see it, and it's not. So it's with the pram, and there's a bridge and trying to find someplace to eat, and it's a holiday, a lot of irritation that has been going on, and there is an argument, and it's like—yeah, it is, you know, it's fun. It's not fun to be there, but it is stupid and funny.

Audience: Could you explain how current cultural contexts and your past have shaped your writing voice and identity?

Knausgaard: Yeah, it is, that's the whole thing with this. I'm exploring my own identity in my own language. Who am I? How did I get here? In the end, I realize, no, it's *not* my language, it was something I was born into, and I'm going to die away from it. It's even not my *culture*, it's not my literature. It's a kind of a collective area I'm entering here. Every single thought in that book, someone else has been thinking. Every single concept, it's in there, so I think it's 99 percent of that is what's in between us—what's in the culture. And I mean I saw that film, and I didn't reflect that I have to go for *that* kind of realism—but it *happened*, and now I can see *that* was one very important influence—and there were several others. And while I was writing *My Struggle*, there was this—what's David Shields—*Reality Hunger*, you know? That's what I'm doing, that's what's going on now, and that's how these things happen all the time, so of course there was a connection.

Audience: Could you explain why you have changed your writing techniques and habits throughout your career?

Knausgaard: When you do something, when you write something, and you have a certain language, or you are at a certain place, you must stop doing that and get to another place. It's very important, I think, because in the end you just start to repeat yourself, and you know what's working, what's not working, and that's not any good. And so *rules* are very good, but just for a short while, and then you can't use the rules. So what I'm doing now, I'm trying to seriously try to get away from that kind of language. I'm writing about objects, one text about one object every day, and I'm going to do that for a year. There is no psychology, and there are no fathers, and the language is very much oriented towards description, with reality, and I'm just doing that to try to escape from that kind of writing, and it is a little bit reminding me of the opening.

Lim: A question about the politics behind *My Struggle* and *The Idiots*—I guess whether there's any *shared* politics in terms of how they are getting away from—

Knausgaard: [*Laughs*] Do I have to take responsibility for everything Lars von Trier is doing? Now of course the title of the book is *My Struggle*, so it's an obvious question, and I have a publishing house. I publish books, and there was a writer we wanted, and he called me, and he was from Switzerland, and he said, "Are you a right-wing man?" And I said, "No," and he said, "Okay, I'll join you." Because there is a certain . . . when you call something "Mein Kampf," which I did, of course, it *is* a provocation, but for me, my writing is the *opposite* of *Mein Kampf*—I mean it's the *exact opposite worlds*, you know? This is an opposition against the ideology and the great visions of the world where the individuality just disappears, and somehow—we live in Sweden, and the rest of Scandinavia, but specifically Sweden, *is* politically correct—and this is an antipolitically correct film in all ways because it mocks also the ones who are antiestablishment. It's also making fun of them too.

But I think the tension between individuality and the social scene is strong in Scandinavia. There is a lot of repression, there are a lot of things you can't do or can't say, and that's one of the most . . . where very much of the energy in my book comes from the *forbidden* thing: "No, you shouldn't go there, you shouldn't talk about that, you shouldn't do that." And that's what *they* are doing, you know, that's where they are going, and I did it by, for instance, writing about people who exist, and my kind of compass—moral compass—was if it hurts too much to do it, I mean physically, I don't. And if I write about something very controversial, if it's too painful to put it down, I can't do it, but I try to push it as far as I can. An interesting thing is of course that in a social setting I couldn't have said *anything* that's in the book. And in the book, there is no one there—I'm free. That's this place I want to be when I'm writing. But I am accused of being right-wing and antifeminist or antiwoman even—all kinds of things—but I think if you read the whole book and see it . . . what I seek is complication. There's a lot of contradictions in the book, and it ends with an essay about Adolf Hitler, where I identify myself with him when he's sixteen. And I'm writing . . . I remember how it was, and he was very much like me, and I guess you too—being sixteen is very much the same. And there's the mystery of what happened, how was this possible to go from there—to love art, to love music, to be in love with someone. You don't dare to tell it to them; you do not dare to talk to them; you know, all those kinds of things. Then it ends up there. But Lars von Trier, he was just rambling, and I think everybody knows that he doesn't mean *this*,[1] but you *want* it to be true in a way, so you could take that provocation, and you can direct your anger towards him, but I think everybody knows that he was just joking. It was in very bad taste, and he shouldn't have done it, but, you know, look at these films. This is serious stuff in a way.

Audience: Would you be open to adapting *My Struggle*? If so, why?

Knausgaard: Yeah, I have got offers, people wanting to make films out of it or to buy the rights, but I have said no. But I think it's really not possible to make a film out of it because it's not a *story*, and it's not a—I mean, it's only ordinary stuff from a life, just thrown out on the pages, and I think a director should do that with his own life and make his own script about it. I mean, it's so specific, these books, but if someone has a very good idea which I trust and believe in, I would of course say yes to it, but for me, literature is what's left when you take out all the things that you can transfer into another art form. So if you can make a film out of it, it will be all the things that's not in the film that is of value for me in the book.

Lim: Is there anyone working in Scandinavian cinema now who you find interesting? We were talking briefly about this young Norwegian filmmaker, Joachim Trier, who is a distant relative of Lars von Trier.

Knausgaard: He's a young Norwegian filmmaker. He has made two films, which I—we are not *used* to good films in Norway—and then this film came, and it had a terrible plot really, a terrible setting. It's two writers, very young people. It's about writing, wanting to be a writer, but it was so fresh in their approach, and it's like, "Wow, this is for real; this is really good." And then he made a wonderful film as a second film about a man. It's opening up with a man trying to commit suicide, and then he fails, and then he goes into the city of Oslo, and you just follow him one day, and it's a beautiful, simple film. And now he has his third film.

Lim: It's an English-language film called *Louder than Bombs*.

Knausgaard: Yeah, and it is in competition in Cannes, and he is absolutely brilliant there.

Lim: The Swedish filmmaker Ruben Ostlund—I don't know if you know his work? He made *Force Majeure*. I know he's a big fan of your work.

Knausgaard: He too is very occupied with shame and with social structure, social mechanisms, that kind of—so, yeah, I feel related to him.

Lim: I've heard—I've read about your phenomenon of slow television in Norway? [*Knausgaard laughs*] It seems a highly particular Norwegian thing. It's conceptual, a Warholian kind of project that seems to—has been compared to *your* private project!

Knausgaard: [*Laughs*] That's insane. Slow!

Lim: Speed seems to be what you were after, right, with this?

Knausgaard: Yeah, but with that slow television, that was that they had cameras on a boat that goes to the coast of Norway, and it was on live television for I think three, four days, and so you saw everything, and people were hooked to it. It became a phenomenon, and people on the places were aware that the ship with the camera was coming. So they were kind of dressing up, and there was a band playing, and it became a kind of an adventure through the whole of Norway, and I can't quite associate myself with that [*laughs*].

Audience: In avoiding artifice, you and von Trier are actually being quite clever. Is this some sort of trick for navigating postmodern literature?

Knausgaard: No, it's a way of getting away from yourself; that's what it is. For me, I'm speaking for me. That's what I'm trying to do . . . What I want to do, I *don't* want to deal with *concepts* or *ideas*, I want to connect with *feelings* and *presence* and those kinds of things that don't have a language, but it's so important for us, and it's so important for the way we see the world. We see the world through our feelings, which a whole academic world doesn't relate to. I mean, they think a thought is clear and kind of untouchable and pure, but it *isn't!* Someone *felt* something when that thought was captured, so that's why I try to get away from thinking, really. That's more like it.

Lim: I want to thank you again for being here.

Knausgaard: Thank you very much for showing that von Trier film.

Note

1. At a press conference at the Cannes Film Festival in May 2011, von Trier made comments about himself being a Nazi. See, for example, https://www.hollywoodreporter.com/news/general-news/lars-von-trier-admits-being-189747/.

Why Karl Ove Knausgaard Can't Stop Writing

Liesl Schillinger / 2015

WSJ. Magazine, Nov. 4, 2015. Reprinted with permission of Liesl Schillinger and *Wall Street Journal*, © 2015 Dow Jones & Company, Inc. All rights reserved worldwide. License number 5342680931418.

One sunny afternoon this August, in the medieval Swedish resort town of Ystad, the Norwegian author Karl Ove Knausgaard appeared outside my hotel to pick me up, a day ahead of schedule, on half an hour's notice. Even if the street had been crowded, Knausgaard would have been instantly recognizable, standing 6-foot-4, with a wolf's mane of silver hair, ice-blue eyes, and craggy woodcut features, but Ystad is a sleepy town, and the street was empty. He stood beside a white VW van, calmly smoking a Chesterfield, dressed in a dark jacket and artfully slashed jeans. Walking up, I felt as though I were stepping into the album cover of *The Freewheelin' Bob Dylan*. It was jarring to think that this unassuming guy, driving a scuffed van cluttered with toys, old CDs, and a baby seat, is quite probably in line to receive a Nobel Prize in literature for his epic saga of what he describes as "the tormented inner life of one male."

The first time I met Knausgaard was in the spring of 2014, after a standing-room-only talk in a cavernous hall of the New York Public Library following the publication of the third volume of his thirty-six-hundred-page autobiographical novel, *My Struggle*. He was so thronged by literati that it was hard to get to him. (This was a big change from one of his prior trips to New York, in 2012, when a small group of early Knausgaard adopters turned up at the tiny 192 Books in Chelsea to hear him. Overcome with nerves, he told the moderator, Lorin Stein, the editor of the literary quarterly the *Paris Review*, "If anyone leaves while we're talking I won't be able to go on.") This summer, I spent three days with him in Scandinavia, amid the church-dotted fields and hills of the village of Glemmingebro, in southern Sweden, where he lives with his wife, the poet and novelist Linda Boström, and their four young children; in Ystad, twenty minutes away; and in Oslo, where I accompanied him for a reading from his newest book, *Om høsten* (*In Fall*[1]). At Oslo's Kulturhuset cafe, he swayed from side to side, barely containing his anxiety while he read from his new book in a deep Norwegian singsong, as the crowd reacted to his text with exuberant appreciation. There was no need for him to be nervous anymore, but he couldn't override the instinct. "The way I am hasn't changed; the way I feel hasn't changed; the success doesn't help at all in regard to that," he says. "A way of being has nothing to do with what happens to you; it's completely irrelevant."

Last year, he reunited with his college band, Lemen ("Lemming"), which Knausgaard writes about in the fifth volume of his six-volume opus, set to appear in the US this spring.

Since the emergence of the six volumes of *My Struggle*, which began in 2009 and continues as the books are translated into dozens of languages, Karl Ove Knausgaard, forty-six, has become one of the twenty-first century's greatest literary sensations. Despite the ominous title—*My Struggle* (*Min Kamp* in Norwegian) is also the name of Hitler's memoir-manifesto, *Mein Kampf*—this is no warlike screed. It is the intensely personal, discursive, and searingly honest story of a Norwegian man's coming of age, of his continuing ordeals as an adult, of his philosophical preoccupations, and of his determination to write the authentic story of his life, as he perceived it, whatever the cost: to "just say it as it is."

The books have beguiled and confounded nearly every critic, editor, and novelist who has read them. They compare him to Marcel Proust for his magisterial evocation of the past (Knausgaard devoured *Remembrance of Things Past* in the midnineties, as soon as it was available in Norwegian, "a brilliant translation," he says) and to the Chilean novelist Roberto Bolaño for his contemporary stream-of-consciousness style. In 2012, when the first volume of *My Struggle* appeared in English, translated by Don Bartlett, Knausgaard's work went global. The critic James Wood, who dubs the reaction "the Knausgaard effect," compares him to the Beats, like Allen Ginsberg and Jack Kerouac, and to the Russian greats: Fyodor Dostoevsky for his "contradictoriness" and Leo Tolstoy for his "utterly prosaic centrality." The author Zadie Smith, upon reading the first two hundred pages, tweeted that she craved the next volume "like crack"; the novelist Jonathan Lethem said, "I'm always putting things off to gulp down another episode."

Alternating between wide-lens and microscopic focus, jumping back and forth between past and present, *My Struggle* relays Knausgaard's everyday routines, terrors, joys, miseries, and hopes—from his adult setbacks and insecurities to the agonies he suffered as a boy in small-town Norway in the seventies and eighties, when his bullying father mocked his speech impediment and his oblivious mother bought him a flower-sprigged ladies swim cap to wear to the pool, to the adrenaline rush he felt when he bought illicit beer with friends, listened to new songs by the Clash and Echo and the Bunnymen, played in rock bands with his older brother, Yngve, and finally figured out how to have sex. In Book One, the focus is the death of his father, in 1998, from alcoholism; in Book Two, it is his *coup de foudre* with Boström and the births of their first three children; in Book Three, his childhood in Tromøya, an island in southern Norway, near the town of Arendal, where his father taught school and his mother worked as a nurse; in Book Four, the gap year he spent as a schoolteacher in a fishing village by the Arctic Circle; in Book Five, his decade in Bergen, Norway, as a university student, self-doubting writer, bad boyfriend, and unsuccessful first husband; and in the sixth and final volume, a meditation on Hitler, the Norwegian mass murderer Anders Behring Breivik and the dark roots of human nature. Four have appeared in English so far; the fifth comes out in the US next spring. In the sixth volume, as yet untranslated, Knausgaard also describes the breakdown Boström suffered after *My Struggle* was published. Writing that section made him cry, he says; but she was "OK" with him revealing their private life in the books, he says. "She says it's not flattering, but it's the way it is," he says. "So I think she accepts it."

Readers have been astounded by the thoroughness of Knausgaard's recollections and the granular detail of his descriptions and dialogue. "The point of the book was not my life but what I made out of it in literature," he says. Explaining his process, he adds, "The recall comes in the writing. I started out with nothing. What went into the book was a few pictures and a few memories; everything was evoked in the process. It was like getting access to that time through writing about it. I think everybody could do it." Most would not dare, not only because of the project's ambition, but because of the intimacies Knausgaard forced himself to violate in pursuit of his goal of scrupulous honesty. Other writers can't help being aware of his confessional innovation, says Geir Berdahl, the recently retired CEO of Forlaget Oktober, Knausgaard's Norwegian publisher. "Many now are writing about themselves, or personal things," he says. "But it's not so easy to write like Karl Ove."

When the first volumes of *My Struggle* emerged in Norway in 2009, they created a national uproar. Nobody was more stunned than Knausgaard that when others beheld his self-portrait they saw their own faces. "It was very shocking when I realized how people read it," he says. "I thought, 'This is so private it's almost unreadable'—but it worked the other way around." He was so convinced that the book would hold no interest for non-Scandinavians that he told a British publisher who expressed interest not to buy it. He was ashamed of the writing. "It's bad," he still says. "I wrote it rather blindly; I didn't think it was exceptional. I thought this would be a minor literary book; I thought it would be a step down from my other books; I thought maybe it was boring and uninteresting and really about nothing." He realized his mistake only when he met Scandinavian journalists for the first time, "and some of them were almost white in the face and found it very hard to discuss the book. I thought then: 'Something is going to happen.'" It did; a new British publisher soon came calling and publishers from dozens of other countries. Now he says, "I think people almost vomit when they hear my name because I'm so often in the news. It's true. Oh, God. I try to keep a low profile in Norway, but it's hard. It's terrible."

At Knausgaard's home in Glemmingebro, three long, low houses enclose the sides of a grassy yard dotted with trees, ornamental bushes, pink hollyhocks, and a rustic old pump. On the fourth side is a trampoline behind an apple tree, closing the rectangle. The back of the main house looks across the lawn to the cottage that holds Knausgaard's writing studio. It resembles an illustration in an old Mother Goose book—cream walls with burgundy-trimmed casement windows and half-pipe tiles on the roof. Boström came to the door of the main house as we crossed the lawn. Petite and daintily built, she held their youngest child, Anne, eighteen months old, on her hip (they also have Vanja, eleven, Heidi, ten, and John, eight). Anne stretched out her arms for her father, and he reached for her. Entering his studio, I saw books everywhere—lined up in shelves, stacked on the floor, propped in piles leaning against other books—hardbacks and paperbacks, galleys and manuscripts, rising in towers from the coffee table. Some came from Pelikanen, the company he formed in 2010, which publishes mostly fiction in translation and contemporary Norwegian literature. The room recalled a postapocalyptic college library. Empty beer cans, Pepsi Max bottles, water glasses, and coffee mugs rose amid the bookscape; and cigarette ash dusted everything, trailing in shallow rivulets between the books, bottles, and crockery. A guitar in a blue nylon bag leaned against a doorway into a den, where I could see speakers, amps, and a drum set. Sunlight spilled through the open door and window, and as we sat down, I heard leaves rustle in the garden and the unfamiliar caws of Swedish birds.

That morning, Knausgaard tells me, he had woken before sunrise, as he always does, to write before his children got up. His task was to produce the final entry for his upcoming book, *Om vinteren* (*In Winter*). Like *Om høsten*, it is part of a quartet (the others are *In Spring* and *In Summer*) of essays on 240 different subjects—his selective lexicon of the universe. He conceived the project while awaiting Anne's birth, wanting "to show her the world she will find, all the objects: This is everything; there's no difference between a toilet seat, vomit, a rainbow, or gold. I wanted to look at everything without prejudice." Before flying to Sweden, I had been unnerved by the prospect of interviewing a man whose every secret had already been printed, published, discussed, and dissected. I confessed these fears to him. "I have secrets, some things I haven't told anyone," he reassured me. "I guess everyone is like that." One of the confidences he disclosed was that, during a recent visit to Tromøya, he met a teaching colleague of his father who told him that his father had been beaten when he was a child by Knausgaard's grandfather. "I also got letters from childhood friends of my father that gave me the same impression," he says. "I was very happy that they didn't tell me these things before I wrote the book because the book is based on my perspective of what I saw."

Knausgaard forced himself to start writing these pages in 2008—the year he turned forty—at breakneck speed, without second-guessing the quality of his output, to break through a long period of writer's block. He had previously published two literary novels: *Out of the World* (1998), which made him the first debut novelist to win the Norwegian Critics Prize for Literature; and *A Time for Everything* (2004), his own favorite, but which "nobody else is interested in because it's the most fictional book," he says. "It's about angels, like angels do exist, they really were around. The mystery in the book is where did they go? It's a retelling of the stories in the Bible." But in the middle of the aughts, a number of distractions, including the sudden onset of fatherhood, with its relentless cycle of diapers, feedings, tantrums, grocery runs, and baby parties, had derailed his vocation. "I felt like I was living somebody else's life, not my own life," he recalls. "I wrote for four or five years with no result, with nothing." In Book Two, he calls this period a midlife crisis. "When you were forty you realized it was all here, banal everyday life, fully formed, and it always would be unless you did something," he writes. "Unless you took one last gamble." *My Struggle* was that gamble.

No other Norwegian writer had dared such full disclosure. France has a tradition of autobiographical fiction, and memoir is common in the United States but not in Scandinavia. Lorin Stein observes, "Norwegians say that the confessional instinct is so culturally alien to them that it was, in a funny way, useful to him." As Knausgaard sees it, "There was a threshold for writing about real people, and it was shockingly open. That was very important to me; it gave me courage."

To heighten the stakes and to increase Knausgaard's resolve, his publisher at Oktober suggested he produce the book serially, "as Dickens did," one short volume a month, then rerelease them as a single, fifteen-hundred-page magnum opus. Knausgaard thought the idea was "fantastic." If he missed a single deadline, he would be publicly shamed, at least in his own mind. "The risk factor was very important," he says. "I couldn't say, 'I need more time.' If you have to do it in eight weeks, you can't care about the writing or composition; anything goes. It's a way of making yourself free." However, once the terror of falling behind on his deadlines had liberated him, Knausgaard wrote so many pages so quickly that he and his editor, Geir Gulliksen, realized a new format had to be devised. They and Oktober's then-CEO, Berdahl, announced that they would publish six full-length novels back-to-back: And thus, *My Struggle* was born. Fed up with the artifice of fiction, Knausgaard decided to use actual names and events to the greatest extent possible. "I felt like I never said what I really meant to anyone; I was trying to please everybody. I felt like a coward, and I wanted to break out of all of that."

Upon the release of the first volume, *A Death in the Family*, in Norway in 2009, Knausgaard's uncle (his father's younger brother) threatened to sue to stop publication. In that book, Knausgaard wrote in wrenching detail of his father's drunken demise, describing the visit he and his brother, Yngve, made to their addled grandmother's house, where their father had died. Finding befouled carpets and sofas, mountains of empty bottles and piles of rotting clothing, "not only mildewed; they were decomposing," they cleaned up the filth, putting on rubber gloves and getting out bleach and Jif cleanser to "scour and scrub and rub and wipe" as if "all that had been destroyed here would be restored. All. Everything." Knausgaard's uncle charged that his nephew had invented the squalid denouement. "The claim was that he died of natural circumstances," Knausgaard says, "that it was a heart attack, and there were no bottles in the room, and so on. I started to doubt what had really happened. I wondered, 'Had I exaggerated because I wanted a better novel? It was like I was going insane.'" When a doctor who had witnessed the disturbing scene wrote a letter corroborating his story, Knausgaard's account was validated. Today, he defends, in absolute terms, the right to free expression: "There's no danger in saying even the most terrible thing," he says. "You must be allowed to say it."

Still, his father's side of the family no longer speaks to Knausgaard. And more controversies were to come. In Book Two, *A Man in Love*, Knausgaard describes his reaction to being rejected by Boström upon their first meeting, in 1999, at a writers' retreat, while he was still married to his first wife, the journalist Tonje Aursland, whom he had married in 1995. When Boström turned him down, he took a shard from a broken water glass and carved long cuts on his face. Seeing him the next day, she cried. When they remet in Stockholm three years later, they fell in love. Knausgaard fainted at their first kiss. Aursland knew none of this history until she read *My Struggle*. Devastated, she produced a radio documentary, *Tonje's Version*, in 2010, in which she confronted her ex; but since then, they have repaired their friendship. Knausgaard dodged awkwardness with the third volume, *Boyhood Island*, by warning his mother, with whom he has a warm relationship, to skip it, fearing she would be hurt by his examination of his boyhood griefs. (She obliged.) She had been so upset by his first novel, *Out of the World*, which draws on Knausgaard's unhappy memories of his father, that she "went silent for two weeks. She was shocked," he says. "She has a very different impression of who I am. That was hard for her."

When Knausgaard first arrived in Bergen as a student, in 1988, at nineteen, he was miserable, by his own account, and he depended on his older brother for his social life. Knausgaard had been accepted to an exclusive writing academy but lost confidence when his teachers and peers did not express admiration for his work. "He was the saddest person I'd ever seen," recalls his best friend from those days, the gonzo writer Geir Angell Øygarden (who volunteered as a human shield in the Iraq War and later wrote about it in his book *Bagdad Indigo*—the first publication from Knausgaard's company, Pelikanen, in 2011). "It seemed like the joy had been sucked out of him." Despairing of a future in fiction, Knausgaard resigned himself to a life in academia and spent a year studying literature in Bergen. Then he took a four-year break, during which he fulfilled his Norwegian national service obligation by working at a campus radio station, then worked briefly on an oil platform in the North Sea, before resuming his studies, this time in art history. But a friend he'd met at the radio station, Tore Renberg, believed in his talent and pushed him to write again. After Renberg sold a book to Tiden in the mid-nineties, he told his editor, Geir Gulliksen, that he ought to publish Knausgaard ("Tore told me Karl Ove was full of shame and doubt about his writing," Gulliksen recalls) and persuaded his friend to submit a story. Gulliksen accepted it and promptly signed Knausgaard up for a novel. Since then, he has edited all of Knausgaard's books. "He has a supreme imagination," he says.

The critic James Wood suggests that Knausgaard may be the first iconoclastic author to have created a genuinely antiliterary work of literary genius. "By its nature, this project can't be well written," Wood says. "There's too much of it; it was written too fast, and he doesn't want it to be well written; the part of him that's actually restless with language and that wants to get beyond it has to in some way demote its importance, and almost demolish it." And yet, he says, in fulfilling this urge, Knausgaard has given something rare to readers: "the gift of universalism."

Stein says he finds innovation in Knausgaard's exploration of the psyche of the men of his generation. "If there's some kind of masculinity that's particular to our generation, we haven't had a writer who got it down before Karl Ove," he says. He detects a broader contribution as well: Knausgaard has restored the authority of the narrator. Stein explains, "Fiction is no longer the central popular art form that it used to be, so the reader tacitly asks: Why are you engaging in this? And that becomes a distraction. Karl Ove seems to have found a way of answering that question. You believe in the urgency of it. You believe that the story needs to be told and that it needs to be told this way." Knausgaard professes himself bewildered by those who extol the originality of *My Struggle*. "Every one of its elements is a very common one," he says. "It's ordinary. The only thing that's new—and that's new in every novel—is the voice." When he writes, even now, he adds, he never has confidence of the quality of his expression. "I don't know when something I do is good or when it's not. It's very strange," he admits. "I have to have someone who says, 'This is brilliant; keep on.' That is freedom for me. You need to get someone who can tell you that it is good."

For Knausgaard, for a decade, that person has been Øygarden. In Book Four, for example, he admits that he did not learn to masturbate until he was nearly twenty. While writing that book, worrying that he had at last exceeded all bounds of decency, he asked Øygarden if he should omit the pages. "Geir just laughed and laughed and found it hilarious. I realized, OK, that was the worst part," Knausgaard says. "It wasn't shocking for anyone."

On my last evening in Ystad, Knausgaard picks me up in his van for the drive to Glemmingebro. We head to Øygarden's house, half a mile from

Knausgaard's, which is set in the middle of a sprawling rose garden. As we talk in Øygarden's orderly studio, the men remember their collaboration on *My Struggle*. During the three years that he was composing the books, Knausgaard called Øygarden each day on the phone—two, four, even ten times, for hours at a time—reading every single word aloud, including fifteen hundred pages that didn't stay in the final draft. "I think Karl Ove needed a space where he could just ventilate everything," Øygarden says. Having absorbed all five thousand draft pages in unexpurgated audio form, Øygarden has never read the books on paper; but he is unafraid to criticize his friend's self-presentation. "I don't agree with the way he read his life," Øygarden says. "In my view, everything was much brighter, but he is of such a temperament that he can't see that." He adds, "You must remember this: Karl Ove has always had lots of friends. He doesn't see it that way, I know, but he always has been popular as far as I can remember. There is no empirical reason for his gloomy attitude." He pauses. "With that being said, so what? That's the way I look at it: It's his book, and it's his story, so that's all."

The next day before we leave for Oslo, I ask Knausgaard if he thinks his kids will look back on their upbringing with more lightness than he did. "There is a lot more love expressed in my family now than there was in my family growing up," he says. "But I have no idea how they are going to perceive their own childhood." Still, he says, he would prefer they not become writers. "In my world there is something wrong with people who are writers," he says. "If someone wants to write, that means there is something incomplete in them; if they're writers, it's a certain sign of unhappiness."

Before Knausgaard sat down to write *My Struggle*, in 2008, he had dreamed of being forever freed of the burden of his literary calling. "I was going to use everything I had, and use it up, so I couldn't use it again, so there would be nothing left to write," he says, comparing the impulse to suicide. He knew the work's last line before he began: "I am happy because I am no longer an author." Since writing those self-annihilating words, Knausgaard has produced four new books. Three other books and a screenplay are in progress. The author is dead. Long live the author. Knausgaard admits he cannot shake his vocation. "I just need to write some books," he says. "I have to write—maybe I can write for twenty more years, that's maybe four or five novels; and that's not much, so I can't waste my time. I know where my fascinations lie; I try to go there. You can write about anything—you don't need a subject or a story. You can just write. Everything will show itself, the story will come, and the things you are really interested in will be in the book, no matter what you are writing about." He lights another Chesterfield and adds, "I'm not looking for something to write about, ever. If it is valuable, it will be inside of me, so I'll write about it one day."

Note

1. Titled *Autumn* in English.

"Babel": Karl Ove Knausgård

Maria Scrivani / 2016

Daily Public, April 13, 2016, http://www.dailypublic.com/articles/04122016/babel-karl-ove-knausgård. Reprinted by permission of Maria Scrivani, freelance writer, *The Public*.

The author of the wildly acclaimed six-volume autobiographical saga *My Struggle* will speak in Buffalo [New York] at 8 p.m. on Thursday, April 21, in Kleinhans Music Hall under the auspices of Just Buffalo Literary Center's Babel series. He's never been here before, and he's looking forward to it; having enjoyed previous trips to the United States, a "fascinating" and "very different" place. What is not so different is the theme of his work; specifically, for Babel readers, in Book One, which ends with the death of his father. In it, Karl Ove, both character and author, struggles to deconstruct their relationship and answer the question of identity and place in a complex world. Today, for a man nearing the half-century mark, with a life story already detailed in six volumes, the question that begs is what next? What about the rest of your life and writing career? In a recent telephone interview, from his current home in Sweden, Knausgård, thoughtful and bemused, gamely struggled to answer all our questions.

Maria Scrivani: You have written many other books, but this is so deeply, painfully personal. Tell us about your writing process and its cost.

Karl Ove Knausgård: It was a very long process. It was 1998 when my father died; he was found dead in my grandmother's home. My first thought was "I have to write about this." I had just published my first novel, but this was what I wanted to write for the next ten years; really, I wanted to write about my father and me, and my experience. I tried it as a novel first, and then, in 2008, I tried to write it as a confessional. My publisher called the writing "manic self-confessional"—he didn't like it. But I was just writing about myself being sixteen, for example, and connecting it to my father's death. I used my own name; that kind of laid out the frame in which I could write about it. All of this, trying to evoke the feeling when I entered the house where my grandmother lived, and how that was . . . I had to say what I really thought; I had to be responsible. I had to be able to look people in the eyes afterward. The hardest part was to write about my brother, who is very generous and accepted what I wrote. I did send the manuscript around before it was published. And my father's family tried to stop the book and threatened to sue me. They were upset at how my father was portrayed, and my grandmother. I was accused of many, many things. Who are you, they said, and is your story more important than our family? To which I reply, "Who are you to say that I cannot write about my father?" This was not a hate or revenge project in any way, rather a genuine quest for identity—who I am; who and how my father was.

Scrivani: There is a biblical quality to your work, with its ancient themes of the human condition. Slogging through daily life and death, suffering and salvation. Do you try to teach through your writing?

Knausgård: No, because you are not free if you write with that goal in mind. My idea was not to care at all what I was writing; to never think of the reader at all . . . That is, I have been reading all my life, and I see that the relationship is between two, the author and the reader, but what is the ultimate value of the work—I could never tell that myself. So I was very surprised by the way *My Struggle* has been received. I think so many things are constant, and the same for all of us. Everyone has a mother, for example, and a father. It is the same to be sixteen in Buffalo as it is in Copenhagen. Perhaps I didn't know before that what is true for me is true for others as well. Now I get letters, from all over. And it is gratifying; that is the best thing for a writer, to know you have reached people. But there are problems, too, like meeting people who think they have a connection with me, and they are complete strangers . . . They may have expectations of you, and what you should be writing.

Scrivani: In Book One, Karl Ove rents a quiet office in which to write but still seems to draw energy from the urban bustle around him. Is that your modus operandi?

Knausgård: I have my own little house on our property where I am by myself to write. When I was younger, I really believed in solitude; I actually went to an island by myself to work. And now I see I have never written as much as I have since I've had children . . . Writing is about life, and so it is good to be close to life. You cannot control everything if you have children!

Distraction is good, but you need concentration as well. But this is not an effort if you want to do it—it has nothing to do with self-discipline, for me anyway.

Scrivani: Your landscape descriptions are poetic and expansive. Is this part of your heritage? And how is that a book so place-specific is universally appealing—translated now into fifteen languages?

Knausgård: I don't know if there is anything cultural here—I have always been attracted to nature in writing. And I need to recreate spaces around me, including interior rooms, to tell a story. That is why I am so preoccupied with landscape. In my book I try to make physical surroundings visible . . . And why so many have read my books, I really don't know. They are so private, so personal, and it was kind of an experiment to write them . . . I was shocked there was so much attention; it was surreal. I thought this was only a thing in Norway, but that was not the case. The books evoke their own memories—that is what people tell me.

Scrivani: And so, next up?

Knausgård: I thought I would never write about myself again, but I am in the middle of a four-book project. This is not about my inner turmoil and problems . . . They are about objects, and my daughter, before she was born, and then at three months old. They are illustrated with original paintings from Scandinavian artists. The books are named for the seasons—first two, *Autumn* and *Winter*, are already out in Norway. *Spring* will be out next; I still have to write *Summer*, but I'll do that soon . . . but I am longing to write a novel; I am fed up with writing about myself. So we will see.

In Which Karl Ove Knausgaard Hangs Out in His Car, Talking on Life, Children, and Not Really Caring What America Thinks

Paul Holdengraber / 2016

Literary Hub, April 20, 2016, https://lithub.com/in-which-karl-ove-knausgaard-hangs-out-in-his-car-talking/. Reprinted by permission of Paul Holdengraber.

Karl Knausgaard: Hello?
Paul Holdengraber: Is this Karl Ove Knausgaard?
Knausgaard: Yes, it is.
Holdengraber: How are you? It's Paul Holdengraber calling you.
Knausgaard: Hi.
Holdengraber: I'm so happy to talk to you. Where do I find you?
Knausgaard: I am in the car in [. . .], driving.
Holdengraber: Where are you driving to, if I may ask?
Knausgaard: I have just delivered my oldest daughters. They are participating in a musical. So they're rehearsing.
Holdengraber: What are they rehearsing?
Knausgaard: It's *Annie* [*laughs*].
Holdengraber: It's what? An Emmy?
Knausgaard: *Annie*. You know, *Annie*, the musical?
Holdengraber: Yes. And do you watch them rehearse, or do you just go to the final performance?
Knausgaard: I do watch the rehearsal, but today I have my little youngest daughter. She's only two; she's in the back of the car. We have to go back home today because I'm alone with all the children. So I have four, you know?

Holdengraber: Yeah. It's difficult, isn't it? I mean, I must say having two felt like a lot. I didn't want to have more because I didn't want to be outnumbered.

Knausgaard: But for me it's actually opposite. I said that we should have three because we need to be outnumbered. It's good for them.

Holdengraber: You think we *do* need to be outnumbered?

Knausgaard: Yes, I do. That was my plan when I had three children. The fourth was kind of outside of everything, but the three first, that was the plan, that they should outnumber us.

Holdengraber: And we need to have them because they need each other so that they can talk about their parents.

Knausgaard: Yeah.

Holdengraber: They can complain. They can love. They can hate *all of it*.

Knausgaard: Yeah, and they are, you know, independent units by themselves, which is good, I think.

Holdengraber: I think it is a good thing. I think it is a very important thing, and they are also part of a collective memory. They will remember things for each other about their parents and about their upbringing, about their trips, going to see—to be taken to *Annie*. Is performing in plays something that happens often? You're in Sweden, right?

Knausgaard: Yeah.

Holdengraber: Is that something that is part of a curriculum?

Knausgaard: I don't know really, but here it is. They put it on every summer and you must go every summer. So my children—this is the third season they are doing it.

Holdengraber: And this is Malmo?

Knausgaard: No, this is *Vellinge* [. . .]. I live in the countryside, and it's a small village called [. . .], which is thirty-minutes' drive away from our house.

Holdengraber: Right. Because I remember going to Malmo when I was in Copenhagen, you know, at the Black Diamond, where I've done a few things. I went to Malmo, and I imagined you walking those streets. I remember coming to one of those squares and—a kind of old square in Malmo which I can't remember the name—but it was very beautiful. And then I went to a sculpture garden near there. I can't remember the name of the sculpture garden either. Do you know what I'm talking about?

Knausgaard: Yeah, I think it's a park, isn't it?

Holdengraber: Yeah.

Knausgaard: I think I know.

Holdengraber: It's beautiful.

Knausgaard: Yeah.

Holdengraber: So the fifth volume is coming out in America soon. And there are two more to come.

Knausgaard: It's one more to come.

Holdengraber: One more to come.

Knausgaard: Yeah.

Holdengraber: Is there any form of excitement in you at this opportunity of another book coming out in America?

Knausgaard: It's much more of a relief that I don't have to actually write the book. They're just coming out with no effort on my side. That's a good thing [*laughs*], if you know what I mean.

Holdengraber: I do know what you mean. The effort has been done. You must be wondering, you know, "So they're coming out, and I didn't even do anything!"

Knausgaard: Yeah, that's right.

Holdengraber: It's all done already.

Knausgaard: Yeah. And that's the writer's dream, you know? To have the books, to publish them and not write them. But it feels good. And there, the book sells different, so I never know what kind of reaction it will get. So this book gives much more of a page-turner than the others somehow. That's the impression from the readings—from other people.

Holdengraber: Do you have a sense what will strike America in this book?

Knausgaard: No.

Holdengraber: No, and you don't care probably?

Knausgaard: [*Laughs*] No, I don't care. That's right. That sounds very ignorant, but I have left the book, and I do that when I publish it, and I'm not waiting for a reaction. I'm not waiting for something to happen. I'm just—it's there, I've done it. It is what it is. I'm happy if people like it. If they don't . . .

Holdengraber: It's fine.

Knausgaard: It's just fine. But I mean, I have changed completely in that aspect during the publishing of *My Struggle*. Because before I was very, very aware of what people were saying, and it was very important for me, the reviews, and, you know—

Holdengraber: —the response.

Knausgaard: It had been so much that it's kind of an overload of reviews and feedback. So it has made me much freer. I'm publishing books now, and I can do that completely differently.

Holdengraber: The response matters. I know that when we met at first, when the first volume came out, it was a whole different ball game.

Knausgaard: Yeah, that's right.

Holdengraber: And you know, I witnessed, Karl Ove, that tipping point with you where all of a sudden—I mean, I don't think in all these years I've ever experienced anything such as I experienced with you. I don't think I've ever told you that, but from a lot of people wanting to come hear you to overnight having *thousands* of people wanting to *see* you. And I became everybody's best friend overnight, and it reminded me of a wonderful line by Rainer Maria Rilke. At the very beginning of his book on Rodin, he says that fame is but the collection of misunderstandings that gather around a new name.

Knausgaard: Yeah, that's a good quote.

Holdengraber: Isn't it?

Knausgaard: Yeah, it is, yeah.

Holdengraber: And I imagine for you, it takes you in a place where there must be just a lot of anguish, because who are they looking at?

Knausgaard: Yeah, but I try not to go there. You know, I'm driving through this landscape, and I stay here most of the time. And I am working very intensely with a book I have to finish in—really, in a week. And that's what I'm doing.

Holdengraber: If you don't mind my asking, tell me about the book, unless you feel it's bad to talk about it. I'm just curious, you know, briefly and schematically, what kind of book is occupying you now?

Knausgaard: Yeah, it's part of a quartet. It will be published, one book in the autumn, one in the winter, and now I'm publishing one in the spring, and then one in the summer. So it's four books, and the first two have been texts: one word, one page, one thing, one page about objects in the world. You know, like everything you can imagine, really: cars, water, vomit, all kinds of things. And they are introduced with a letter—which is authentic—which I wrote to my daughter when she was unborn. So it's really the appearance of the world as I see it: "This is awaiting you." And there are all these texts, and I really love the format. You know, the short texts where you start the day writing about the toothbrush, and you have nothing to say about toothbrushes, but then in the end of the day, it's one text about toothbrushes. That's an exciting way to work. So it's no psychology in it, but then . . . are you there?

Holdengraber: Yes, I'm listening carefully.

Knausgaard: Yeah. And then these two first books, it's 120 texts, 120 objects. But in Book Three I felt I needed some movement, and then my daughter was born. So that book is kind of a narration of a day in her life.

And this is—was—very difficult to make. So I've been struggling really hard with it. It's been meant to be very light, but then there is some dark stuff that has been going on. So I need to write about that, and I don't want to go into *My Struggle* again, so I try to make it differently somehow. And this is a short story that is—maybe it will be sixty, seventy pages, something like that, a hundred in a book. And then the fourth book would come with short texts again. The seasons are very important in it, and it's very much winter in the winter book and very much spring in the spring book.

Holdengraber: But, you know, brevity seems to me an important choice for you now, considering that that was hardly the choice for *My Struggle*. And I'm reminded by what I think was a very good question from Ben Lerner when he spoke to you in New York about your origins as someone who loved and had such a good poetry teacher.

Knausgaard: Yeah. This is related to that. Are you familiar with the French writer Francis Ponge?

Holdengraber: Am I familiar with him? I so adore him! And I have a story to tell you about him before you tell me anything—if you don't mind, forgive me. I just have to tell you this, Karl Ove, because it is incredible. I love Francis Ponge. I love particularly one of his texts on the need that architects should pay attention to homes that have enough plugs for electricity because they so often don't have enough electrical outlets. [*Knausgaard laughs*] And it's highly comical. Ponge, like [Georges] Perec, had an incredible, serious intent but was very funny at the same time. And a friend of mine was writing in the days when I was a pretend academic. I had friends who were writing very serious dissertations, and he was writing a dissertation on Francis Ponge, and he called him up. And Ponge said, "Excusez moi, monsieur, I'm so sorry, I am not well, I am sick. I would love to see you. Of course, I applaud your effort. I'm not sure that the choice you have made of me as a subject is the right one, but good luck." And my friend said, "Monsieur Ponge, before leaving you, if you had to write a book now about a simple object, let's say a toothbrush, if you had to write a book about—a *poem*, I think he called them—about a simple object, what would it be?" There was a silence on the phone, much like our phone call now. And Francis Ponge said, "I would write a poem about a thermometer." [*Knausgaard laughs*] Because that's what was in his life. What was in his life was a *thermometer*. And that was it. But tell me, you were going to say something about Ponge.

Knausgaard: Yeah, it was just his texts. I read him, and there was not a very good translation in Norwegian in the early nineties when I read them. And I really, really loved the texts and everything and the objects he writes about then. And I, since then, I thought I should do something like that one day, you know? This is a very Ponge-like book I've been writing.

Holdengraber: Well, it *felt* like that to me. And, you know, there is something in the extreme concentration, where you're squeezing things down to the essential.

Knausgaard: Yes, and when you are completely free—and he's completely free—you can write about, you know, a loaf of bread, and it's just wonderful, wonderful prose.

Holdengraber: But because also, who but you—and by you, I don't mean just Karl Ove Knausgaard—I mean, who but you, in the sense that very few people do pay attention to things sufficiently. I mean, you know, there's a—I'm sorry to sound so highfaluting—but there is a gesture here which really reminds us of the origins of phenomenology, of [Edmund] Husserl and people of that nature who were—Ponge himself was deeply influenced by the object in itself, looking at it really with concentration, attention and maybe even a form of love, simply by virtue of giving it time.

Knausgaard: Yeah. It's true.

Holdengraber: Do you know, by the way—I'm sorry, this is leading us in directions which are tremendously esoteric—but do you know a French philosopher by the name of Henri Maldiney?

Knausgaard: Maldiney?

Holdengraber: Yeah.

Knausgaard: No.

Holdengraber: M-A-L-D-I-N-E-Y. I will send you a reference. It's a book called *Le legs des choses*,[1] *The Legacy of Things*, and it's a book written from a philosophical point of view on the work of Francis Ponge. And for some reason, I think you need it.

Knausgaard: [*Laughs*] That sounds wonderful. Thank you.

Holdengraber: You know, it's really about common things. And I think the other person I mentioned who I so love, Karl Ove, is Perec.

Knausgaard: Yeah, I know him. He's wonderful too.

Holdengraber: You know, he talks—

Knausgaard: But in a completely different—

Holdengraber: —completely different way.

Knausgaard: Yeah.

Holdengraber: Maybe less disciplined.

Knausgaard: Yeah. And less of a poet.

Holdengraber: Yeah, maybe *not* a poet.

Knausgaard: No.

Holdengraber: So, was Ben Lerner right when he said there is this pull back in you towards poetry?

Knausgaard: I don't really know. I don't read much poetry anymore.

Holdengraber: You don't?

Knausgaard: No, I don't. But I don't read much at all, really. But he is somehow right.

Holdengraber: You don't read much anymore? Why?

Knausgaard: It's just I don't feel I have the time, and it doesn't feel like work anymore. It feels like leisure. And I can't. I mean, it's like I don't find time and I've so much to write and to do, but I did read an absolutely wonderful book, which is well known. You know the Nobel committee in Sweden?

Holdengraber: Of course.

Knausgaard: He was the secretary for them. [. . .] And he writes too, and there was an interview with him on Swedish television, one hour. And he said, yes, he'd been in a war and in a true crisis. And he was talking about the darkness and how miserable he was, and it seems like he was on the brink of suicide— . . . Excuse me. I just have to fix something.

Holdengraber: Take your time.

Knausgaard: Yeah. Yeah. Just two seconds. . . . [*Knausgaard's voice in the distance, speaking another language*] Sorry about that!

Holdengraber: Not at all. It's part of being on the phone.

Knausgaard: Yeah. So he was talking about that. So lucky. But then he said he read something, and it saved him, and it was like—then the interviewer tried to make him say what book it was, and he didn't want to say it. And then in the end he said it was Turgenev. You know, *The Hunter's Sketchbook*? And they asked, "Why, why did that book save you?" And he said, it was no answer to it, but he never thought that literature would hold the whole way through. And the interviewer [said] into where it was real, real life, so to speak. I can't say it in English properly, but as, you know, that it was good enough. And then I thought I just have to read this book, and I did, and I completely understand what he meant. It was such a wonderful book. It was one of the absolutely best I've read ever.

Holdengraber: I have to make an admission here, which is I have not read it.

Knausgaard: No, because it's completely unambitious, and there's not even a project. It's just him wandering around writing about the people he meets, and the nature, and that's it. And it's like these sketches, but it has this power of presence. It's like you are in 1840 in Russia, and I read Tolstoy at the same time and that wonderful, wonderful novel. I read *War and Peace* again, but it still, it lacked that presence. And I saw it immediately when I read through Turgenev. And then I read *Fathers and Sons* and his other stuff from then. It was not even close to where he was when he wrote that, and it's so unpretentious and easy. Like I said, it's really like a really, really great painter doing something with no effort at all, but it still is magical in a way. So that's the last thing I read that made an impression on me.

Holdengraber: Well, and what an impression! And, you know, it strikes me as we grow older, how many of those kinds of experiences, such as the one you described, do we have left in us?

Knausgaard: [*Laughs*] That's a good point.

Holdengraber: You know, to be so overcome by something so powerful is rare. I mean, one has to be present to *that* presence. One has to be present to Turgenev describing things that make you feel as though you're right there.

Knausgaard: Yeah. I think you must need it. That's what's it takes. And if you need it, you are open to it, and you can take it, but you really need to need it. And I did, when I read it.

Holdengraber: Do you watch movies?

Knausgaard: Very rarely now. I'm sorry—there's someone knocking. [*Short but audible non-English conversation with the person at the door*] . . . I'm sorry!

Holdengraber: Not at all. I wish I knew what you said, but I agree. People are speaking a lot, and now about that book, which is so extraordinary—and reading an article yesterday in the *New York Times* about how this Anders *Breivik*[2]—I think you say—he's feeling that the prison is not treating him well.

Knausgaard: Yeah, I know.

Holdengraber: It's wild.

Knausgaard: It is insane.

Holdengraber: And saluting, you know. He came into the courtroom, doing a Nazi salute.

Knausgaard: Yeah.

Holdengraber: It is frightening. It really is. And, you know, here we are talking about that. And then thinking about books that may save us in some way.

Knausgaard: Yeah.

Holdengraber: You know, one thing I would love to do one day is bring you together in conversation with Lars von Trier.

Knausgaard: Yeah. We talked about that when I saw you in New York.

Holdengraber: I think it would be—

Knausgaard: Do you know him?

Holdengraber: I don't, but you know when . . . This little program I've started now with the Literary Hub called *A Phone Call from Paul*. It simply is doing something very old-fashioned, which we don't do very much anymore, which is speak to each other on the phone. People actually don't particularly like it. They like to text or to email because, I suppose, it keeps a distance; it interrupts, but in a different way. And so, my guess is I would try to find a way of calling him and saying, "I have an idea and I'm not even sure why it's a good idea, but I imagine that you and Karl Ove would have things to say to each other that you don't even know you have to say to each other."

Knausgaard: That's very optimistic. I'm a bit afraid of him.[3]

Holdengraber: Are you?

Knausgaard: Yeah.

Holdengraber: You have *not* met him.

Knausgaard: No, I've never met him, no.

Holdengraber: Well, we should try one day. We should definitely try. I will, with your permission, I will just see if I can get somewhere. I don't give up easily, as you may know.

Knausgaard: I know.

Notes

1. *Le legs des choses dans l'oeuvre de Francis Ponge* (1974).

2. A Norwegian mass murderer, who is one of Knausgaard's subjects in Volume Six of *My Struggle*.

3. Regarding Knausgaard's artistic admiration of Lars von Trier, including introducing and discussing a screening of von Trier's *The Idiots* in New York on May 9, 2015, see pages 66–77.

"Literature Should Be Ruthless"

Kasper Bech Dyg / 2016

Louisiana Channel, Aug. 19, 2016, https://channel.louisiana.dk/video/karl-ove-knausgaard-literature-should-be-ruthless. Reprinted by permission of Louisiana Museum of Modern Art.

[For the transcription of this video, translated from Norwegian, the editor of this volume has largely used Louisiana Channel's captions, except for punctuation. Long pauses are rendered as ellipses (. . .).]

Karl Ove Knausgaard: [*Reading*] "The person you are in private doesn't demand any insight because there is no distance, no way in to traverse; only your self is what there is. But when you go on to another situation, there's a distance, and the objectification turns the self into something else while it remains the same. These tiny differences grow over time into conflicts to an extent where the self can't bear it without becoming dysfunctional because the self is also our frame of action, and that makes it necessary to repress and forget but also to remember. Memories make up our own narrative, maybe the most important part of our identity. The string of memories holds it together, and repression and forgetfulness keep the string of memories clean, noncontradictory and manageable."[1]

[*Black screen*]

When you write, you're looking for something that's hard to define. You're looking for a means of expression, I think. An outlet for saying something meaningful, a form that enables you to say something significant—in all kinds of ways. I didn't find that form until I latched onto what has been dubbed autofiction or autobiography or whatever. . . . I don't know why I did it, but it ignited a fire in me. It was almost like it was forbidden or dangerous. You had to cross a line, so it was . . . It was exciting to delve into it. But it didn't spring from a theoretical interest in the self or myself. I was interested in writing, and I've always written, but it never felt like it was my own. It felt like it came from the outside. This gave me a means of expressing things in myself, that I met in myself, but that I wasn't aware of. *My Struggle* showed me the richness of the self. There are no boundaries between the self and culture. The self is saturated with all kinds of literary and cultural impulses—friends and family. There are no boundaries, just a voice. That voice can be close to your identity or not. The literary voice enables you to offer fragments of your identity, fragments of a conception, what I call "strings of memories"—and the narrative of the self, because there is so much more to it.

[*Black screen*]

[*Reading*] "Writing about oneself is to some extent the opposite of insight because insight is directed inwards, and writing about oneself is directed outwards. Yet both processes strive for intimacy and then understanding. If you write about yourself, you see yourself from the outside and gain a strange objectivity that is both tied to the inside and the outside, and this objectivity allows you to go into your self as if it were someone else's. And thus, you've gone full circle because that movement demands insight—or empathy, as it's called today."

[*Black screen*]

The difference between *My Struggle* and my new seasonal work is small—and hard for others to see. It started out as two things. One was short texts about objects, the material reality, very inspired by Francis Ponge. The other was a letter, or rather a diary, that I wrote for my daughter. I describe reality from an external perspective. I project myself outwards. There is no introspection. I'm not interested in myself but in the object. The dynamics are different. I try to push the psychology aside. It's there, but it's not the main thing. The diary to my daughter is also addressed to her, and it's not directed inwards. It ends up as the novel, the third book in the series, *Spring*. I cut out 90 percent of myself and describe a day in our life: what we do, what it looks like, the various moods on this spring day, what I feel, and so on. But I never explore *why*, in the introspective manner of *My Struggle*. The book is much more extroverted. I leave most of my inner self out of it. The book revolves around a traumatic experience that happened before my daughter was born. I had to write about it in this book to keep it truthful. But I didn't want to write about how *I* experienced it. I wanted to describe the impact it had on my surroundings. Almost—well, much more objectively.

Kasper Bech Dyg: Try to elaborate on this style of writing in great detail. What kind of reality does such detailed description open up?

Knausgaard: It opens up a nonexistent reality. You evoke it by writing or thinking about it. But it's also true, because you write about things that exist. It's this impossible conflict between objectivity and subjectivity. A classic issue. I have a favorite quote by Pentti Saarikoski: "I don't write about the world and its places but the places and their world." That is true of all of these texts. Every little dot opens up a world, a world that relates to other things and phenomena. But you can't see the world in that manner when you live in it. But the possibility is there, and that's where literature or art comes in. It becomes extra hard if it opens up for introspection. I wanted these static objects that open up tiny worlds—and a dynamic movement. In the third book, that puts the objects in motion. This again renders them insignificant, just fleeting objects. And the interhuman relationships are all-devouring. That's what being human is like: We are focused on other people.

[*Black screen*]

I think less about autofiction than anyone else. We have so many narratives about reality today—and so many images—and they're all structured in the same way. It's as if we have the whole world inside us. If you say Brazil, I know what it's like in Brazil. If you say . . . Sri Lanka, images pop up. But the tactile sense of intimacy is gone. If you've witnessed an accident, you know the smell and the setting. But if you see a picture of it, you take out reality—and you're left with a narrative, *fiction*. That creates a longing for something else, something here and now that doesn't push us away but pulls us in. That's what I long for, anyway, when I'm writing. I think it's important because in this age of many narratives, fiction can't offer a proper take on reality anymore. . . . You could say that autobiography doesn't differ much from fiction—and it doesn't. But I've tried to break down these narrative structures by doing away with the narrative altogether. The second volume of *My Struggle* hardly has any narrative at all. It's a sequence of events, but it doesn't lead anywhere. I wasn't aware that I was doing that, but I see it now. The same thing goes for my new books: texts about objects aren't narratives. It's just reality devoid of a narrative. But in order not to lose the readers, you must have some kind of narrative to capture them.

Dyg: These very detailed descriptions, do they evoke some kind of intimacy?

Knausgaard: Yeah. To me they do, but it's not a conscious move on my part. It just interests me, that's all. But you could write a work of fiction that way as well. Take the last book by Bolaño. It doesn't offer a linear narrative.

[*Black screen*]

[*Reading*] "It's the narrative's possibilities, against which concepts such as fiction and nonfiction are inadequate. They are too coarse-meshed or irrelevant. They're not the bone of contention. Some say fiction is more true than reality, truth having a lofty significance as crystalized and universal: artistic truth, as they called it once. That the truth of reality, the incident as it played out, is tied to the narrator, with all the implied limitations. I believe that the poetic truth is if not bigger, then more important than that of reality. But it doesn't take a lot of autobiographical writing to realize that it's governed by the same principle. Not in that you embellish or fabricate, but in the way the story is formed, which version you go with. It's like an equation. If the universal truth rises, the personal truth drops. More than anything, it depends on the setting, how much is revealed around the 'I'—and how much the narrator identifies with the 'I.' Total identification promotes the personal truth at the expense of the other, and from that springs the old rule of thumb: that literature should be personal but not private. Private things are only relevant to the writer. Herein lies the paradox that the author must compromise his own truth; that is, create an 'I' that the he or she doesn't fully identify with to express something that may be true to others."

[*Black screen*]

I read manuscripts by other authors because I am a publisher too. Many of them are first-person narratives about their own lives. The poor ones are those that offer only themselves. That's all they write about, and it's only interesting to themselves. I know it sounds funny coming from a guy who's written three thousand pages about himself! But I thought I could do it. But there are layers of distance, irony, and openings when you write. There's an objectivity in the literary form—the limitations also included. When I wrote *My Struggle*, I had a specific focus throughout the books, which eliminated all other versions which were continuous. You must impose limitations on yourself when you write—in order to say *just this*. Other limitations mean you can only say *this*. So it's crucial. On the other hand, the concept of the narrator must be pulverized—or at least afford you the space to express something else as well. It's unbearable to listen to someone who *knows* what happened. The reader should understand that the narrator is in a context—with many other versions—and this should be incorporated into the text, not to play it safe, but because it's part of the meaning.

[*Black screen*]

[*Reading*] "So towards others, the self is constructed as an address, rather like the basic figure of language is an address, while by itself the self is structured like a story made up of a string of memories, rather like the bond between couples. They too share a story that constitutes their identity as a couple, and if it strays too far from reality, that too is bound to collapse. A couple's story needs constant affirmation; the self's story needs constant affirmation for both the couple and the self hold so many contradictions that they have to boil them down to a few simple maxims: This is us, this is me. So if the self is a narrative, it's only one of many versions."

[*Black screen*]

You don't realize it until many years later what inspires and impacts you. You can't see it. You can't plan your style. . . . But you do have a certain affinity for someone. I had a strong affinity for Marcel Proust at school. I never thought about why; it's just always been there. Then I read Gombrowicz's autobiography—no, Gombrowicz's *diary*. And that really appealed to me. Before I wrote my first two novels, which are fictional, I read Swedish author Stig Larsson's *Natta de Mina* [*Goodnight, My Dears*]. It was a shockingly raw read and had a huge impact on me—and on all my friends in the Bergen literary community in the nineties. It shocked us all—everyone I knew, anyway. I never thought I'd go down that path, but it remained in the back of my mind as something very powerful. If you remove a filter, it opens up for another force than fiction offers. . . . But after I'd written the first book, I moved to Stockholm, and for six years I couldn't write anything. There were two options: one was my autobiographical notes from my time in Bergen, and the other was a novel about angels, and I chose the latter. But in the back of my mind was writing about things as they were. But I didn't actively decide to do it at some point. It was just an option that emerged.

Dyg: You have a passage about Flaubert and his book *Madame Bovary*. Why did it make such an impact on you? And what have you learned from it?

Knausgaard: [*Knausgaard smiles, laughs*] I've read it three times in my life. First as a child, I found it in the bookcase. I loved *The Three Musketeers* and *The Scarlet Pimpernel*—French adventure novels—so I read it in continuation of those. The 1800s, horse-drawn carriages, romance—it fascinated me. I reread it as a literature student in Bergen in the nineties—as an example of realism, at a time when realism was considered naïve. The concept of doing away with lavish language in order to represent reality authentically. At that time, we were very much into language, so that's why we studied it. And then I read it again later. I also read Flaubert's letters. In them, he opens up about his own life. It's like being backstage in Flaubert's life. They're very good, but not like *Madame Bovary*. In *Madame Bovary*, he concentrates this huge reality into one person, and it's just fantastic. In my opinion, it's the best novel ever written. . . . It's hard to say anything new about it, but it still has a freshness to it. This controlled perfection—that I usually don't like—elevates it. Maybe because it's about imperfection. I love this meeting between the romantic concept of life and life itself. His realistic style is superb. I write at the end of the text that it's like looking at the world—and suddenly someone wipes the windshield and you see it clearly.

[*Black screen*]

[*Reading*] "Even though my current texts *are* autobiographical and about my life, life in itself is another matter. It unfolds somewhere else behind the text, a dark mountainside of which only glimpses are seen as if in the light of a flashlight. We've talked a lot about how to recount an experience you've had, without offering your own version of it, one which doesn't focus on the narrator but on the experience itself. It sounds like we're splitting hairs, but no, there's a big difference, and when my editor first mentioned it, it opened up a room of narratives."

When I wrote it—I wrote that in my diary—but I'm referring to a conversation with my editor. He asked me, "How's life?" It's a throwback to a conversation we had while I was writing *Spring*, which is about me and my family in a somewhat dramatized fashion. "How do I tell that story?" He said the redeeming words: "It doesn't have to be your version. Recount the events, but don't invest your own." That was the background for this train of thought. He writes too, so he knows very well that writing about yourself is a tiny path through a huge forest of other things—or other perspectives. Literature offers a form for all this, but only a small part of it. In *Summer*, I've written a fictional text. It's a diary entry that evolves into fiction like this: "In the next sentence, this narrator will be replaced by another narrator. This narrator will be filled with another—a seventy-three-year-old woman from Malmo." And then the other narrator takes over. They are my words, of course, but I had a vague sense of her that made it a little bit different. I wrote thirty pages, her narrative, which I told with my words, but there was a difference. I put her into situations I haven't experienced, but I invest all my feelings in them and identify with them. Sure, I haven't met the woman, and she's very much me, but it channeled a part of me to another place. It's not so unlike writing about yourself. If you were to write about your seventeen-year-old self, so much is gone that you'd have to do it in the same way, channel yourself into another "I." And all the time the author is hovering above, judging it, at a distance. In my experience, there's not much of a difference. They are just different means of expressing different sides of what a person contains.

[*Black screen*]

[*Reading*] "The story that is my identity, this crab-like shell, this set of conceptions that I don't challenge, contrast with literature. For while I'm not interested in my personal freedom, and haven't been since I was a teenager, literary freedom means everything to me. It is the essence of literature, and that's why I wrote 'Ruthlessness is the justification of literature.' Because freedom and ruthlessness are two sides of the same coin."

[*Black screen*]

I think when we look at something—film or pictures or whatever—they are conveyed, and we form an opinion. "Distance" is the key word. When you read, there is no distance. You take in strange things that you otherwise distance yourself from, compelling you to articulate them with your own voice. I have my own opinion about gender, about man, woman, and family. If I see something on TV that doesn't fit into that—I just turn it off or I get mad, you know. But then I read a great book by American author Maggie Nelson, and her view of the world is far away from my own. But when I read it, I articulate it with my own voice, my own feelings, and I'm compelled to think about it in an intimate way. I like it, but it's also a struggle—so many things go on. And that's because there's just me and her. I don't know her, but she wrote this in her language, and I read it. Only literature can pull you in like that. But it can be exploited as well. Hitler knew that literature was a bad medium for propaganda. Literature disintegrates and breaks down and isn't as effective as visual impressions that enthrall you. You always put yourself into literature. It's an important part of it. But that's just my . . . I've always read. My children don't read much. I try to encourage them to read, but it's easier to watch TV or a film. . . . There's an intimacy to literature that no other art form offers, as far as I can see.

[*Black screen*]

Dyg: If you were to give young writers a piece of advice, what would it be?

Knausgaard: I have only one thing to say: Sit down and write. If it doesn't work, just keep on. That's my experience. If you're willing to do it for ten years and pay the price for it; your parents and friends may think you're an idiot without any talent . . . If you're willing to endure all that long enough, something is bound to happen. It's not very hard to copy something else. You tend to mimic your idols. But then it's not meaningful. You just want to publish a book. But if you keep sitting there, sooner or later it will become meaningful. It has to be like that. If not a matter of life and death, then at least the main thing in your life. So just sit and sit and sit and write.

Note

1. The readings in this conversation are apparently from Knausgaard's otherwise unpublished diary.

"My Munch"

Alf Marius Opsahl / 2017

This is an English translation of the Norwegian cover story "Min Munch" ("My Munch"), originally printed in *D2* magazine and published by *Dagens Næringsliv*, March 29, 2017. (The excerpt from *My Struggle One* is from Donald Bartlett's translation.) https://www.dn.no/d2/profil/dvard-munch/karl-ove-knausgard/munch-museum/my-munch/2-1-54607. Reprinted by permission of Alf Marius Opsahl.

He is standing against the sunny wall outside the Munch Museum and receives the question: "Do you ever miss the time before *My Struggle*?"

"No. Not at all. No," he replies.

"Why not?"

"No, there's just no way. I'm much happier now."

"You're happier now?"

"Yes, absolutely more happy. Of course."

The last time I met Karl Ove Knausgård as a journalist was on a September day in 2009. This was before anyone had read about his premature ejaculations, his alcoholic father, diaper changes, and life as a father of young children. He was already a well-known author at that time, but not yet a literary rock star. On this September day, everything was still on its way out into the world: six volumes about the author himself and the people closest to him. *My Struggle* in its entirety would become the longest novel in Norwegian history, and Knausgård was kneeling before the scaffold. Would he be received as the next Hamsun? Would it all drop to the earth like a dead turkey? He came slinking out of a flat in Malmo, located between a clothing store and a Chinese restaurant on Triangelen square. We went to a nearby café.

In May the author will also publish the book *So Much Pain on So Little Surface*.[1]

In the book the author interviews artists about their relationship to Munch.

"The closer I get to the present, the more dangerous it becomes," he said.

Friendly, but also uncomfortable. From time to time, he spoke in long tirades, as if his thoughts were flying in all directions. But he then would also suddenly become introverted and silent, as if what he wanted most of all was just to disappear back to where he'd come from: the balcony, chain smoking in solitude.

Afterwards he sent me an email: "It became a claustrophobic experience; it wasn't your fault. When I left, I thought that it is almost impossible for me to move in that direction: from the book and out into reality. It was written inside a secluded space, and it is actually only in that space that what I say can be said. I was like an animal trapped in headlights."

Eight years later, the *My Struggle* books have made him an international star. He receives accolades all over the world—most recently the Swedish daily *Expressen*'s Björn Nilsson prize in February. He is interviewed by the major newspapers, and he has started his own publishing house (Pelikanen). The American director Alexander Payne is working on a film based on the travelogue he wrote for the *New York Times*.[2] And now he has been invited by the management of the Munch Museum in his native country, Norway, to curate a special Munch exhibition, which will open in May.

Black boots. Black trousers. A dark jacket, a gray scarf. Almost a decade has passed since he wrote: "In the window before me, I can vaguely make out the reflection of my face. Apart from one eye, which is glistening, and the area immediately below, which dimly reflects a little light, the whole of the left side is in shadow. Two deep furrows divide my forehead, one deep furrow intersects each cheek, all of them as if filled with darkness, and with the eyes staring and serious, and the corners of my mouth drooping, it is impossible not to consider this face gloomy. What has engraved itself in my face?"

He will soon be fifty years old. The furrows are deeper; his hair is grayer. Otherwise, he has at least bought himself a bit more expensive clothing. But there is another change that is more conspicuous as he comes strolling into the tiny cinema in the basement of the Munch Museum in Oslo. His face is possibly still mask-like, to use Knausgård's own words, but that can have just as much to do with the fact that for several years he has been traveling around the world, been interviewed on stages in Berlin, in New York, and acquired a practiced manner of being. The point is, here comes also the personality Karl Ove Knausgård. The author, who previously used to stiffen when he entered a room of people, has learned to play this role as himself, as a professional.

"Karl Ove," he says and greets the others firmly before sitting down.

Along with the Munch Museum's own curator, Kari Brandtzæg, he takes his seat more or less in the middle of the sloping auditorium, where also other representatives from the museum and a team from Snøhetta's design department are present. They are in the home stretch now: Knausgård will choose the colors for the walls on which the approximately 150 works he has selected will hang. The designer Henrik Haugan from Snøhetta moves to a spot furthest down, on the floor by the screen, where he begins to show the preliminary color samples from a projector.

"They can tolerate quite a bit of color, I believe," Haugan says about Munch's paintings and explains further: "Many modernist painters require a little surrounding breathing space in order for the work to function, while Munch is a bit more like the old masters. In a way, the force of the paintings is enclosed within the frames, they can be hung against virtually anything at all," he says.

For the first of several rooms, the proposal is a shade of blue. It is shown on the screen.

"It's a little too melancholy," Knausgård says. He continues: "I believe it can work with blue there, but it has to be a strong shade."

"Not so bright?" the Snøhetta designer asks.

"More intense, is what I'm thinking," Knausgård replies.

He calls himself an amateur curator, but there is nonetheless no doubt about who is the focal point around which everything revolves while he is here. It is the last day of a week the author has spent in Oslo. He has gone through these more practical aspects of the exhibition, but he has also taken small journeys in Munch's footsteps, to both Åsgårdstrand and Jeløya. Parallel to the exhibition, the author is working on another book, about Munch, which will be entitled *So Much Pain on So Little Surface* (*Så mye smerte på så liten flate*). In the book, which he estimates will be about 150 pages long, he also reflects about the essence of art in general and interviews Munch experts and a series of artists—among them Vanessa Baird and Anselm Kiefer.

"And then I also have David Hockney on my list," he states.

"Has he said yes?"

"I sent him an email and asked if he would like to come to the opening and that I was thinking of doing an interview with him about Munch. Then he said that he was interested in principle, but that he is eighty years old, and his hearing is poor, and he's not very fond of traveling and a lot of such things. Then I thought that I would email him and instead ask him to answer questions."

Together with the director brothers Emil Trier and Joachim Trier, Knausgård is also involved in a new film—this one also about Norway's most famous artist. The rest is apparently a bit unclear, for the time being: "A lot of it is Joachim Trier and I walking around and talking," he explains.

"What kind of film will it be?"

"Nobody knows how it will turn out. We were down in the storeroom filming yesterday. We just film and see what happens," he says.

After going into a hallway to look at some fabric swatches in the light from a window, Knausgård sits down together with the curator Brandtzæg in the museum café. They are apparently supposed to agree upon some dates for the upcoming time period. They will have lunch—sandwiches and coffee—before I will also receive a little time alone with Knausgård, for an interview.

As Kari Brandtzæg also says: "Karl Ove is the boss. He is the one who is supposed to shine."

He has also received assistance. In the past year, these two have together worked their way through all of the Munch works in the cellar, chosen around 150 of them—the majority of which have never been exhibited before.

"We have not placed importance on chronology or biography. There will be neither titles nor dates. It will be a much freer and more emotionally charged path into Munch's artistic world," Brandtzæg says.

"There must also be a reason why many of these paintings have never been exhibited before?"

"No," she says.

"There has long been a very narrow, tacitly agreed upon, biographic focus on Munch, with these early Frieze of Life paintings that reappear over and over in relation to different themes. With Karl Ove, it is a fresh and new narrative that is generated."

The exhibition has been titled *Mot skogen* (*To the Forest*), after one of Munch's paintings. Few of the artist's iconic works will be included. In other words, a tourist looking for *The Scream* will be disappointed.

"I had a pretty clear idea with regard to not showing any of the famous Munch paintings, that it almost shouldn't even resemble Munch," Knausgård says.

It is the "dust gatherers," Munch's lesser-known works, which will dominate.

"The idea is to try to bring these into the spotlight, try to give them meaning, give them relevance."

The author connects the idea to a collection of books he received when he turned forty, containing photographs of Munch's entire artistic production.

"It was the first time I began looking at him properly," he explains.

"I was surprised about how much there was, how different everything was, how distant it was from the image we now have of Munch. Some of the paintings were almost the complete opposite of this, aesthetically speaking."

"In what way?"

"If you look at *Vampire* or almost any one of these paintings, they have no relation to *place*, to the here and now. They are related to an idea he has had, or a perception, of a woman, for example, something that wasn't there, something he created. Which is very powerful. The paintings we have chosen can be of a barn in a garden, painted right there and then. And that's it. There's almost no intensity at all. It is more material, more materialistic, in terms of the technique," he says.

Knausgård maintains that precisely by removing the icons, one is obliged to address the qualities of the paintings in their own right.

"If we hadn't known about *Madonna* or any of these other famous paintings, who would Munch be then? I think that this is an important exercise to carry out because we have such a clear image of Munch. When we see *The Scream*, we are unable to see it as a painting. We just see it as an icon. But one must see these paintings as paintings because one hasn't seen them before."

"Do you identify with Munch?"

"I have thought about that quite a bit—while I've been writing about him, while looking at the paintings. I see something of what I personally want: to create without thinking about creating a masterpiece, just taking it as it comes, being in that flow. Although it is of course difficult to compare writing with painting, there is an aesthetic in Munch that I am especially fond of."

He adds: "I am also fascinated by his savageness, his rawness, by how he wasn't concerned about finishing things. There is something of a very rough quality and a powerful intensity in everything he has done."

"What about the existential sadness? You have said yourself that you scarcely have any joy in your life?"

"That's true. Yes, he was known for being dreary. But what I identify with is his temperament. I don't identify with Munch, in other words. I believe he was a very unusual guy. But there are elements there that I can relate to. And then there is something in his art that I can relate to. But that is true for everyone, of course."

He draws a connection between Munch's *The Scream* and an exhibition he recently saw in London of the work of the German artist Anselm Kiefer.

The German's apocalyptic sculptures and paintings caused Knausgård to think about how one looks at a painting today.

"Why do we look at pictures? How do we look at pictures? *The Scream* was a radical painting in its day. At that time there were also realistic paintings that depicted trauma, difficulty, and the speculative. Death, sex, disease, etc. But there was always a space to be found there, which could open up for something else. You could contemplate it, feel compassion, and so on, but there was also a distance there."

When he saw Kiefer's exhibition, he also saw an artist who does the opposite of Munch's *The Scream*. While Munch depicted humans at extremely close range, through his images devoid of humans Kiefer creates a distance, a space—and as such, also a contrast to today's world.

"Munch simply closed up that space. There is no space in *The Scream*. There is no reconciliation whatsoever. There is an immediate emotional impact. When I saw Kiefer in London, there was *only* space. There wasn't one human being there. Then I thought that it is because the distance to our emotions is like that."

He snaps his fingers above the tabletop.

"When something happens in the world, we have an emotional reaction right away," he says. "We live in Munch's world. We live in *The Scream*'s world."

He goes outside to smoke a cigarette and sits down with his cell phone on one of the chairs at the café tables in the snow outside. Afterwards he and Brandtzæg trudge in through the corridors. She is apparently going to find the calendar; they must meet again before the exhibition is finished. She fetches more coffee. We are shown into a room, he and I, a kind of meeting room. There is a table there surrounded by some chairs. A window faces the park outside; otherwise it's rather empty. When Brandtzæg shuts the door, Knausgård sits down on the chair at the end, with his back to the window. He remains seated like that, drumming his fingers against the table while I ask him about his new life. He still struggles to find the peace of mind to write, he says. At the same time, it is becoming increasingly important to him.

In the future he wants to return to writing novels with fictional characters, in a fictional universe. About *My Struggle* and the subsequent books, the author says: "Now I know very well how to write in that way. I have done it so much. So I must try to move away from it. There's also a hype, right? And the air always goes out of a hype. Then you land somewhere else. I've just tried not to think about it. Just write and work with what emerges," he says about his new existence.

He is in the process of getting divorced, and a former life is also slowly creeping back: He recently bought himself a turntable, and has started buying vinyl records again.

"I'd completely forgotten the pleasure of it. I was just in London and bought LPs there also. It was incredibly fun," he says. "Or not incredibly fun, actually. But it was like a kind of back-to-basics feeling."

"Before all the soul-baring of *My Struggle*, before it came out, you were very nervous. How has this changed? Do you mind less? Have you acquired a thicker skin?"

"I have acquired thicker skin, yes. Plus, I've accepted the consequences of that. I can't think about how it looks from the outside any longer. I've completely stopped doing that. I do what must be done and don't think about the consequences of it."

"Do you manage to do that?"

"More or less. But now and then, things will get to me. But it's a matter of protecting oneself. Now I'm actually just talking about the media and the public sphere, the role there. But I'm very much at home in the tiny village where I live. I don't see anyone, I'm just with my family, or sitting and writing. That's what I want, and that's what I must try to protect. More and more, that's the way I think: that's what it's all about."

"But when you sit and talk about Karl Ove Knausgård in these interviews everywhere, is it like talking about a character, almost?"

"No. It's like *being* a character. It's like going into a character. That's how it is. But it's not who I genuinely am. For me it's only a very unnatural situation, to sit there and talk about myself, particularly on a stage."

"You've become more professional?"

"Yes. But it's also true that to do it well, I can't play it safe, either. I just have to talk and take some chances. And then it also becomes exhausting in a way."

A few days before, Knausgård was interviewed by the Swedish newspaper *Expressen*, in conjunction with his being awarded the newspaper's Björn Nilsson prize. Things worked out as they tend to do, when one has reached a certain level of fame. Other newspapers pick out a few quotes they find to be sensational and write articles that are based on these. In the newspaper *Dagbladet*: "Knausgård lashes out at Norway in a new interview: 'Norwegians lack professionalism, they are a little more childish.'"

I ask him if he has heard about this.

"I heard about it. I haven't read it. I don't want to know anything about it," he says and immediately afterwards asks me: "I have no idea what they have used, but I assume that it was negative?"

"So you don't read such things?"

"No, I really don't. Then I would have in fact been destroyed, I believe. It's bad enough knowing that it's out there."

"*Norwegians lack professionalism, they are a little more childish.*"

He releases a kind of sigh.

"What did you mean, really?"

"I was speaking about the differences in the cultures. The Swedes have an extremely formal culture, where everyone knows what they are supposed to do, and there are roles for everyone. And then I come to Norway, and it's not like that. Then it seems as if they are unprofessional and a little childish. But that is really a good quality. Unlike the Swedes, who are very stiff and formal. Norway isn't like that. It wasn't anything more than that," he says.

He sits in silence for a while. He looks out the window. He drums on the table top a bit. Then suddenly he starts twisting in his seat.

"Oh," he says, and: "Ohhh."

"What is it?"

"But what does this say about me? Why have they written this? Good God. That isn't what I think of Norwegians. It goes without saying. In relation to the Swedes, everyone is unprofessional." He looks up. "You see? Oh, dear me. That's how it is." Still troubled. "Little things that I actually shouldn't care about can completely dominate my state of mind. For me it's very much about getting away from it, and to do that I must get away from myself. Then I can read or write. When I am with the children, it's also different because then it's about something besides me."

He no longer reads interviews of himself, after a writer colleague recommended that he stop. "It was during a tour with some Norwegian and Swedish authors in connection with my being nominated for the Nordic Council Literature Prize. The Swedish author Majgull Axelsson noticed how disturbed I was by what was written about me, how much anxiety I had in relation to it. She said: 'Never read it. Never watch yourself on television. Never listen to yourself on the radio. Just be yourself and talk.' I have tried to follow her advice. Sometimes I have a relapse. I read Norwegian newspapers and suddenly something is printed there. I don't *read* it, but maybe I see a headline ... But I try to stay away completely. It was very good advice," he says.

There are still members of his family with whom he doesn't speak, after the publication of *My Struggle*. All four of his children have also appeared in several of his books. The eldest are now about to become teenagers. They have Google.

"Are they prepared for what is found there?"

"They know a little bit," he answers.

"I have always talked about it with them, so they know that it's there. That I have written about myself and about us. But they don't understand the consequences of it, as such. They are sheltered."

Last autumn the news that he and his wife Linda Boström Knausgård (forty-four years old) had separated became public knowledge. They now live in their respective houses in a small village of three hundred residents, on the outskirts of Ystad, in Österlen in southern Sweden.

"How are you doing now?"

"I feel good," he says and smiles. "Of course, it's been full of conflict and all that. But it's very much about the children, how to get them through this without it having any consequences for them. That is something everyone who gets divorced is familiar with. That is the number one priority. It's also a cliché, but it is what is most important."

"Do you see them often?"

"Yes, absolutely."

"It's a kind of every other week set-up?"

"It's the best of both worlds," he replies.

He can still become nervous, but a lot has changed since as a thirty-nine-year-old he sat there at the window in Malmo, looking at the shadowy reflection of his face, while he wondered about what had engraved itself there. Little things he shouldn't care about can still bring him down, things that can "totally dominate your state of mind."

"But I'm no longer afraid," he says. "That's the big difference."

Before, when he entered the Oktober publishing house, in the time preceding publication of *My Struggle*, he didn't speak. "I would come into a room and say nothing. I went out for dinner and said nothing. I was completely closed-off," he explains.

The books based on the four seasons of the year will now be published in England and the USA. In the end of May, *My Struggle VI* will be launched in Germany. He had actually planned to stay home. "I'd planned to say no since it's about Hitler, and . . . yes, everything that entails. But then I found out that that's not an option. I have to go there and take it. Take the heat."

Success has never been a goal for him, but even an occasionally tormented man deserves to have his moments.

"And it's fantastic," he says about his ongoing success. "No author can ask for more than this," he continues. "I have been given the chance to curate an exhibition at the Munch Museum. I would never have received the chance before. And never had the chance to write for magazines and newspapers. All my books are published. I must enjoy it while it lasts, because it will come to an end one day."

Once again, he sits in silence, drumming with these fingers of his. What is he thinking about now? His next novel?

No. He turns back from the window and asks: "What do you really think about the colors?"

Notes

1. The 2019 Penguin Books edition, translated by Ingvild Burkey, is entitled *So Much Longing in So Little Space: The Art of Edvard Munch*.
2. This project was not completed.

"The Innocence of Things": A Conversation with Karl Ove Knausgaard

Srikanth Reddy / 2017

The Point, Sept. 11, 2017, https://thepointmag.com/dialogue/innocence-of-things-karl-ove-knausgaard-srikanth-reddy-in-conversation/. Reprinted by permission of Srikanth Reddy.

Srikanth Reddy: *Autumn* is strongly framed by the second person. And that must have felt like a big change for you after writing the *My Struggle* novels, which are so bound to first-person narration. How did that feel? Was it weird?

Karl Ove Knausgaard: It was very much a relief. And the reason to do it was exactly that, that *My Struggle* is six novels, and it's very much introspection, and it's very much my interior life, and it's very much psychology. It's very much emotions, and it very much analyzes. And these books are the opposite.

This is a book about objects and things and the material world, the things that are around me. I go maybe ten meters away from where I am and write about that world. But it still is a huge, huge difference. And there's a logic to it. It is a kind of encyclopedia of things. I love encyclopedias. I think it's a great concept: you have the whole world in writing.

But if you try to write your own encyclopedia, something else shows up in the text, and it changes; it isn't objective anymore. It is a kind of personal thing, and then it looks different. Who's talking? Who's seeing?

Reddy: It's interesting that you were describing that as a question of who's talking because to me, throughout the book, I kept asking myself, Who was the listener? It's framed as an address to an unborn daughter, but the daughter kept disappearing into a second-person plural. A "you" that was more than just the unborn child, but rather, the future. Did you find that to be a technical challenge as you were writing the book, or something that was exhilarating?

Knausgaard: Well, this book—first of all, it's four books. So this is the first. And the first two books are texts about objects, and then the third book is a novel, and it is directed to "you," my daughter, who is unborn.

And then there is a fourth book, which is more texts and stuff, but the thing is that it is two different modes of writing: one, directly to her, and then those texts. And the book to her was something I did privately; we were expecting a baby, and I thought I should—for some reason, I don't know why—write to her, about who we were, about the world that she was coming into, and it was partly a letter and partly a diary. And it's about a hundred and fifty pages. But it was all meant for her. I thought I should give it to her when she turned eighteen as a present, but then I started to write those short texts as a different project. And then somehow they merged. So I took some of the pieces written to her, put it into this. And it changed the book completely, and made it into a book, somehow.

Reddy: I'm surprised to hear that there's a novel in there somewhere. A second-person novel.

Knausgaard: Yeah, it is a day in the life of her. And she is three months. And me, from the sunrise 'til the sun sets. So it's a classic narrative about nothing, basically.

[*Laughter*]

Reddy: Great, so we'll talk about that, sometime. But the encyclopedia aspect of the book I found very interesting, and I kept thinking about it as an encyclopedia, or a dictionary, for a future person. How do we organize a dictionary, or encyclopedia? Alphabetically. And because my Norwegian is a little rusty, I was wondering if the entries that I was reading were alphabetical in Norwegian but not in English. Or how did you put this book of lots of moveable parts together?

Knausgaard: [*Laughs*] I was curating an exhibition in Oslo earlier this year, but I'd been working on it for two years. And that was the question, you know. There were like a hundred and fifty paintings. How do you set them together? How do you structure something like that? And I went for a very intuitive way of [doing it]. What belonged to each other and what could add something to each other. And the book follows that logic: just, what works.

One of my favorite books is called *The Order of Things* by the French philosopher Michel Foucault. It's about how the organization of all elements in the world creates the world. But you don't see the organizing principle behind it. So he uses an example in the foreword, a short story by Borges, and it is about an encyclopedia, where the words are organized by a completely, completely different system, which has nothing to do with rationality at all, and when you read that, you see the world is completely changed—it's not even our world anymore.

Something I discovered by writing this book is . . . the hierarchy we have of things. We organize them in a hierarchy, and *that* hierarchy we don't challenge. We challenge social hierarchy, we challenge all sorts of hierarchies, but we don't challenge the way the things in the world are organized. And when you do something like this, you see that. It wasn't intentional. It was just kind of a side effect of the project. But it was very interesting. If you focused as much on, you know, vomit—if you give it as much attention, and care, and intensity as you do, for instance, to something like war or love—then something happens in the relationship between things.

Reddy: So, for example, there's a section called "Lightning" that's about the sublime, terrifying experience of lightning that kills cows and flashes on you in the middle of the night. And that's followed by a section on chewing gum. And there's a section called "Silence" that's followed by a section called "Drums." And then my favorite one was a section on *Madame Bovary*, followed by a section on vomit. Each of those sequences gave me a different feeling—and maybe you can do that in narrative, but I'm convinced that you were exploring *poetry* in this book. Was there any one principle that was guiding you as you were putting it together?

Knausgaard: No, it was basically an emotional composition. But it also has the subject of the season. It goes more and more towards winter in the book. And the winter is much, much darker and has much less life in it. And it's more of a speculation, much more like the texts of Borges, Calvino, and then summaries, just bristling with lots and lots of different things. So there wasn't any principle guiding it. But it is poetry, you were saying? I was thinking . . . paintings.

Reddy: Curation.

Knausgaard: Yeah, but also in the writing. I had rules for myself when I was writing it. It should be one word, one text, in one sitting. And as soon as I picked a word, I couldn't escape it. I had to do it. I had to force myself, even if it was the most uninteresting word in the world, to do it.

Reddy: Like "thermos" . . .

Knausgaard: Yeah, for instance. Or "toothbrush." And the thing is that if you do that, then things start to come. I mean, I start every day thinking I have nothing to say. I don't know anything. And I don't think much. But then if I just start to say, no, I'll write a page about one thing, something just turns up. And *that* is writing for me. That's why I'm writing. Because it opens up the world.

It isn't my thoughts because if I just look at something and should try to say something about it, I wouldn't be able to say anything at all. But if I write about it, it's different. And that is very interesting.

But I think the form of literature and the language are outside of us, and if you pour yourself into it, something else comes back. You can plunge into what is collective, what is between us, which you can't do alone. So all of these texts are about connecting to the world, somehow, for me. It is magical to write when you lose yourself. That's what writing is, for me.

Reddy: I found myself laughing again and again as I was reading the book and then feeling like I wouldn't know if you had wanted me to laugh.

Knausgaard: What do you think?

Reddy: [*Laughs*] Well, so, would you be willing to read a section?

Knausgaard: Yeah, of course.

Reddy: The section about mouths. There's a very direct description of a mouth.

Knausgaard: So, I should just read something of it?

Reddy: Maybe just the description of what an actual mouth is. I think it's toward the beginning.

Knausgaard: Yeah. [*Reading*] "The mouth is one of the five body orifices, and thus a site of exchange between the body and the world. The outermost part of the mouth is made up of the lips, two relatively long and narrow pads which lie horizontally against each other on the forward-facing side of the head, in the lower part of the face, below the nose. These pads are distinguished from all other visible parts of the body by being reddish, in contrast to the white, yellowish-white, brown or black skin stretched over the rest of the face, and by being moist. Both the moistness and the color are characteristic of the interior of the body. This is so because the lips belong at once to the interior and to the exterior: they form the orifice."[1] And so on . . .

Reddy: Yes, so, I loved that, but when I read a description of the lips as being two horizontal pads on top of each other toward the front of the face, you know, underneath the nose, I wasn't learning anything new; I was just amused. The book is full of these kinds of descriptions of things we all already know. Were you amusing yourself when you wrote that?

Knausgaard: Of course I was. To describe something everybody knows as if it has never been seen makes a distance, and that's what makes it funny. You also have this scientific approach to it, which also creates that distance, which is ironic. It is an ironic text. But it starts there, and it goes somewhere else, almost all the time.

To gaze at the world, as if you had never seen the world and have no idea what it is, and just describe it—then maybe you could see it. Because you don't really see the lips or the mouth. I at least don't. I don't think of it. If you do that, it comes up. Even though it is very well known.

Reddy: There's a kind of parody of objectivity, but also it felt like—to use a kind of literary geek term—a defamiliarization of the everyday. This happens again and again in the book. Here we're being made to feel the wonder and the mystery of lips, which are deeply part of the poetic tradition: describing one's mistress's eyes, etc. . . . To feel humor in that moment was exciting to me. But you use the same approach to describe things that oftentimes are considered quite ugly, like plastic bags. There's a section called "Plastic Bags." I think there's a section called "Oil Tankers." So why did you bring this to bear on things like plastic bags or petroleum spills in this work?

Knausgaard: There is a book I read when I was twenty, by a French poet called Francis Ponge. He writes about the material world, and he does it beautifully. And I was completely blown aback by it when I read it. It was *so great*. And I didn't know that could exist, a book without people, only things. I tried then to write like that. And I couldn't. Then when I tried later on, I could. But I didn't want only the natural world. I didn't only want the beautiful part of it. I wanted the more realistic part of it, and the more everyday-life part of it, which is our world. Things that are very much a part of our world, but not often written about in *that way*.

I think it was fifteen years ago, I was writing on an island off the coast of Norway, by the sea, and I was alone there. And there was snow, and it was an exceptionally beautiful place. And the water was green—I was in a bay—and deep down in the water, maybe three meters down, there was a plastic bag. It didn't move at all, it was just hanging there, suspended. And I think it was one of the most beautiful things I've ever seen. I don't know why, but it was completely magical. And I want to write about *that*. And then I have all the other aspects of plastic bags, you know. But I really just wanted to write about that site, and the feeling of *being* you have, to exist, when you see something like that. You don't understand it, but it is sublime. And I found that interesting, that a plastic bag could be sublime. But I mean, of course it could be sublime.

Reddy: Would you read that section?

Knausgaard: That section? After calling it sublime? [*Laughter*]

Reddy: Yeah, maybe not. Fair enough. Let's skip over it—you guys will read it later. The thing about the plastic bag was, to me it was terrifying also. Because whenever we hear the words "plastic bag" the footnote for that is "evil, horrible, destruction-of-the-planet" bag. And so you are looking at it in this scene, in this memory, just under the surface of the water. It's not floating up into a tree; it's there. And you have a section later in the sequence about jellyfish. You're imagining the life-world of a jellyfish, and I kept thinking about the plastic bag when I was reading about the jellyfish, and it made me feel like there was a kind of undernote of dread.

Knausgaard: Yeah, but the plastic bag text ends there, with exactly that. When it's in earth, in soil, at the end there. What it is. What it represents. But it is also beautiful. It is both.

Audience Questions

Question: In *Autumn*, there is often a decentering of the human world by a sudden intrusion of cosmic time, or of geological time, or of nature. But in *Kamp*—the *My Struggle* series—maybe the most startling and uncanny intrusion in the entire book is your encounter with your father's journals, which, if anything, seems like a transmission from another planet, suddenly. So, just an invitation to respond to that.

Knausgaard: Yeah, that's true. It is a part about loneliness, I think, and about what it is to be alone. That's what it is. I didn't intend to write about him, but I did start with just how good it is to be alone, to shut the door and be alone. And then I just remembered his diaries that I had gotten hold of, and I started to write about him. After writing six novels that are all about him, in this [new] form—one page, one subject—I made a completely different thing about him. He is very different in that text. It is an extremely frightening text. I am discovering something about him, about his relationship to others, when I am writing the text, and you can see that when you read it. It's like I am thinking about it and realize that's how it is. I can't say more than that.

Reddy: There is one moment from *Autumn* where you mention that the two things you've kept of your father's are his boots and his binoculars.

Knausgaard: Yeah, people think that's symbolic: binoculars and Wellingtons. Because those were the two things that I got from him when he died, and I used the Wellingtons, but it never occurred to me that I'm walking, you know, in his boots . . .

Reddy: Or looking through his eyes . . .

Knausgaard: . . . I didn't think of it. I just wrote it because it's true, and it's there, and they're things, you know.

Question: I have a question that has to do with your relationship with Marcel Proust in the retrospective project of *My Struggle*. How much do you feel your shift from a retrospective to a prospective project reflects his influence? So much of both projects, both in this seasonal form and in the retrospective project of *My Struggle*, has to do with an immediacy . . . that is so much of what went into the early volumes of Proust. So I'm wondering what your relationship is to these same sorts of Proustian projects.

Knausgaard: When I was in my twenties, I wanted very much to write. I wanted to be a writer. And I just couldn't. I didn't have the language, or the form—nothing. It was like I had this inner life, and what I was writing was just . . . little nonrepresentative things that looked like literature.

Then, in this phase I read a lot of books, and they were all very influential: Michel Foucault, as I was saying, was one of them. Then when I was twenty-six, I read Marcel Proust. It had just been translated into Norwegian, and I read it intensely. And then I stopped reading it. And then two years later, I could write, and I published a novel. It took me many years to see the connection.

I get so much from Proust, so much from that book, so much of his way of thinking of literature and thinking of literary form—I just took it. But I thought it was myself. I completely integrated it into my own writing. The way he uses metaphors, for example, where he opens up the world through a metaphor, so many parallel worlds at the same time—I just took that. And his concept of memory and time—I just took that too.

But when I started to write *My Struggle*, I was aware of this, and I was writing about my own life, and I *couldn't* do it the way he did. I had to do it differently. So it *is* very different, but it is also related to him because it is a kind of anti-Proust book. He is there all the time. He's in my blood, so to speak.

In this new project, I don't know what the relation is. But I think what I want to do when I'm writing is to make things or episodes or people *present*. That's what I try to do. When it comes to reflections or digression I always want to get back to that presence in the world. I don't know if that's . . . an answer to your question. I hope so.

Question: You've talked about how with *My Struggle* you wrote very quickly, an amazing volume of pages per day. Could you talk about the process with the more recent books? Was there more self-editing?

Knausgaard: The concept for the new books was, as I said, one text, about one thing, in one sitting. And I did that. I wrote one text every morning. And I kept every one. I didn't really edit them—some a little—but the whole point was that it should be in one go. That means that there are some very good texts and some not very good texts. But I just wanted to capture the process. I could have taken out many of the weaker texts, but I think the number of them has a function too.

But I'm not sure if that worked. . . . I never read reviews, but there was a review in *The Guardian*, and it was so horrible that it was . . . translated into Norwegian newspapers, so I accidentally saw the headline. It was: "This Book Is a Pile of Shit." I hope no one from my publishing house is present—I shouldn't say this. [*Laughter*] But it is something that interests me a lot. Just the question of quality—what a good text is.

For me, the notion of quality is . . . I don't care for it. There is always something else that I hope for, that I want, in a text. And *that* makes it possible for me to write, and it makes it possible for me to find things. . . . Naïveté, if you don't go there, there are so many things that would disappear. And I'm not saying that to defend myself. I'm saying it because I believe it.

It's the same thing with music, or with paintings. When I did that Munch exhibition in Oslo, I chose many of his paintings that had never been shown, and they haven't been shown, maybe, because they weren't that good. They weren't masterpieces. But if you have many of these paintings side by side, something happens. And you can see something that you can't see in the masterpieces.

Question: I teach creative nonfiction and the essay. Many of my students are engaged in memoir projects or personal essays, and I wonder if you could talk a little bit about if you think there's a particular proclivity for autobiographical work in the last thirty or fifty years, and certainly going back to Proust.

Knausgaard: I don't really know. When I started the project, *My Struggle*—my editor recently reminded me of this—I didn't want to do it. I was very against it because it was so of the time. At the time, everyone was doing this. I didn't want to go there. I remember we had this discussion about it, but then I had to do it anyway.

I read a book—it is, maybe, a different literary climate in the US than it is in Scandinavia—but I remember reading a book in the nineties by a writer called Stig Larsson (not the crime writer but another one), a collection of poetry. It is about him, obviously, and his friends. It had a huge impact on me; it was so powerful. I think the thing was that there was no God. There was nothing in front. You just had access to him and his thoughts directly. And that's what I love in literature. That's why I read diaries and other stuff that isn't fiction but isn't nonfiction either. But I didn't write [*My Struggle*] because I wanted to tell a story about my life; I did it to make literature. Somehow, I wanted that. It was not a memoir to me. It was a longing for authenticity, and I don't mean that in any other way than that I wanted to explore the things that are underneath the concepts we use to hold ourselves together, underneath the concept of difference, underneath the memories and what makes us.

Question: I noticed that from [Knausgaard's second novel] *A Time for Everything* (2004) to these texts there's a sense of innocence when you look at the world. This wonder that comes not from seeing things naively but from a sense of openness and freshness, and then, when you're confronted with the violence in Cain and Abel, or your father, or vomit, or things like that, the world becomes open and universal. I picture the painting *The Fall of Icarus* when I read your work sometimes. Because it's all regular life happening, and then this little tragedy in the corner. Do you think about innocence when you write it?

Knausgaard: Yeah, that's a very good question. No, I don't. [*Laughter*] Because I see it almost as a personal weakness, the naïveté, that I don't understand things that are going on around me. I don't understand people's motives because I don't even know that they exist, you know. And that is a weakness. It is also a weakness for a writer, because I can't write *Macbeth* or anything— that's out of the question. I can describe things, and I can write about myself.

But I do think about it, because when I read my work, that's what I see, that it is innocent. It is also a matter of having no God, but I think you can get the innocence away, somehow.

When I started to write my first novel, I gave it to my editor. The things I was most ashamed of, and that I thought he would never work with me because of—those were the things he liked about it, the things that were so extremely naïve but that open something up.

It's hard to talk about yourself in this way. Book Three in this series, which is called *In Spring*, is a novel. It is about very dark things because dark things happened around the birth of this child. That's why I couldn't publish more than several parts of the diary, because things happened. And in that book, I deal with it, I confront it, and it is not innocent. But then the opposite thing arose: I wanted it to be about *life*. Because it is for my daughter, and it is about spring, so it has both elements. It's very, very simple. So I think the way of wanting to get away from the innocence, somehow, made it even more innocent. I'm not sure what I'm saying—this was a very difficult question to answer. This can't be the last, can it? Can we end there . . . innocence?

Note

1. From "Mouth," *Autumn*, translated by Ingvild Burkey (New York: Penguin Press, 2017, 73).

"You're Not a Real Writer until You Have Enemies": *The Millions* Interviews Karl Ove Knausgaard

Alexander Bisley / 2018

The Millions, Oct. 26, 2017, https://themillions.com/2018/10/youre-not-a-real-writer-until-you-have-enemies-the-millions-interviews-karl-ove-knausgaard.html. Reprinted by permission of Alexander Bisley.

"Many writers are very bad communicators in life, but they are great writers. The writers I know are fucked, wrecked, destroyed: Not all of them are aware of it themselves," Karl Ove Knausgaard says, over a midafternoon glass of water at an Auckland [New Zealand] hotel. Not just Scandinavian writers? "No, there's a lot of fucked up people all around the world."

Despite the unrelenting detail of his thirty-six-hundred-page "indiscreet" memoir *My Struggle*, Knausgaard has a rep for being less than forthcoming in conversation. The "existential loner hero with four children," Zadie Smith said, has "many contradictions." "I tried desperately to think of something to say. We had to have something in common," Knausgaard recalled his awkward lunch at Jeffrey Eugenides's home. "But no, I couldn't come up with a single topic of conversation."

Knausgaard is jaggedly handsome and sharply dressed, six feet, four inches tall and firm of handshake. Scandinavia's leading literary figure of the last decade has things to say, seasoned with gesture and glance. He can be minimalist with his responses, though. Some questions and observations elicit "Yeah" or "Yeah. That's true," accompanied by a nod, a raised eyebrow, or—most tellingly—an affirming smile or laugh. Knausgaard is a fine exemplar of Scandinavia's dry, deadpan humor. In *My Struggle*, he can be very funny. He writes about being a teenager doing a creative writing course, surreptitiously looking at Peter Paul Rubens and Eugène Delacroix nudes in a library art book, the comedy of trying to get laid for the first time, and dealing with premature ejaculation, and writing graffiti like "U2 stops rock."

Knausgaard is attracted to New Zealand (and the Auckland Writers Festival) by the remoteness and the similarities with his native Norway. "The fjords look the same." His frankness writing about everyday challenges through *My Struggle*'s six volumes and the Seasons quartet—someone close to you being seriously depressed or an alcoholic—resonates with many readers worldwide. "The loving care she sought was bottomless," he writes of his Swedish ex-wife's depression in *Spring*.

Spring, and its lyrical descriptions of nature—"the smell of wet snow in winter," "the beauty of the world means nothing if you stand alone in it"—aims to inspire. "The great and terrifying beauty does not abandon us, it is there all the time," Knausgaard concludes, "in the sun and the stars, in the bonfire and the darkness." He is passionate when asked to elaborate about *Spring*'s message. "Life can be incredibly hard, life can be incredibly difficult, but it's always worth living. That's the book's essence . . . Writing a novel is nothing other than making a place where it's possible to say something simple and true. That message is such a true thing, it's very banal too, you need a novel to say it so then it becomes true, you understand what it is."

The forty-nine-year-old father of four says *Spring* is especially for his youngest daughter, who was in utero when her mother attempted suicide. "It was such a fantastic, idyllic summer. The sun was shining every day. The children were laughing and swimming. My then-wife was so depressed that she was in bed all the time, and drew all the energy in there. It was so hard to understand, how is this possible to be so disconnected from the world? To not see that happiness and joy, that it just does not mean *anything*. I have had friends and people I know been depressed and kill themselves. If you just stay there for three more weeks it would be OK. Your life would have been better."

Knausgaard confides that he himself can still find life a profound struggle. "Life is so hard that you think, 'What's the use? Why should it be so *fucking* difficult, everything?' I want my daughter to know that life is always worth living."

Humor is one of the things that can make life worth living, the drummer and soccer enthusiast agrees. "Books Four and Five are especially funny to me, tragic but in a funny way. It's a deadpan humor. I have friends who think *Book Four* is the most terrible thing they ever read because they identify so much with it they don't see the humor. My editor always says to me: In life and in writing, take one step aside and everything looks differently. And humor is that step. When you are there, it's not funny at all, but it *is* funny. And it was fun to write about."

In *Summer*—among odes to "Barbecue," "Dogs," "Ice Cream," "Bicycle," and "Repetition"—he praises Monty Python. "A [teenage] revelation," he adds. Further comedies enjoyed include Louis-Ferdinand Céline and *Seinfeld*. Like *Seinfeld*, *My Struggle* is about everything, though it has been said to be about nothing? "Yeah, that's true. I've also thought that about *Seinfeld*, that there is a relation somehow," Knausgaard smiles.

Though his English publishers describe *My Struggle* as autobiographical novels, the self-dubbed workaholic ("writing to escape myself") says that they are "novelized autobiographies," poetic truth. Literature should go for the hurt and fear and be ruthless, Knausgaard adds. "You're not a real writer until you have enemies."

My Struggle: Six, released in English translation during September, caused controversy in Scandinavia for its coverage of Adolf Hitler and Anders Breivik. Knausgaard—now in a relationship with his UK publisher Michal Shavit—counters that he dislikes Sweden's journalistic and academic cultures. "It's so monological. It's very one-sided. I wrote an essay about it called 'In the Land of the Cyclops.' There's a monopoly of meanings. If you have an opinion outside of that it's impossible. I'm being compared to Nazism and Breivik because of that. It's very different than Norway. My English is not good enough to explain. You can see it now in the crisis about the Swedish [Nobel] Academy. That's a very interesting thing that's happening. It's only one version [of events] that's dominating. There are other possible versions, but they're just not present."

Knausgaard (recently in *The Other Munch*) is currently adapting his debut novel *Out of This World* for cinema, and greatly likes films such as Ruben Ostlund's *Force Majeure* and *The Square*. He is intrigued by Lars von Trier's serial killer movie, *The House That Jack Built*. "One hundred people walking out [at Cannes debut]. I think he's a genius, absolutely brilliant. I hope I will never meet him." He double-checks a new von Trier quote on his phone: "I've never killed anyone myself. If I do, it will have to be a journalist." That sly smile again. "I don't think he means journalists like you."

Karl Ove Knausgaard Looks Back on *My Struggle*

Joshua Rothman / 2018

New Yorker, Nov. 11, 2018, https://www.newyorker.com/culture/the-new-yorker-interview/karl-ove-knausgaard-the-duty-of-literature-is-to-fight-fiction. Reprinted by permission of Joshua Rothman, the *New Yorker* © Condé Nast.

The sixth and final volume of *My Struggle* was published in English this fall [2018]. But it came out in Norwegian, in 2011, three years after Karl Ove Knausgaard began writing the first volume, in 2008. The person who wrote those books both is and is not the man who, last month, came by my office to talk about them. He is now, for one thing, famous in an unusual way, having shared a remarkable number of intimate and embarrassing details with his readers. ("I have to hide from myself how much people know about me," he said.) He is divorced from Linda Boström, to whom he is married in the novel. He lives in London and has quit smoking. He seems to be happier.

To some readers, these changes may feel almost like a betrayal—as though "Karl Ove," the character, has walked off the page, gone rogue. But if the passage of time has made the man a little blurrier, it's also brought the novel into greater focus. Over the course of an afternoon's conversation and a subsequent e-mail exchange, it became clear to me that I had not quite understood Knausgaard's book. What I'd taken for a self-portrait was more like a snapshot, and what had seemed like a monument was actually something stranger—what Knausgaard, in our conversation, called a "cave in time."

This interview has been edited and condensed.[1]

Joshua Rothman: Is it true that *My Struggle* was originally going to be twelve books?

Karl Ove Knausgaard: Yes. In 2008, when I wrote Book One and Book Two, the head of the publishing house suggested twelve books—one each month. For practical reasons, that didn't work out. But they said they could do six. All the books were to be published in a year, from 2009 to 2010. It would be more like an art project, almost, than a novel.

I had to decide how to write four more books. I already had one about my father's death and a second about the present, with the children. The obvious thing was to go back in time. Then I thought that Book Five could bite Book One in the tail—a circle. And Book Six could be outside of that circle, dealing with the consequences of all of it. In the end, I did write Books Three, Four, and Five during that year.

Rothman: How did you write so much, so fast?

Knausgaard: I wonder about that, too! It's strange that, with three small children and limited time, I wrote so many pages a day while, before, when I spent all the time I wanted on writing, and even lived on isolated islands and in remote lighthouses, I hardly wrote anything. But writing *My Struggle* was all about lowering thresholds—between what was in my head and what was on the page, but also what was in the novel and what was in my life.

When I wrote my first novel—I was nineteen—I did it very quickly. If you write fast, you feel like you're entering something not yet familiar—a world rather than thoughts about the world. The novel was crap, unbelievably silly and stupid, but at some point, speed-writing became like reading, a place where I disappeared. When the novel was rejected, I lost belief both in myself and in speed. I started to polish the car instead of driving it—and, obviously, when you polish your car, you don't get anywhere, no matter how nice the car looks.

I spent six years after my first novel and five years after my second without getting into a new book. That was what I was longing for, just to write at full speed. Book One was written slowly, in something like eight months. I spent oceans of time on the opening pages—the sentences were written and rewritten—but the rest of the sentences were written just once. Book Five was written in eight weeks. When the books started to be published, I had incredibly tight deadlines, which was a great help. Then I couldn't afford to think about quality, only quantity mattered.

Rothman: So you were cruising—until Book Six.

Knausgaard: I failed with Book Six. I had to bury that book, and I took a break and wrote a new version that was finished six months later.

Rothman: What happened?

Knausgaard: I knew so much about what people liked, I completely lost authenticity in the writing. I just mirrored and repeated things. It was awful—really awful. So I decided to just write about what was happening at that moment.

Rothman: Book Six is almost like a blog, with time stamps ("It's the twelfth of June, 2011, the time is 6:17 a.m., in the room above me the children are asleep...."), whereas the previous volumes often focus on specific days or weekends. How did you choose those moments?

Knausgaard: In the beginning, the method was different. We moved stuff around and took things out in order to make it into a novel. The first book opens with a reflection on death, and then it's the father-son thing, and then the being-sixteen-years-old thing that has been in my notebook since I started wanting to be a writer. It said, you know, "A bag of bottles of beer in the snow." I always wanted to write about that.

But from the second book on I never thought, "I have to write about that moment." I would just start writing, and then I remember something, and then I write about that, and then I remember something else . . . and I like that, because then the moments will maybe not always be the important moments but could be the moments that are just beside the important ones. There's a freedom in that.

Rothman: In Book Six, on the other hand, you're not journeying through the past. You're describing things that have just happened.

Knausgaard: The events I'm writing about are much closer to now, so they are much more precise. If I were to go back to the hotel and write about this encounter with you, I could write fifty pages about it, but if I were to recall when we met—like, two years ago?—it would be more vague. In that case, I would already have selected what was important. It's two very different modes of writing.

Rothman: In Book Six, you call *My Struggle* an "experiment" that has "failed." What did you fail to do?

Knausgaard: Well, you can never reach an authentic "I," an authentic self. I think it's impossible to free yourself from the social being you are. I remember seeing an interview with Ian McEwan where he used the word "selflessness," and I really understood what he meant: that's the dream for a writer. That's a precious place to be—and if you are there then you are authentic.

But it's not often that the writing goes there. I think of this book as many different modes and many different levels, and some are very close to me and authentic, and some are distant, and they contradict each other, and there's a multitude, and that's a self. I think I came as close as I could.

Rothman: Was that the experiment? Getting closer to the self?

Knausgaard: I had felt for many, many years that the form of the novel, as I used it, created a distance from life. When I started to write about myself, that distance disappeared. If you write about your life, as it is to yourself, every mundane detail is somehow of interest—it doesn't have to be motivated by plot or character. That was my only reason for writing about myself. It wasn't because I found myself interesting; it wasn't because I had experienced something I thought was important and worth sharing; it wasn't because I couldn't resist my narcissistic impulses. It was because it gave my writing a more direct access to the world around me. And then, at some point, I started to look at the main character—myself—as a kind of place where emotions, thoughts, and images passed through.

Rothman: Does storytelling itself—one thing, then another, then another—exert some falsifying force?

Knausgaard: Yeah. I'm reading now a very interesting book I should have read many years ago: Frank Kermode's *The Sense of an Ending*. Have you read it?

Rothman: Yes!

Knausgaard: He explores the idea of all the stories that are around us, and then you have the real world as something almost outside of that. So the notion of Tick-Tock, if you remember it. . . .

The idea is that, if you isolate any span of time—even the span between the tick and the tock of a clock—that duration acquires a narrative structure: a beginning, middle, and end.

I mean, *My Struggle* could have gone on and on. I have a colleague—Thure Erik Lund, he's a really great novelist—and he said, "If you want to make this really original, you should just keep going, keep doing it for the rest of your life!"

But, no, what I like is that it's very much about those years. That's why I dated it—because if I had started two weeks later or two weeks before it would have been different. It's more, like, This is a block of time. That was me.

Rothman: Do you still feel like the same person?

Knausgaard: No. At an event in Edinburgh about Book Six, I started to read the essay part in the middle, and I couldn't recognize the thinking. It's like a cave in time that I made.

Rothman: You write, in the new volume, about a book by Peter Handke called *A Sorrow Beyond Dreams*, from 1972. It's about Handke's mother's suicide, but it describes her life entirely from the outside, unemotionally. You describe Handke's writing as both beautiful and "merciless." Is there some part of you that wishes your writing had been more merciless?

Knausgaard: That's a good question. Handke's book is about the death of his mother, who committed suicide. My book is about the death of my father, at the end of a destructive period that I think of as a slow suicide. But Handke never represents his mother in the text, while I describe my father, his movements; I re-create his speech. Which text is more truthful? Obviously, Handke's. I think I could have been braver, gone further in that direction. The question is whether, like Handke, you can represent the world more truthfully when you don't use the conventional tricks of the novel. When I was writing, I felt very strongly that I had made my father into something like a character in a novel and that I had manipulated people so that they could feel what I felt, or what I wanted them to feel, in relation to him. I felt that I was cheating.

Rothman: So you wish that you had been more objective?

Knausgaard: I think "objective" maybe is the wrong word—and objectivity is impossible, anyway. What I admire in *A Sorrow beyond Words* is that it's uncorrupt. We have expectations about how a good novel should look, how a good sentence should look, what quality is, what a story is, what a life looks like.

That's why not fulfilling expectations is so important in literature and art. It makes it possible for us to see ourselves because we're no longer inside the expected but somewhere else—and from there we can see the world as we think it is. Art is a form of negotiation between our ideas of the world and the world. I had many ideas about what death was, like we all do, but then I saw the dead body of my father, and it was something else completely. I tried to represent that insight, or feeling, or whatever it was, and I failed, I wasn't even close, but I realized that there was a gap, and through trying to fill that gap the novel was written.

Rothman: In writing about yourself, were you also negotiating a gap between what you thought you were like and what you are actually like?

Knausgaard: In other people, I can see how suppressed anger, or suppressed jealousy, or even suppressed hate—and also, of course, class and gender and geography—play an important role in what they do and express, without those people knowing it themselves. I can't see that in my own opinions and views, but the mechanisms have to be the same.

An important part of my books is that they want to find out how a particular view of the world comes into being. For Heidegger, the mood or state of mind always came first because that is what you think through—your mood is always there. No document states it, it's in no archive, you can try to describe it, but the point is that we don't think about it; it's just there. In these books, by writing about so much that I don't control, I hoped that all this would somehow become visible.

Rothman: Heidegger thought that some states of mind could make it harder to see the world clearly, while others could open it up. Often in *My Struggle*, you write about seeing the "divinity" in the world. In Book Six, you write, "All it takes is one step and the world is transformed." Are there spiritual possibilities that we can grasp if we approach the material world in the right way?

Knausgaard: Yes. Otherwise, it would be meaningless for me to write about my life. The last time I was in New York, I bought a book: Kierkegaard's *The Lily of the Field and the Bird of the Air*. It's about, what do you call it—Jesus's Mountain Sermon?

Rothman: The Sermon on the Mount.

Knausgaard: Jesus says you should be like the birds, and then you can enter the kingdom of God. And Kierkegaard writes about how if a bird's nest is destroyed, the next day he's happily rebuilding it. The future just doesn't exist if you're a bird. And I read this with, you know, such an incredible desire. A friend of mine has wood pigeons who build a nest, lay eggs, have chicks, and there's a hawk that comes and takes them. That's happened four years in a row. But the pigeons still go to the same place because, for them, the future doesn't exist. Maybe they're in what Kierkegaard would say is the kingdom of God.

And then you've got Heidegger's view on the birds, which is that they have a poor existence—they don't really know anything. Two positions about being in the world. I mean, your baby is in the world. [*New Yorker* ed. note: He's four months old.] He's not aware of himself or who he is. It's probably wonderful to be him! But would you go back there and renounce everything you know now? We're not in the world—we're looking at the world, longing for it. Do we want in there? Is that where God is?

Rothman: In Book Six, you describe how, at your father's funeral, the priest drew a lesson from your father's life: "One must fasten one's gaze." You write, "Everything is there, the houses, the trees, the cars, the people, the sky, the earth, and yet something is missing because their being there means nothing . . . We have not fastened our gaze, we have not connected ourselves with the world, and could just as well, taking things to their logical conclusion, depart from it." You write that we all have an "obligation" to find meaning in the world—even though, "objectively," it's meaningless.

Knausgaard: My father, I think he always wanted to be in another place—always wanted to be another person, to have another life. He had no presence, and sometimes, it seemed, even no awareness of us. I think it must have been painful to be him, and drinking was a way of getting away, of getting out.

And there's also a pull in me—away from home and into art, for instance—that I fear. It's much better now—I think I've managed to fasten my gaze somehow—but I've struggled with that throughout my life. Because nothing is as defined in life as it is in literature or in art. If everyone fastened his gaze on life, there would be no art.

Rothman: Do you consider yourself a religious person?

Knausgaard: I don't. But I brought up Kierkegaard's discussion of the birds because I think the same: being present, being present in a moment, that's the beginning of the kingdom of God. In that sense, I'm religious. You know, recently, someone else asked me if I believed in God. It was a very young person. And I said yes.

Rothman: There's a connection, in Book Six, between the desire to get beyond the rules and patterns of social life—to get "outside," to the sublime—and Nazism. Did you always plan to end the novel with a long essay on Hitler? Is that why you called the book *My Struggle*?

Knausgaard: No, no, it was nothing to do with that. I thought it was suitable because that's what the book was: my struggle. It was also a provocation—the perfect title. I didn't actually plan to write about Hitler at all. But then it came to feel like an obligation. Using that title for your own purposes, it left me with a bad taste in my mouth. I thought that I had to go there.

Rothman: You did find a Nazi pin in your father's belongings after he died—a souvenir of some kind. Maybe it was in the back of your mind.

Knausgaard: Yeah, that's true.

Rothman: Was your approach to writing the essay different from your approach to writing the rest?

Knausgaard: No. I started reading, and then I started to write about it. The thought was that now you know this man; you know all his flaws and shortcomings and interests, and now you see he's reading about Hitler—what will happen? This is a novel written from inside of one person. But also the things we've been talking about, about cheating—those things become acute when you write about the Holocaust. That's where you really have to think about what it is to make something "appealing." Because when you write about even the most horrible thing, there can be something appealing about it—an attraction, an artifice. That's why *Shoah* is such an absolutely amazing film.

Rothman: Because it's completely concrete.

Knausgaard: Because it doesn't pretend to give a picture of the past, because that's impossible—it's just the present. Just the people you meet. It's just what is, now.

Rothman: In the history of the novel, there's long been a connection between a kind of concreteness, or aesthetic reticence, and an idea of "manliness." In Hemingway, for example, there's a distrust of language, and that distrust is linked to a desire to break out of the social world, which is seen as feminine, and into something more "pure." Did you see masculinity—which is a major theme in *My Struggle*—as connected, somehow, to these kinds of questions?

Knausgaard: No, no. Anyway, it's hard to say because being a man is such a big part of my identity that it's invisible—it's obvious if you read the book, but to me it's just how the world looks. I'm interested in masculinity, but I've never thought about whether masculinity has anything to do with the desire to get out of the world and out of one's social circumstances.

I do feel that there is an incredibly feminine side to the book—but, then, if I start to talk about it, I'll end up defining what's "feminine" and "masculine," and people will get angry. It's almost impossible to discuss these things outside of a novel—although, in novelistic terms, it's a great subject. It has to do with identity and with what it is to be "something." And, for me, masculine identity was something that I was standing outside of when I grew up. I was bullied because of the ways I was "wrong": I liked flowers, and I liked to read, and I liked clothes and to dress up, which was completely wrong where I grew up. And then there was the feeling that I had no will of my own, that I didn't stand up for anything. That had nothing to do with being feminine—just with not being a man. And all the emotions I had, the crying: it was everything a man shouldn't do.

Rothman: There's a moment in Book Three where your brother tells you not to worry—he says, "Think about David Bowie. He's androgynous. It's a good thing in rock, you see. David Sylvian as well. Ambiguous sexual identity. A bit woman, a bit man."

Knausgaard: Yeah, exactly. . . . But, still, it's very much read like a man's book, and men relate to it. And in Sweden there's a provocative masculinity in it somehow. It's very strange, because I think that it's exactly this area that's very complicated in the book, because there are so many different layers and contradictions.

Rothman: But there is in *My Struggle* an idea of representing attitudes that are forbidden today—the way you represent the homophobia you felt when you were a teenager, for example. Right now, there are a lot of disaffected men who feel that their attitudes are unspeakable. Were you thinking about the politics of your own thoughts?

Knausgaard: For every thought, you reflect: "Is this what I am? Is this what I thought?" But that doesn't mean that there's a political view connected with it. Like, in the book, when I'm walking in Sweden with a pram, and looking at a woman, and feeling all kinds of things—or when I'm at a children's singing class and feeling undignified, intimidated, minimized—that was how it was. It felt like a shock! A year later, I was fine; my masculinity wasn't caught up in that. But then I felt it very strongly. People say, "Oh, that's his view." But it's more about the feeling of being a teenager and being a failure; of growing up, being in your twenties, and being a failure; of feeling so many pressures about how you are supposed to be. Being outside of things. And that is a dangerous feeling.

Rothman: You say that feeling outside of things is dangerous. But in *My Struggle* you often write about wanting to get outside of everything—outside of yourself, outside of life, which can feel narrow, constricting—as a kind of spiritual longing.

Knausgaard: It's very much about ideas of art and the sublime. The sublime is the perspective outside of us, which I feel is more and more lost in our time because we're more interconnected and less outside, and there's no God anymore. Nowadays things are less and less things in themselves—they are in a position, you know? And I think there is a longing in *My Struggle* to get to the things in themselves. It's the same with the self. I think that's why the self is so huge in the book—because there's a feeling that somehow it's disappearing.

Rothman: Is there a connection between the spiritual aspects and the political aspects of this idea? Today a great many people feel as though they're outside of their societies—on the fringes. And they also feel trapped in systems, maybe of oppression, maybe of bureaucracy, or economics, which they feel keep them from living authentic lives.

Knausgaard: I grew up in one of the most homogeneous countries in Europe. My family was middle-class—my father was a teacher; my mother was a nurse—and in my lifetime the country has been deluged with money. Schools are free; hospitals are free; if you lose your job, the government will support you. So, when I'm writing about the feeling of being "outside" society, it's very far from the direction your question takes us, toward the name of Trump and the rise of populism, or toward what I can see in Sweden, for example, where the integration of immigrants has failed completely, so that you have a generation living on the margins of the society—meaning that they don't identify with it, that the police are not their police, the politicians are not their politicians, the teachers are not their teachers, and so on. The rise of the populist right, and the rise of terrorism, is of course always connected to poverty and to hopelessness, and to the feeling of not belonging. It's about economic inequality. That is what we should talk about, nothing else.

But I'm not a historian or a politician or a social scientist, and I have nothing insightful to say about this. There are a lot of brilliant analyses of our time—Timothy Snyder's great book *The Road to Unfreedom*, for instance—but they are by nature about the big picture, the general structures and the long-term tendencies. What a novel can do is the opposite—it can go into the particular, into the concrete, singular life. That's the only thing that really exists. The Rust Belt, the joblessness, the poverty, the opioid epidemic—they only exist as seen or experienced by particular individuals.

Rothman: And that's what you're interested in.

Knausgaard: A novel is the only place where it's possible to explore that. That is what makes literature so important. I mean, the two best books I have read about contemporary America are Rachel Kushner's *The Mars Room* and Maggie Nelson's *The Argonauts*. If people two hundred years from now wanted to reconstruct today's USA, they would come a long way by reading those two books. Central in them both is the feeling of being on the outside of the society that they're, at the same time, embedded in. As a reader, you identify with them, and with identification, a certain form of insight comes, filtered through your emotions rather than through your thoughts.

Now, this starts to get complicated because what populism and the far-right offer is exactly that—an emotion-based belonging. A common history, a common culture, a common people. It is "we"; it is "us." But that "we" is general—it doesn't really exist; it's a fiction. So the duty of literature is to fight fiction. It's to find a way into the world as it is, to open a road we can glimpse for a second or two before a new fiction has covered it again.

Rothman: You write about how, as a child, you played in a Nazi bunker near your house. At that age, the Second World War felt completely abstract—like a story you'd read about. And then you found your dad's Nazi pin; you heard your grandfather make an anti-Semitic remark. It turns out that the Nazis inhabited our reality. And yet their way of viewing the world was completely wrong; it was a fiction.

Knausgaard: There are so many fictions about the world, and what happens in those fictions is important for our view of the world. Maybe that's why Handke, in *A Sorrow Beyond Dreams*, didn't want to evoke feelings through representation. It's one thing to read about the myths of history, to feel their pull, and quite another to see those myths unfold in the real world, as Handke's mother did, being Austrian during the war. I assume—but I don't know, of course—that Handke's way of writing that book, of withholding all manipulative power, was a reaction to growing up in the shadow of Nazism.

Rothman: I keep returning to the moment when your discussion of Hitler ends. It's gone on for hundreds of pages. Suddenly, we're on the balcony outside your apartment. You hear a child laughing and a man's voice, and the laughter is so infectious that you look over the railing, but you can't see them. And that's how this long contemplation of the Holocaust ends. Why did you choose to end it that way?

Knausgaard: That was how it was when I was writing about all of this. I was on the balcony, writing, and I heard this child laughing, and I couldn't see anyone. And I was filled with the feeling of having dealt with all of this, and now I don't know—I have no idea. I didn't plan anything. That was how it was.

Rothman: That was part of real life, too.

Knausgaard: Yeah.

Rothman: Now that we're talking, I remember that, when I came to that moment, I was at home, reading, and I looked up and saw my wife and infant son. I didn't think that juxtaposition was very remarkable. But in your novel, it feels that way.

Knausgaard: What did you feel, when you read it? Did you think that it didn't belong there?

Rothman: In the novel, it feels like a shocking juxtaposition: the Nazis and a child's voice. But not in real life. In general, I found Book Six—the last part of which deals with your then-wife Linda's nervous breakdown, which is brought on, in part, by the publication of Book One—to be almost uncomfortably real. You write, "Linda isn't a character. She is Linda. Geir Angell isn't a character. He is Geir Angell." And so on.

Knausgaard: Someone was talking to me about the book, and she said that when my father's name first appears, it's almost shocking. His presence is different when he has a name—it's a connection to the real world. And literature always has a gap, a veil between it and the real world. It has to be like that, and it should be like that . . . and then I took real people and put them behind that veil, into this closed world. Seeing their names, it's like a glimpse of their real existence.

Rothman: Toward the end of the book, you write, "This novel has hurt everyone around me, it has hurt me, and in a few years, when they are old enough to read it, it will hurt my children." And, on the last page, you write,

"I will never forgive myself. . . . In two hours Linda will be coming here, I will hug her and tell her I've finished, and I will never do anything like this to her and our children again."

Knausgaard: I felt very bad at that moment. It was a guilt-ridden ending.

Rothman: That was seven years ago. You and Linda are now divorced; you've moved from Sweden to London, where you have a new partner. Do you still regret *My Struggle*?

Knausgaard: I don't regret it. I think it was hard to see then, and easier to see now—people were hurt, and it was terrible for them when it was happening, but, still, it wasn't the end of the world. There's the guilt for my children, which is constant, which has to do with how I gave our story away to everyone. But, on the other hand, there's a lot of love for them in the book. And when I'm gone that story will also be there for them.

I can't, if I'm honest, think that it could be wrong to add a book to the world. How destructive can that be, really?

Rothman: Are people still angry with you?

Knausgaard: Yeah, yeah. That will never go away.

Rothman: Is Linda still angry with you?

Knausgaard: Linda? No. She read it and accepted it.

Rothman: Reading about Linda's breakdown made me feel guilty for enjoying *My Struggle* so much.

Knausgaard: Really? I never thought about that happening.

Rothman: It made me think about the novel as a whole. It starts by reckoning with your dad, who felt trapped in his life, and who did what he needed to do to feel freedom, and it tallies up the costs of what he did to you and other people. And then it becomes about you, his son; you also feel trapped, and you do what you need to do to escape, and that also has costs, not just for you but for others.

Knausgaard: I agree. I think it's true. I never drew that parallel. But I think it's right. That's a very accurate way of saying it.

Rothman: Looking back on the whole project, what surprised you the most?

Knausgaard: One thing is just how much is in a mind, you know? The past, memories, books. But what also surprised me was that what I thought was idiosyncratic—what I thought was for me and me only—connected with other people. That surprised me very much and still does. I think we are much more alike than we normally think we are. I think that's a fact. It must be a fact.

Rothman: You're back to writing fiction again. Has *My Struggle* affected how you experience that?

Knausgaard: It has. I feel much freer. The hard thing is to find the sense of obligation. Because you're free—you don't have to be true. And it still needs to be.

Rothman: What about from the perspective of craft?

Knausgaard: I have no idea what craft is—and I have no idea what writing is. That's true! The more I write, the less I know about what it is that makes something good. I normally think, you know, "This is complete shit." And I send it to my editor or someone else, and sometimes they say, "No, this is alive." Maybe two or three months later I can see that it was good. But I don't know why. Really, I've developed a method, which is being in the present, sitting here, drinking some coffee, thinking of a memory. That's the only way I know how to write. I don't know how to write a novel. But I know that if I just try, something might happen.

Rothman: Suppose you were to take Thure Erik Lund's advice and just keep going. Just write *My Struggle*, Book Seven. Reading it, would we encounter the same "Karl Ove"? Or a different you?

Knausgaard: When I wrote *My Struggle*, I was very frustrated; I felt trapped in my life. Before, the only way of escaping I knew of was through literature. That had always been my way—escapism. But in *My Struggle*, I used literature to confront my life, instead of running away from it. It was obviously a midlife crisis; every sign is there. Now I'm in a completely different place. I live the life I want to live. I am the same, of course, but maybe I am looking in different directions. My father is no longer a haunting presence in my life, and my childhood seems very remote compared to when I was forty and everything seemed recent, in an almost acute way. Now I'm much more interested in what I see, more than how what I see makes me feel.

Rothman: In Book Six, you write that when you started *My Struggle*, you had "nothing to lose." Looking back, do you feel that you made a decision to write it?

Knausgaard: No.

Rothman: Do you feel like you made artistic choices during it?

Knausgaard: No, not really. I was just looking for a way to make it possible for me to write about my father.

Note

1. That is, edited and condensed by the interviewer and the *New Yorker*.

"Rejoicing to Heaven, Grieving to Death": An Interview with Karl Ove Knausgård

Anders Beyer / 2019

Anders Beyer: Influencer of European Art & Culture, Jan. 2019, https://www.andersbeyer.com/publications/interviews/rejoicing-to-heaven-grieving-to-death/. Reprinted by permission of Anders Beyer.

The director of the Bergen [Norway] International Festival, Anders Beyer interviewed Knausgård in London. The interview was translated by James Manley. (An edited version of this interview was published in *Norsk Shakespearetidsskrift* in January 2019.) "Waiting" by Calixto Bieito (director) and Karl Ove Knausgård (libretto) had its World Premiere on May 22, 2019 at the Bergen International Festival. See also Beyer's article "Solveig Will Wait No Longer."

Anders Beyer: You have recently written an essay about how you found your voice and started writing. Can you expand on that?

Karl Ove Knausgård: It's about creating a space where it's possible to say something. For me it's very much about a kind of emotional truth. Everything is emotionally charged, philosophy too. A great deal is missing for me when I read philosophy, or when it's supposed to be about existential questions, and the reality isn't involved, the space we live in. The quite simple and banal things, or things that are just silly, they have to be said too since that can give life a kind of weight, a new truth. I already knew when I began to write that this is what it's about, this is the way it is.

But it's difficult to write. You have so much to say, and then nothing seems to come. But suddenly there can be something that opens up, and then you can say everything. The truth may still be relative. My truth doesn't have to be everyone's truth. But it's possible to say something true.

Beyer: What made you think you had to do just that: write?

Knausgård: I read a lot when I was growing up. For me it was very natural to think that was what I should do, that I should write, as I had such great experiences in connection with literature while growing up. When I was sixteen, I began reading books by Hemingway for example (*The Sun Also Rises*) and Jack Kerouac, which made it cool to be a writer, more of a lifestyle and a way to be; that's what was interesting to me.

Beyer: You also thought about becoming a musician?

Knausgård: Yes, but if a writer was what I became, it was very much because I wanted to *be* a writer. I sort of had nothing to say or anything like that. But something happened when I began on my first novel at the end of my twenties—reading and writing became more or less the same for me; they fused together. Then a space arose that I could go into every day, and be in and come out of, which wasn't me but which wasn't out there either, it was somewhere in between. It was very much about disappearing into it and about creating, about something being created there. I suppose I had experienced it in flashes when I was in my teens and wrote, but never that way. This is what I always try to get back to when I write. I don't write because I want to say something in particular or because I want to do something important. I write because I want to be *there*. There, everything that is important comes out. But it isn't such that I go around thinking that I have to write about this, or that now I have to write.

Beyer: So what is important comes, and you write about what you experience as true. The starting point is often the personal, your own reality. Is that where you find the fuel for your writing engine?

Knausgård: No, but I appreciate what you mean. That's what is so treacherous; it's so easy to think that writing is a self-absorbed activity, or that it's about your own problems, that it's the place you have to go because it's the only place the writer really has access to. It's the individual viewpoint; it's the subjective; it's where you see the world from; you can't see the world from some other place. But then the thing about literature is that it's collective after all, it's for everyone, relational. That's what makes literature so special, for the moment you begin to write literature, it's no longer about yourself or about your own problems; it's about something else. It's as if you latch on to something else that is much more, you get into a current that has flowed there for hundreds of years and that you become a part of. But you so clearly use yourself and your own experiences to get in there, for you have no other experiences, they don't exist. I can't think of a writer, or an artist or a composer, who doesn't use himself or herself to go there.

Beyer: You experience that you come in and sort of become part of a current, of something that has been there for an endlessly long time?

Knausgård: Yes. And that's exactly the same as you do when you read. You become part of a flow that exists everywhere around us and has been going on since time immemorial. When you write, that's also what happens.

Beyer: So you don't think there's such a big difference between being a reader and being a writer?

Knausgård: No, I don't think so. When you read, in the best case you disappear completely. When you write, you also disappear completely in the best case. And then there are areas in between, of course, When you write, it's as if you make your own choices. You do it this or that way because you think it's best, but the reason you choose exactly what you choose is that there has been a huge amount of literature before you and behind you that makes it possible to go there or there. In a way it's as if the more you've read, the more you've taken in something from others. The more unoriginal you are in a way, the more personally you can write and do your own thing as a writer, I think. But this is maybe both true and not true.

Beyer: During the reading of the first volumes of *My Struggle*, it becomes clear that you very much want to be recognized. You want to be successful and become known. You had problems at the writing school since there were some people who wanted to control you too much, and you had difficulty finding your own voice. But little by little you found it. Both in your books and in the way you are as a person, I experience a great humility, which makes you always try to understand the surroundings. But in parallel with this there's an element of megalomania. Can you say something about this?

Knausgård: To be able to say or write anything at all you must have self-confidence one way or another. Just having to hand over a novel to someone, to my editor, is a huge step. Why should he read it? Why should I have something that others want to read? It's a quite absurd and quite terrible thought, actually. All the same, I've always done what I've done with an inevitability, while at the same time I seem to have had no self-confidence at all. I still don't, although I've had lots of success. When I write a text now, I send it to my editor in exactly the same way I've always done and think: "This is quite hopeless; this is terrible." That's how it is every single time, every single day. So that's one side of it—yes, I don't like myself, I don't like what I manage to produce. At the same time, I have an opposite side since

I also think what I do is quite fantastic. This is probably a quite simple psychological mechanism.

Beyer: On the one side, on the other side. If I had to compare your *magnum opus* to something, it would have to be Wagner's *Ring of the Nibelung*, Stockhausen's *Licht* and Proust's *In Search of Lost Time*, works that took several decades to write. It's as if that was the format you decided on?

Knausgård: But it was exactly the opposite I wanted. I thought, "Now I'll have to write something small and stupid; now I'll write about my own life, and it mustn't be big; it mustn't be great literature; it must just be simple." It was only then I began to write so much.

Beyer: And *My Struggle* developed into a gigantic work.

Knausgård: Yes, but it's small, even though it's long. It isn't big because it's only about one life. I've always thought of it as small, never thought of it as big. But it is long. What made it possible was that I didn't think about writing great literature. My problem now is that I have to write great literature, and that won't work; it's quite impossible. So I have to get back to where I was and just try to sort of scribble something down on the page.

Beyer: So the triggering factor was that you just managed to get writing?

Knausgård: Yes, that was the triggering factor.

Beyer: That you discovered that you should just get going and write?

Knausgård: Yes, yes—not make something; it didn't have to be anything. I just had to write. That's how it was.

Beyer: When you had finished the major work, were you firmly resolved not to write anymore?

Knausgård: Yes. But there was a kind of loophole I had. Since I wrote about myself, and since it became so long, I had to find a way out, and that was the way out.

Beyer: What significance does your reading of Proust's *In Search of Lost Time* have?

Knausgård: I read Proust for the first time in the summer I turned twenty-five, in Bergen. I was a student and had little money, and since his novel series was on sale, I bought it. I remember I sat out on the wharf and drank water in the café there and read Proust throughout the summer—that was what I did that summer. I thought it was quite fantastic. It was as if my childhood experiences disappeared into Proust's novel, and I just wanted to be there. I read and read. At that time, I couldn't write.

But two years later I could suddenly write, and then I wrote a novel. I never associated the two things with each other, but now I do; now I see how much I learned from Proust, how much Proust there is in my first book;

not in *My Struggle*, but in the one called *Out of the World*. I seem to have taken it all in, absolutely everything, quite uncritically, and then just poured it out again, entirely without knowing it. The whole understanding of time and space, and the whole architecture of the novel, where a metaphor can sort of build one space here and another space there, and where the past, future, and present are also spaces in a kind of novel architecture, I just took that straight in without knowing it came from Proust. So he has meant an incredible lot.

But when I wrote *My Struggle*, I thought that wasn't how I would do it for I knew after all that it was autobiographical, so it had to be quite different. No metaphors, not that type of construction, not the elegant and sophisticated type either, but much, much simpler. And now I seem to have exhausted that possibility. I could have spent twenty years writing *In Search of Lost Time* all over again, and might have written a fantastic book, but I can't do that any longer. And it became what it became.

Beyer: You have said that your subject or your ideas must come to you unawares. What do you mean by that?

Knausgård: It's difficult to formulate, But I'm not interested in what I can do and what I know because I *can* do that, and I *know* that. I'm not interested in showing off what I can do for then it's already finished, but I'm extremely interested in what comes into existence while I'm writing. And I think there's an energy for the reader too in the fact that the writer in fact doesn't know where he's heading, that there's a kind of voyage of discovery at the same time, where you feel that you're seeing the world in a new way or from a new angle. What is so nice is that it's fine to write about yourself and not know what will come on the next page, not know where it's all going.

I think we have a version of ourselves that is quite fixed. If you have to introduce yourself, you'll say that you're called this and that, you work with this and that, you grew up there and there, your dad was like this, your mum was like that. Then you can expand on that, but there'll always be something tangible that is your character, that is your identity. And that's quite OK; that's what you live with every day and think about yourself. But you're so incredibly much more than that. And one way to get hold of it is to begin to write about yourself and just see what pops up, instead of sticking firmly to this or that identity. For example, you can write very close to a particular day, about what happens in one day, about all kinds of thoughts and feelings that come up, so that who you are in a way loosens up a little. But you can only do that if you don't know in advance what you want and where you have to go; you can't plan it. If you plan it, you shut it in. What you are interested in is opening up.

Beyer: So in principal anything can be done, and new paths can arise without you actually knowing that it's happening?

Knausgård: I can also write for example about an episode I've written about before, but begin in a different way, and then disappear into it. Then it'll be different, will be about other things. This is the opposite of having a plot. With a plot it's a bit the same as with an identity; it shuts the writing up in something in particular and in a given pattern. We see the world in categories and in boxes, and we have to do that so we can live here and get through it and handle it. But actually, these are just our inventions, for in reality everything is very fluid and chaotic, and in a way, I always think that's what I have to get into when I'm writing. I never get in there in an elegant sort of way, but the fact that there must be something, a window, into what I don't know anything about, is what drives me on.

Beyer: A few years ago, something came to you unexpectedly that you couldn't predict; that is, an approach from the Festival in Bergen about something you hadn't tried before.

Knausgård: Wow, was that so long ago?

Beyer: I asked you whether you would write a libretto for a stage version of Grieg's *Peer Gynt* suites for orchestra. The idea was to create a kind of symphonic passion in a dual sense of the word: suffering and strong emotion, and wanted to focus on Solveig, not on Peer. Tell me a little about how you received my proposal and about how you got started with his work.

Knausgård: I like *Peer Gynt* very much. That was the first thing, and I came to think about Tom Stoppard's film *Rosencrantz and Guildenstern Are Dead*, which is about the two secondary characters in *Hamlet*. You hardly see the action itself, for it takes place sort of somewhere else. When I got the proposal, I had the feeling that one could go into *Peer Gynt* but be inside Solveig, and then everything would look different and change the whole play in some way. It was almost a spatial understanding of it, and I thought it could be fun to try that, so I said yes.

I was given deadlines but couldn't write anything for a very long time. Then I met the director Calixto Bieito. He said what he wanted; he wanted a monologue by a woman but didn't want it to be Solveig, and it shouldn't be Peer either; it was to be a woman who is waiting, just as Solveig waited. And he said: "You can write as you want, write as you usually do, as you always do. I don't want a text that rhymes." It was very liberating that I could just do as I usually do. I had an idea that Solveig in *Peer Gynt* is someone who stays where she is and shows endless forgiveness and endless patience, which for me is very much a mother's kind of love. She is the one who stays, but also the one who gives, while Peer, he is the one who leaves and the one who takes. That rhymed in Norwegian—I hadn't thought of that. That was the second thing I thought of.

At the same time, I was in New York, and I began to read a Kierkegaard text of all things: *The Lily of the Field and the Bird of the Air*. I thought it was a quite fantastic text, and then I thought that it's about being exactly where you are, that life can be quite insanely rich and intense and meaningful here and now. The question on the whole isn't what you do or where you go. What it's all about is a sort of approach to the reality you have. You can sit here or there and live a totally valid life. I had a lot of thoughts like this. And then I thought about what it is she should talk about, this woman. After that I thought I should just let her sit and think about Søren Kierkegaard, and that should be my text. But then there was the other matter about giving and forgiving, and I asked what it really is, to give and forgive. So I was suddenly in a situation with a woman with her mother on the one hand and her daughter on the other—three women.

Beyer: It became a novella, a family saga?[1]

Knausgård: Yes, and it became a novella that is about three women, where the youngest, the Solveig character's daughter, is just expecting, and the third, her old mother, is waiting for death, while she herself, in the middle, is in a waiting relationship with the other two. It's sort of three different ways of waiting. It's the Solveig character who is giving, but that doesn't really help. There are no limits for someone who gives—giving is a boundless activity. Now it sounds as if this is very big, but it's very small. It's a little story about three women.

Beyer: Why should the Solveig character work in the health care sector? Should we regard her as a kind of Florence Nightingale?

Knausgård: All I was thinking about was giving. That's what I was thinking about. And that those who give are not seen, but those who take are seen.

Beyer: At one point in the novella, Solveig says that she came to think about Kierkegaard. She says that she was on a Kierkegaard course in Lystrup in Denmark. For me that is such a presence that I almost feel I've been there. Do you know whether such a place exists?

Knausgård: No. But my mother is a nurse, and I remember that in the eighties and nineties there was a lot of talk about Løgstrup and Denmark, and Heidegger in fact, in the nursing sector. My mother started at the university and talked about it. So I had Løgstrup and Denmark in mind, and then I also put Kierkegaard in it, and so it became an echo of the eighties and nineties, nursing, Løgstrup, Denmark and Kierkegaard. Then it all fitted, and that's what it became.

Beyer: When your Solveig figure had read Kierkegaard's text, she felt as if she was standing at the edge of the kingdom of God, you write. In connection with your novella, as with several of your other texts, I'm reminded of a formulation in a Goethe poem: "Rejoicing to Heaven, grieving to death," I think it can be translated. I think your text lives and breathes in such a tension between the exalted and the everyday and trivial, with melancholy undertones. Do you recognize yourself in what I'm saying here?

Knausgård: Yes. What I'm trying to do is challenge the space I feel I live in, and have always lived in, which is the very trivial one. Where the fantastic only exists as some sort of construct, or in texts you read, and that you try to integrate. You try to get the sacred into your life. That was a feeling I had when I read Kierkegaard, the feeling that life can open up totally. That's something very radical in Kierkegaard and in religion, which there's a little of in my text. But it's something I want to try, going into that space.

Beyer: Kierkegaard's text takes on great significance for your novella, it's quite central, and it has given you the title.

Knausgård: Yes, what I really want in my text comes from Kierkegaard, for whom I sort of make a space. And I want it to be true. I try to say it in a way that makes it true.

Beyer: So Kierkegaard becomes a kind of recurring motif.

Knausgård: Yes, he does. But his text is very strange too. It's a sermon; it isn't a philosophical text, but a sermon. It's quite fantastic. I can't say why it's so fantastic. But when I begin to talk about it, I get tears in my eyes. There's something incredibly appealing in it, with the lilies in the field and the birds in the air appearing again and again.

Beyer: How did you arrive at the title?

Knausgård: It says what my text is about.

Beyer: You listen to music when you write. Can you remember which music you listened to when you wrote this text?

Knausgård: I listen to pop music when I write. I always play the same record—for three months at a time, it's the only one I play. I'm quite sure I played Father John Misty, his last album, when I wrote the text we're talking about.

Beyer: So music is a kind of backdrop for you? How does it inspire you?

Knausgård: When I began to write, I put very loud music on—sort of to get into something else. I don't do that anymore; now it's a lot about feeling safe. Writing is about getting into something that's a little unsafe, and maybe a bit dangerous. With the same music all the time, it's like a house I'm in, like a home. I get up in the morning, put on the headphones, then the music comes, and then I'm home. Then I can do anything I want since it isn't so dangerous anymore. There's some safety in that.

Beyer: Maybe you also want to shut something out? The noise that surrounds us?

Knausgård: It's very much about making a space that is my own.

Beyer: The text, as we have discussed before, is about human relations and giving. But also about humanity's place in a larger context, in Nature, in the Creation, about the transitory and the new life that arises in defiance of normal programming. But perhaps it's also about human limitations, about what normal Scandinavian life has become in the 150 years or so that have passed since Ibsen's drama was written. Can one say that you make Solveig into a present-day character?

Knausgård: Yes. I take her qualities. There isn't so much about *Peer Gynt* in my text. It's Solveig's qualities I transfer to our time.

Beyer: So the postmodern Solveig isn't sitting waiting for Peer? She's the mother of her child, and she helps her daughter and her mother, while at the same time she has to take care of her professional work. Can one say that your Solveig figure is in a process of becoming, while Ibsen's Solveig has been deprived of her own existence?

Knausgård: That depends on what you mean by being deprived of your own existence.

Beyer: I mean that she has more or less deposited her creative energy with Peer, and just waits.

Knausgård: Yes, yes, that's true. But at the same time, in the purely literary sense, you remember Solveig just as much as Peer. Peer saw clearly too, but Solveig in particular did.

Beyer: The personal, or autobiographical if you like, is often pivotal in your texts, but here it seems to be absent.

Knausgård: I've been very interested in what happens when you write "I" and are someone else. In whether it works to come out of yourself, especially because I've written so much just about myself. In a way this new text has been a little experiment for me. But what I wanted wasn't to try to think like a woman, to create a woman. My thinking was: OK, here I have a situation with a main character who isn't me. But at the same time, I've used my own self, sort of poured in the other self and thus made something happen.

What I was wondering about was credibility: Is my Solveig character a credible woman or not? I still don't know. After all, she isn't me. All the same, there's a lot of me in her, obviously, and a lot of me in the text, but the purely factual has been taken out, so it isn't so easy to see. Emotionally, it's just as much there. And then there's the way I write, for I write just as I always do. That's why I wondered what it would be like when it's a woman who writes like Knausgård—what would people think? I don't know, but it isn't me, that's obvious, that's what writing is. It wasn't me either when I wrote *My Struggle*. It was bits of me, but it wasn't me...

Beyer: What I think is so inspiring when I read your texts and other great literature is that there are always some secrets there, that the text never reveals its inmost being, but remains enigmatic. I came to think about the brooch in the drawer of the woman who is waiting for death, and picked up several associations, for example with Munch's painting *The Brooch* from 1903, one of his most beautiful and most acclaimed representations of woman. The brooch takes center stage and creates a fine balance in the picture, emphasizing its mysterious aspect. What does the brooch mean for the woman in your text?

Knausgård: I can't really say.

Beyer: But it means something?

Knausgård: Yes, obviously it does. But it's not a riddle. There's nothing in the text to be solved. There really isn't.

Beyer: The reader is left unresolved, you could say.

Knausgård: It's often like that in the world too. There are very many things that are not cleared up and resolved.

Beyer: Has the novella given you any ideas for further writing?

Knausgård: Yes, yes. Absolutely. There's something there I want to go further with. Not least the thing with the birds. A friend of mine, who is called Stephen Gill and lives in Sweden in the village where I have lived, is a photographer. He's had a project going for two or three years where he's been photographing birds. He sticks a pole in the ground and a camera with an automatic motion-triggered shutter release right beside it, and then birds start coming down from the sky—all sorts of birds. He gets quite fantastic pictures, and one of them is in my novella, the picture of him when he sticks a pole in the ground and attracts the birds down from the sky. This is something I've thought of going further with.

Beyer: What interest or energy is involved in this stuff with birds?

Knausgård: For me the magic is in the fact that it's so exceptionally specific, so exceptionally physical—it just is. It's so extremely material, it's worldly, or earthly, it's flesh and hunger and survival. It's existence, the struggle to survive and all that—while at the same time there's a kind of metaphysical sky above it all, which the birds are part of. I always want to penetrate to the real, the way things actually are, the way the birds actually are. And the way life actually is. We humans are also physically specific, fleshly creatures. But at the same time, we live amidst all the rest. I'm very interested in these two levels—they always meet. They also do so in both Kierkegaard's and my own text: Kierkegaard's birds and the birds of the Bible, Stephen Gill's birds and the birds of reality.

Beyer: And now you've handed over your work for someone else to do something with it. How do you feel about that? You don't usually hand over a work that way.

Knausgård: When I delivered this text, I thought maybe the director couldn't use any of it, and that it will be Solveig and songs and a setting he creates out of his own mind. Or maybe he'll use some of it? Then my text will be a kind of echo in what he wants and in what he creates. I'm very, very excited about what the director will and can use and how he sees it in his own setting. Here I have no prestige. I've just written the text. It was interesting in itself, and very fruitful.

Beyer: Now we're talking about Calixto Bieito. And he's given you some feedback. What did he write to you?

Knausgård: My impression was that he liked it and was moved by it, but that so far, he didn't know how he was to use it. But he's used to taking texts that exist and working with them and making something of his own out of them. That's what he does, that's what directors do, and to be exposed to this is quite simply a privilege.

Beyer: So you don't see it as an intrusion?

Knausgård: No, absolutely not. I have no ownership of what I have written. You can't have that as a writer, for people read it, say what they like about it, think what they like about it, and write what they like about it. There have been dramatizations of my books that I've never read and never seen. I've said, "Do what you want; it's quite fine with me; it doesn't matter." After all it has to be alive. The more rules you have, the less alive it becomes. It will be really intriguing for me to see how he can use my text. In a conversation, he said, "You can write a whole life; you can write two minutes." When I'm set completely free, then it's fun. And the same must go for him. He can use just two of my sentences if he wants. That's entirely up to him. It'll be exciting to see what he does.

Note

1. This work has not yet appeared in English.

Conversations with Tyler: Karl Ove Knausgård on Literary Freedom

Tyler Cowen / 2019

Conversations with Tyler (podcast), March 15, 2019, https://conversationswithtyler.com/episodes/karl-ove-knausgard/, produced by the Mercatus Center at George Mason University. Reprinted by permission.

Tyler Cowen: Hello. I'm here today with Karl Ove Knausgård, one of the great writers of our civilization. He also has a new book coming out—which I enjoyed very much—called *So Much Longing in So Little Space: The Art of Edvard Munch*. Karl, thank you for coming.

Karl Ove Knausgård: Thank you for inviting me.

Cowen: In Book Six of *My Struggle*, you mention René Girard, and that mimesis is a useful concept for understanding human behavior. How do you think about who or what you're trying to copy?

Knausgård: Who I'm trying to copy?

Cowen: Yes. If you believe in mimesis.

Knausgård: That was a tough first question, I have to say. How can I have come to that? I think there's several levels you could reply to that question.

Cowen: Sure.

Knausgård: First level would be whatever's related to literature, to the art of fiction—how to tell a story—which is something you learn through reading. And you have to have that for writing. There are several ways to tell a story, several ways to enter a scene, several ways to write realistic prose. For me, almost all reading I've done has, I think, subconsciously sunk into me in my own world and in my own writing.

When I, for instance, read Marcel Proust for the first time, I absolutely loved it, and I read it like I was drinking water or something. But I wasn't aware of me soaking it up at all, and I couldn't write at that time. Two years later, I wrote a novel. It is incredible—many similarities with Marcel Proust, but I wasn't aware of it. It was just something that happened. That's one level of mimesis.

The other level is the opposite. It's unlearning everything you know to be able to access what I like to think of as the world—the world we live in—because sometimes fiction can be so mechanical and so locked into certain ways to look at the world that it's more like you're looking through literature than through the world.

That was what I was struggling with in *My Struggle*: trying to find a language for my experience of the world and not . . . I wasn't interested in writing a novel. I was interested in trying to get the language from my experience of the world.

And I think *that* is the key to Edvard Munch—what he did as a painter. Very much so because he grew up in Norway at the end of the nineteenth century in a kind of a certain pictorial language, which was realism, which was naturalism, and which was a national romanticism. You know, the glossy images of mountains and flowers and that kind of thing.

Cowen: Yes.

Knausgård: That was what he had available when he started. He wanted to paint. That was what he had available.

Cowen: And he described his art as an act of confession, as you know. Is that true of yours? Are you fundamentally in the confessional tradition?

Knausgård: Yeah, I think so. But what Munch wanted . . . I think what Munch had was some experiences, very strong experiences. He lost his mother when he was very young, and then he lost his oldest sister, which was even harder for him. I think what he lacked when he started to paint was a language to express that. Couldn't do that through glossy, nice romanticism. So he had to break down everything he knew about painting to try to get that through what he had experienced.

That's the same thing with writing. That's what you want to do—get that personal experience. The thing that only you feel. The thing that only you see. The thing that you know. Get that through. If you do that, you realize, "No, that's how everyone sees it. That's how everyone feels." But that's kind of the thing you have to try to reach, to tap into.

When I started to write *My Struggle*, I didn't know that existed. I just wanted to do it for my own sake, more or less. And yeah, it was confessional.

Cowen: I reread a lot of your work in the last few months, and what struck me more is what a—in a sense—conservative writer you are. At first, I thought of you as a radical. But if you think of this long-standing pietistic, religious tradition of self-scrutiny, you have Rousseau, Goethe, even

Swedenborg, August Strindberg. I now see you as very much in that tradition—that you're the next Nordic confessional, and quite religious as a writer, in a way. Would you accept that characterization?

Knausgård: Pietistic I will accept, and a part of that Nordic tradition I will very much accept. Religious? That's a bit more difficult to relate to, I think.

Cowen: But you wrote a whole book about angels, and it's striking: Swedenborg, Strindberg—they were obsessed with angels.

Knausgård: Yes, true.

Cowen: You're obsessed with angels.

Knausgård: Yes, true.

Cowen: Why the combination of angel obsession and confessional from the Nordics, including you? What's the unity there?

Knausgård: The obvious thing in regard to that is that a pietistic Christianity is a very personal relation to God, a very intimate relation to God—much more than a collective play like a religion as Catholicism would be. Much more internal than external. And as a novelist, that's the confessional path, so to speak. But these things you don't think about. These things you just do.

If you are born into a culture, that culture becomes part of you. That language becomes part of you. And something of that you have to challenge. Something of that you are not aware of. It's just part of you. There's certain writers I do really love, and I think that is part of my culture. And I think I'm similar to them because of many different things.

But these things you are talking about are kind of more cultural, deep-layered things, the pietism. These are not things you think about. These are things that just happen, I think. But it's very unmodern. That's true.

Cowen: Yeah.

Knausgård: It's very old-fashioned.

Cowen: Arnold Weinstein has a book on Nordic culture, and he argues that the sacrifice of the child is a recurring theme. It's in Kierkegaard's *Fear and Trembling*. It's in a number of Ibsen plays, Bergman movies. Has that influenced you? Or are you a rejection of that? Are you like Edvard Munch, but with children, and that's the big difference between you and Munch, the painter? I told you we ask different questions.

Knausgård: Yeah, yeah. You just said different. You didn't say difficult.

Yeah, because there was a lot of grouping together. Here you had Kierkegaard and the sacrifice of Isaac and the biblical story, which basically is a story about faith, and what it is to believe in God, and what it demands to believe in God—the completely irrational level it takes to believe in God. The leap out in the unknown which you have to take.

It's an interesting thing going on in that essay, which is a wonderful essay about Abraham sacrificing Isaac. It's that it also has some small parts about breastfeeding in between, which is *incredibly* strange, and I've been thinking a lot about that. What is that?

But it's moving away from something. It's going from a mother into society, and the leap of religion is going from a society into the unknown, into the things we don't really know about, the things we don't have language for.

There is another very interesting Norwegian poet—no, not Norwegian, but Nordic poet—called Inger Christensen. She wrote a collection of essays which is really brilliant, and she talks about those kind of border areas. It's a matter of language—what we can express and what we cannot express. In science, those are the string theories. That's the things we don't know. That's the unknown.

And the border is the language. We don't have language for it. We *can't* really. She also said that—like a letter in a book cannot read what's around it, cannot read the book—we are the same in the world. We cannot read the world. We're part of it.

But that was Kierkegaard. Yeah, I find it hard to connect Kierkegaard in regard of children, sacrifice of children. And Bergman? Bergman is completely different somehow.

Cowen: But children are abandoned, both in his life and in the movies.

Knausgård: I know. Bergman's workbooks just came out in Sweden. It's not his diaries, and it's not his plays, but it's kind of an in-between state, all notes he took when he was working with things. And it's incredibly interesting because you can see how a film surfaced from almost nothing and just became a film. And you see all his struggles, and you see all of that.

But then in one particular passage, he wrote about a film he wanted to make, and then he said, "Today, my grandchild died." And that was it. Just a little passage, like he really didn't care. In a normal person, it would have filled that person completely. And then that little episode turns up in his next film, that the child is drowning.

There is another episode from Bergman's life, that when his son was lying on his deathbed, he refused to have his father come there, and that's a very, very strong statement.

Cowen: Sure.

Knausgård: You have this almost archetypical artist putting his art before his children, before his family, before everything. You have also Doris Lessing who did the same—abandoned her children to move to London to write.

I've been kind of confronted with that as a writer, and I think everyone does because writing is so time consuming and so demanding. When I got children, I had this idea that writing was a solitary thing. I could go out to small islands in the sea. I could go to lighthouses, live there, try to write in complete . . . be completely solitary and alone. When I got children, that was an obstruction for my writing, I thought.

But it wasn't. It was the other way around. I've *never* written as much as I have after I got the children, after I started to write at home, after I kind of established writing in the middle of life. It was crawling with life everywhere. And what happened was that writing became less important. It became less precious. It became more ordinary. It became less religious or less sacred.

It became something ordinary, and that was *incredibly* important for me because that was eventually where I wanted to go—into the ordinary and mundane, even, and try to connect to what was going on in life. Life *isn't* sacred. Life *isn't* uplifted. It is ordinary and boring and all the things, we know.

You have these myths, and they work for some. They don't work for some, but you can relate to them. I have a friend. He's a brilliant writer, and he always says, "Yeah. When you want to create something, you have certain . . ." I don't know the English word. You have certain things that's fixated. What do you call them? Premises? Or—

Cowen: Assumptions? Axioms?

Knausgård: Yeah, you just have to accept them and work inside of them. That's the only way. If you can't write, then you have to start right out from that fact.

I think that's the best advice I ever got—to accept everything that happens. So if you have many children, it's a good thing. If you don't have children, it's a good thing. You have to embrace it because that's your life. That's where you are, and writing should be connected to that—or painting or whatever it is.

Cowen: Your focus on Nazi history in part of Book Six of *My Struggle*—is that a kind of confessional for Norway and Knut Hamsun? Or the parts of Norway that were attracted to Nazism? How is that connected to the fact that you wrote a confessional about your own life?

Knausgård: Yeah.

Cowen: Since clearly you have no sympathies for a Nazi regime at all, but there's a connection between your culture, history?

Knausgård: Yeah. It's many connections. One would be that when my grandmother died, we found *Mein Kampf* in the chest in the living room. What was that book doing there? Had they read it? And I realized it was kind of a common thing to have that book. It was kind of a common thing to cooperate with the Nazi regime.

When I grew up in Norway, the story we were told at school was the heroic one: the resistance and how every able civilian resisted. But the fact is that Norway was ... The wheels were rolling, and the society was working, and there *had* to be a lot of cooperation with the Nazis.

My other grandfather—he befriended an Austrian officer that was posted by where he lived. When I grew up, there were remnants from the war, like bunkers we were playing at. And it was like war was, in one sense, incredibly distant but, when I start to think about it, incredibly close. It was my grandparents', parents' world, really.

But that wasn't the reason why I started to write. The reason was coincidental, basically, because I called my book *My Struggle*, which is the English translation of *Mein Kampf*, and then I had to read it. And then I realized Hitler's book is his writing about his own self. I'm writing about my own self. It's the same title.

I started to read him, and I got incredibly intrigued by what I read because there was so much—not that he was lying, but it was so much that was unsaid, so much that he twisted his life into something completely different. Couldn't be true. And I just dived into that and started to read more about it and try to find out what kind of man he was and how all this could happen.

Well, it started out like it started in the book. It's a reflection about names because I couldn't use my father's name in the book. My family forbid me that. So I started to be interested in and look around—what names really are, what they signify. Then I stumbled across a Romanian poet who wrote in German, called Paul Celan. His parents died in the Holocaust, and he was Jewish. He wrote postwar in the language of the Nazis.

Cowen: Best poet of the twentieth century, perhaps.
Knausgård: Yeah. And the rest is—
Cowen: Maybe Rilke.
Knausgård: No, I think Paul Celan ... Yeah, maybe.

But anyway, he wrote this incredibly, incredibly, incredibly intriguing poem where almost nothing can be named. There's no names. And it's like it's almost impossible to say anything. It's like the language is completely, completely broken, so there's no connection between the element and the language. And I read that, and I wrote about it, and I realized this is—and it's about the Holocaust, of course—this is the end of what was started with *My Struggle* (Hitler's).

And then that was the moment in the book ... because Hitler also wrote in German, and he also wrote ... You could read it. It's bad. You can say whatever you want, but the fact that you could actually read him is intriguing. And you can see everything he wants to do is in the book.

So I wanted to describe that path from Hitler to Celan. It's the only part in the book that's not about me. But it is, of course, about me. And it's the only part that's not about our time. It's about the past. It's kind of a place, kind of a dark mirror in the book where you could see everything be . . . get a perspective to everything.

And it's the only part I found really pleasure in writing because there was *so* much I discovered during writing. That, and it wasn't about me, which is a burden to do, but that was different. It's about the generation that grew up with the First World War and made the Second World War happen.

Cowen: So many great Norwegian writers—Ibsen, Sigrid Undset, Knut Hamsun—there's nationalism in their work. Yet today, liberals tend to think of nationalism as an unspeakable evil of sorts. How do we square this with the evolution of Norwegian writing?

And if one thinks of your own career, arguably it's your extreme popularity in Norway at first that drove your later fame. What's the connection of your own work to Norwegian nationalism? Are you the first non-nationalist great Norwegian writer? Is that plausible? Or is there some deeper connection?

Knausgård: I think so much writing is done out of a feeling of not belonging. If you read Knut Hamsun, he was a Nazi. I mean, he was a full-blooded Nazi. We have to be honest about that.

Cowen: His best book might be his Nazi book, right? He wrote it when he was what, ninety?

Knausgård: Yeah.

Cowen: *On Overgrown Paths*?

Knausgård: Yeah.

Cowen: To me, it's much more interesting than the novels, which are a kind of artifice that hasn't aged so well.

Knausgård: Yeah.

Cowen: But you read *On Overgrown Paths*, you feel like you're there. It's about self-deception.

Knausgård: It's true, it's a wonderful book. But I think Hamsun's theme, his subject, is rootlessness. In a very rooted society, in a rural society, in a family orientated society like Norway has been—a small society—he was a very rootless, very urban writer.

He went to America, and he hated America, but *he* was America. He had that in him. He was there in the late nineteenth century, and he wrote a book about it, which is a terrible book, but still, he was there, and he had that modernity in him.

He *never* wrote about his parents. *Never* wrote about where he came from. All his characters just appear, and then something happens with them, but there's no past. I found that incredibly intriguing just because he became the Nazi. He became the farmer. He became the one who sang the song about the growth. What do you call it? *Markens Grøde*.

Cowen: *Growth of the Soil.*

Knausgård: Yeah. Exactly. It's like he's fist-fighting himself, doing that. So he's not your nationalist. He's incredibly complex, and the interesting thing is that you can see that struggle in his writing.

Cowen: Is your own American travelogue a revision of Knut Hamsun's in some way? Like, "Well, Norway's going to get it right this time"?

Knausgård: [*Laughs*] No, but actually, I have thought about doing that — go in his footsteps because he was there for quite a long time. He drove a tram in Chicago, did a lot of things, and it's an exciting story, really.

But anyway, the thing with writing in his case is that he's getting so close to the world and to the people in his writing. It's so complex that he is not a Nazi in his writing. But in his essays and in his speeches, there's a big dissonance. There, he's a Nazi.

And that's what a teacher can do, is to get you so close to these things that nationalism just disappears because they don't exist on that particular level. You have to move away from the world — to be able to establish a distance — to be able to talk about these things at all. Norway is a nationalistic country, but it's not in any bad way at all, really. It's a very innocent country.

Cowen: What's the worst thing about living here in London?

Knausgård: The worst thing?

Cowen: The worst thing.

Knausgård: I think it's — to me, being an outsider, it's both the worst and the most interesting, and that's the huge difference between the classes. It's the extreme poverty, and then you just walk up a hill, and it's incredibly rich.

It's not only a matter of classes, but the area I live in is a rather poor area. It's a black area. And then you go up the hill, and it's a white area. I think it's a kind of hopelessness, really, to be here because you can't do anything about it. It's in the structure in the society.

But then also, it makes it incredibly — the variation incredible and the richness incredible, and so it's very much an alive city. Coming from Norway, it's very different. It's like all kind of things going on simultaneously, which is incredibly interesting and nice to at least—I know I'm not a part of it—but to see and to be around.

But it has that backside with the privilege being . . . going around and around and around and around in the same kind of class and the privilege the same; you can't move from one to another. The Scandinavian society is much more egalitarian in that sense.

Cowen: As you well know, Hans Jaeger was a seminal influence on Edvard Munch, and you can think of him as a highly intellectual, cynical nihilist. Munch knew him in his early years. Has there been a Hans Jaeger figure in your life who's a formative influence? It doesn't come through in your books.

Knausgård: You mean personally or through reading?

Cowen: Personally. Who's your Hans Jaeger?

Knausgård: [*Laughs*] I don't have a Hans Jaeger, but I have this writer I really admire, and he's really something.

Cowen: Who's that?

Knausgård: He's called Thure Erik Lund. He's not translated into English. He's very wild—wild as a person, wild as a writer. He has inspired me a lot and showed me what's possible to do in writing. But he's so particular that it's hard to translate him. If it had been written in English, he would have been, I guess, level of Thomas Pynchon or whoever. He's that good. But he's so idiosyncratic that it's hard to translate him. He's not my Hans Jaeger, but he's an influence.

Cowen: Edvard Munch—he was known for beating his paintings, abusing them, not treating them very well.

Knausgård: Yeah.

Cowen: Have you ever done the same with your books?

Knausgård: Yeah, I'm kind of a careless person. I don't take backups, and I have a window open—it's raining on my computer. I have lost a computer down on the tracks of trains, and I have lost them, you know, but it always turns out well.

But that's not the same. I don't care about how a book looks. I don't deal with that part of it at all. When I'm done with a book, there's hardly any editing. I just leave it and publish it, and I want to move on because it's the process of doing it that interests me, not the result. I really hate it when a book is done because then I know it'll take a few years before I will get into something else.

In that I can recognize Munch. He hardly finished a painting in his life. And he was very reckless with his paintings. It is a certain aesthetic in that as well.

It's like in writing. It's like the difference between Dostoevsky and Tolstoy. Dostoevsky really didn't care. He just didn't have to describe it fully. Just a few sentences, done with that, and go on and go on and go on, looking for something, like a flame or something burning or something, the intensity of something he was looking for.

Tolstoy—he wrote about everything and painted it fully and did so wonderfully, but it is completely different aesthetics, and they reach completely different places. When I was young, I thought Dostoevsky was the primary, the one that had reached the front. Now, I'm older, it's Tolstoy, really.

Cowen: Edvard Munch—he stuck with Dostoevsky as an influence.

Knausgård: Very much so. The day he died, in the afternoon the day he died, he read Dostoevsky, and then he died. So he just followed him throughout his life. I think Dostoevsky was part of forming his identity as a painter—exactly what's unfinished, exactly what's raw.

Cowen: Is *The Scream* a self-portrait of Munch? And is he wearing a mask or a death mask?

Knausgård: Yeah. *The Scream* is based upon an experience he had walking up the hill outside of Oslo, seeing what you see in that painting, hearing the nature scream. So in a way, it's a self-biographical painting, but the radicality of that painting—it's hard to get a grip on now, I think. We are very much used to that kind of distorted way of depicting the world.

That's a long story about . . . I write a lot about it in the book because it was fun, because that's a painting that everyone knows, and everybody has a thought about it. I tried to write about it afresh. What is this? What did it do? I can talk about it if you like, but it's a long, complicated story. I don't know if I can do it.

Cowen: Let me ask you about *Between the Clock and the Bed*. Jasper Johns's paintings are often mysterious, but he chose to redo *Between the Clock and the Bed*. What is Johns on about? What is Munch on about in that painting?

Knausgård: I don't know about the Jasper Johns. Using the pattern on the bed, isn't he?

Cowen: Right, yes.

Knausgård: Yeah. Munch made some remarkable self-portraits, I think. He did so throughout his life. He started at eighteen, nineteen, and they were all very different, and I think they were all very good. I think this is one of the very last ones.

The thing with this is, it's so incredibly simple. It's just a man standing there, and it's like he's showing us that. This is it. There's no posing. There's no defense, and Munch was a man full of defense. I think painting was a way for him to get *under* the defense and reconnect with the world. In this painting, that's what it does. It's like the guard is down. This is what it is.

Cowen: Is autobiography a kind of defense or protective strategy for you, a way in which life cannot be a disappointment? There's always something happening you can write about. In that sense, your portfolio, so to speak, is very diversified.

Knausgård: Yeah, it is a place to hide. That it is, I mean, that's obvious. There's that wonderful sentence in Witold Gombrowicz, a Polish writer. His diaries are, I think, amongst the masterpieces of the last century. It really is brilliant. He published his own diaries when he was alive. When they were published, he said, "You know, I just have to retreat one step inside myself."

That's what you do when you reveal so much about yourself. It's like you could just take a step back, and it's all right. It's not even connected to you if you do that. It's like, "Okay. I never think about what people know about me." The act of writing is, for me, a place I can go to and where I am protected somehow.

Publishing books is a different thing, of course. I try to disconnect from that. Don't think about it—the publication of it. What I want to do is to be in the space where I'm writing. It's also a way for me to understand what's going on, to see things that I normally don't see because I'm very much enclosed in myself and in my own space, and I don't really notice things, and I'm kind of closed off to the world. So writing is a way of opening up, also.

There's a lot of things, but I've been writing for so long now that it feels like a place I can go to. Go into that place and sit down, and I will be at peace as long as I am there. Even though I write about terrible and heartbreaking things, it still is a place of peace.

I do find reading the same thing. I've always done that. I think that was why I read so much when I was little and when I grew up. I think I became a writer the moment I realized that that space is the same. The reading space and the writing space are basically the same, and you do the same things there in those spaces.

Cowen: Why does Munch have so many mediocre paintings, some might even say bad paintings?

Knausgård: He didn't really care, I think. He wanted to capture something, and if he didn't do that at the first instant, he moved on. But he kept all the bad paintings, too. I find that also very interesting. [*Laughs*]

Cowen: Is that a model to emulate or a cautionary tale for you?

Knausgård: I was curating a Munch exhibition in Oslo at the Munch Museum, so they gave me access to the magazine in the basement. I was shocked because it was . . . You know, you pull out these enormous kind of walls, and it was maybe ten paintings or five paintings or seven paintings or fifteen paintings on them. And it was a complete mix-up, with masterpieces, *terrible* paintings, sketches, mediocre things, old things, new things.

It was like being in a work of progress. If you go to museums, you see everything finished. Everything is almost stylish. Then it's everything is art. This was completely different. This was entering into a process because the paintings they have are the paintings Munch had when he died, everything he kept, everything he didn't sell.

When I did that exhibition, I thought that was an opportunity to try because . . . In Norway, at least, you can't really see Munch because you've seen it. He's so big, and you see all the paintings so many times that you can't really experience them. So I tried to use other paintings to give a new access to Munch, what he was doing. Amongst them were sort of bad paintings.

Cowen: You've bought a Munch, right? *Head of a Woman*?

Knausgård: Yeah, yeah.

Cowen: Why buy only one? Why not buy a second? What is your thinking on the matter?

Knausgård: It's expensive.

Cowen: You enjoy it, right?

Knausgård: Yeah, yeah. It was expensive.

Cowen: They're capital assets. You can resell it someday. Your heirs will have real value.

Knausgård: No, no. It was hard for me to buy that one. Having a Munch in Norway is very bourgeois, and you're very settled when you do that. My excuse was that I got a fee for the curation of the exhibition, and I thought I could use the fee for buying a Munch, so that's what I got.

It's just a drawing. It's nothing, really, but it's incredibly nice. To see anything with a good work of art is that you can see it every day, and you don't get tired. It's like it gives endlessly. It's very simple, extremely simple, but it still comes something from it every day, actually, which is what you want from a piece of art.

Cowen: You showed up seven minutes early for this interview. Do you think of yourself as ultimately a defender or a critic of bourgeois culture and bourgeois virtue?

Knausgård: When I was a teenager, I was very much in opposition to it then.

Cowen: But that's the typical pattern of someone who's older, right?

Knausgård: Yeah, but you know, I don't really care. That's true. I'm too busy raising children. I'm too busy trying to survive that I can't really afford to think in those terms. I remember when I got my first daughter, and I was full time with her. I thought, "This is very unmasculine, and this is taking away my identity."

But then I had three children and then four children, and who *cares*? You just deal with them and try to be good and go on. It's the same now. It's about that. If that's bourgeois, if that's what it is, I don't care.

Cowen: You've written in great detail about raising your children, but looking back, what is it you feel you understand now that you didn't then? If you were to add in a footnote? Because retrospective memory is quite different from experience in the moment.

Knausgård: Yeah. That's hard. I mean, there are so many things I did that I wish I hadn't done. But that's life.

Cowen: Most of them don't matter, right?

Knausgård: Yeah, yeah, but that's life. That's how it is, and you can't undo it. You *do* have to experience things and learn things. I can't tell a young father what to do, what to not do. You have to find out yourself.

The thing about the book, which I'm happy about, is that it covers the process. I wasn't aware of that, really, but a very short period of time, really. I wrote it in two years. As you say, I've forgotten everything now in my head, but it's in the book. It's captured in the book—to see how I was thinking, to see, yeah, mistakes I did or not did or whatever. But still, it's like a slice of life that's in those books.

Cowen: Is it possible at all to enjoy your works on audiobook, or is the use of voices different from yours too discordant for stories that are so personal, that are so you, so confessional?

Knausgård: No, I don't read my books, and I don't listen to them. In Germany, they have readings very different from here. It's readings, so you have an interview with the writer for maybe five minutes, and then it's one hour of reading. When it's a foreign writer, they have actors reading. There have been some incredibly nice experiences if there is a good actor reading. It's like he makes the book into . . . has nothing to do with me—

Cowen: Is it better than you?

Knausgård: Yeah, yeah, yeah. But then it becomes proper storytelling, and it becomes literature, and that's very strange to witness, but also very nice.

Cowen: You're obviously very fluent in English. What do you feel the English-language reader loses in the translation from the Norwegian?

Knausgård: I think the translations are excellent. Donald Bartlett—he translated five and a half of the six books, and Martin Atkins did the last part of Book Six.

He asked me in the beginning how hands-on I wanted to be in translation, and I said, "You can do whatever you want to. I don't want to have anything to do with it." Then I remember getting Book Five in the mail, and almost accidentally, I started to read, and I just kept on reading because it was so well done. It was in English, so it was kind of removed from me, but still I recognized everything, and I think he's a world-class translator, Donald Bartlett.

But an interesting thing in that regard is that I have another translator for my other books. She's a poet. She's half Norwegian, half American, called Ingvild Burkey, and she translates my language completely different. It's a completely different feeling of her language than his language.

Both are brilliant but in very different ways. He's much more translated it into an English novel, and she's much more translating into a Norwegian-feeling English. So she's much more close to my language, and he's much more above, and both come from the same writing. Very different, both very good. They have different qualities, so to speak.

Cowen: Why do we put dead bodies in the basement rather than the attic?

Knausgård: Yeah, good question. [*Laughter*]

Cowen: You asked it yourself in Book One.

Knausgård: Yeah, but that was a long time ago.

Cowen: To pursue your father's question, how many people in solo car accidents are actually suicides?

Knausgård: Yeah, exactly.

Cowen: Are all Swedes crazy?

Knausgård: Not all.

Cowen: Not all?

Knausgård: No.

Cowen: Which Ingmar Bergman film has influenced you the most and why?

Knausgård: Sitting here with you, I can't really think of any Ingmar Bergman film.

Cowen: You once said *Wild Strawberries* was your favorite, but favorite may not be the same as influence.

Knausgård: No. I think *Scenes from a Marriage* is incredibly good, to be serious.

Cowen: That's the best movie ever made if you watch the whole thing through, I think.

Knausgård: Yeah, yeah. I think that's his richest and best. Yeah, I think so. I love *Persona*, and I do actually—even though I know Lars von Trier hates it, I do like *Fanny and Alexander* also. It's such a fairy tale touch to it, which I like. But no, it is *Scenes from a Marriage*, I think.

Cowen: I like *Smiles of a Summer Night* very much, the Mozartian feel, the Shakespeare connection. It's a very alive movie for me.

Knausgård: Yeah. Yeah.

Cowen: Peter Handke—what kind of influence have his novels had on you?

Knausgård: That's a hard . . . I'm discussing him and his influence in Book Six, actually because he is a writer I absolutely admire, and I think my writing doesn't reach up to his knees, [*laughs*] his writing's knees. But *My Year in the No-Man's Bay* is a book that I read—must have been in the nineties when it came out—before being a writer myself. Or was it exactly that moment I started to be a writer, I think. That was very influential.

And his writing about the things that don't belong in a story and the things that really don't belong in a landscape—the areas between the city and outside of the city—the railway tracks, the grass, the fences, kind of the world as it is outside of the story, I think. He's just . . . I don't know, and the book about his mother is absolutely fantastic, I think.

Cowen: Is Elena Ferrante the main contender for having bested your achievement? For handing out lifetime achievement awards for contemporary serious fiction?

Knausgård: I've only read one Ferrante book, and that was *Days of Abandonment*. I would have cut off my left arm to write that book. I think it was so absolutely brilliant.

Cowen: Try *The Neapolitan*.

Knausgård: I know, I know, I know, I know. As I say, I have a problem with things I know are very good, to enter it, because I'm not a jealous type, but I feel I will in the end. But that book, *Days of Abandonment*, was really, really outstanding, good.

Luckily, there's no competition here, so there's nothing to . . . I do what I can do. You have incredibly good writers everywhere, in every country, and when I'm outside of a novel, I just look at them, and I think it feels so hopeless. How are they doing this? How are they managing to do this? And if you think like that, you can't really write. It has to come, has to be personal, has to come from inside, has to be *within* something without looking out. What you're talking about is outside of books. Then you can start and be jealous and, "Oh, no." Or, "Why did he get that grant and I not?" And "Why did I get so bad reviews?" And stuff. That's worthless. It's completely worthless, and I try to stay away from it as much as I can.

Cowen: But we know Ibsen was obsessed with medals and honors, right?

Knausgård: Yeah, he was.

Cowen: Was that a character flaw?

Knausgård: It's very funny, a very funny flaw, I think.

Cowen: One you share or not?

Knausgård: I don't share that, no. But he had also a mirror in his hat so he could take off his hat and look at himself, which is also very funny. And he was a very little, very little man, loving medals and having a mirror in his hat. That's funny.

Cowen: From another literary tradition, take Calvino, Borges, Cortázar. Are they, in your view, in some ways overrated, and is your objection to them ultimately a political one?

Knausgård: No.

Cowen: They're running away from life in a way. Correct?

Knausgård: No, no. I feel quite comfortable in Borges. I think he's superior. I think he's a master, really a master, and an author I've learned a lot from, not in ways of telling a story, but what the story tells you about the world. He has been very influential in my worldview, basically, especially one called "Tlön, Uqbar." It's a short story.

Cowen: Sure.

Knausgård: It's just the best short story ever written, I think.

Cowen: We agree on that, actually.

Knausgård: Yeah. Calvino is less . . . Calvino had . . . yeah. Cortázar is also very good, but he's not Borges, I think. And Calvino, I love. *The Baron in the Trees*—what it's called—is one of my favorite books.

If I could write like them, I would, but I can't. Every time I have something fantastic, I mean in that sense, something that really could happen, I try to write it. I can't make it work. Just don't have it in me. Has to be some sort of realism. I have to believe in it myself. And the magic with Borges is that you believe it completely. He makes it completely believable.

And his essays are absolutely wonderful. And in every little essay, every short story almost, you can pull something out of value. So he's absolutely one of my favorites.

Cowen: Is Magnus Carlsen going to withdraw from the World Chess Championship cycle?

Knausgård: Chess is not my world.

Cowen: Has liberalism exhausted itself?

Knausgård: Maybe not liberalism, maybe capitalism.

Cowen: There's something about the aesthetic people in the early twentieth century—Hamsun included—seemed to think that a vital sense of the aesthetic—maybe it didn't quite have to be fascist, but it had to move the artist somewhat in a direction which we, today, would mostly consider unpleasant. Do you think a strong notion of the aesthetic and liberalism are totally compatible?

Knausgård: Good question.

Cowen: T. S. Eliot would be another example of someone who moved in a quite unsavory direction.

Knausgård: I don't know, really. I wonder if fascist literature—if that's even possible? It's like those two concepts are not able to—

Cowen: But liberalism in literature is also tricky. Take Romain Rolland, who is a great classical liberal. He wrote books that everyone read at the time, but they're mostly forgotten. They're seen as a little flat.

Knausgård: I don't know, what do you mean by liberalism in this?

Cowen: The notion of a particular neutrality across values, which government then enforces by having impartial laws, and people believe strongly in some underlying notion of neutrality. Doesn't that clash with the aesthetic impulse at some level?

Knausgård: Yeah, of course. Yeah, if that's what you meant. Yeah, definitely.

Cowen: In your own thought, how do you reconcile those two things?

Knausgård: What I'm struggling for in my writing is what I call literary freedom, and it's a space where I can be free in every sense, where I can say whatever, go wherever I want to. And for me, literature is almost the only place you could think that that is a possibility.

My fear is that that space has come closing down on you. You're closing it down yourself and becoming more afraid for what you're saying. "Can I say this? Can I do this?" And this power is also strong, you know? It's *so* hard to go somewhere you know is wrong, or this is . . .

I did it with *My Struggle* because I wrote about my family, and I *knew*, of course, I shouldn't do this, and really it is immoral to do this. And then I did it because I wanted to say what I wanted to say, and I wanted to be free to talk about, to write about my own life in a complete and in a free way.

That's also why I admire writers like Peter Handke. He had the Yugoslavia controversy around him, and you have a lot of controversies around him. But what he does is, he's there. He's hardcore, saying what he thinks and stands for it, no matter how ugly it looks from the outside. And that's what you can do in literature and no other place, I think.

This is an internal struggle in every writer, I think. And it goes in almost all levels of society. I find it hardest to go into the private places that belong to my family and my life, but you have all the political topics. You have a lot of things you can think of. But it's good that it's a struggle, and it's good that there's an arena where we can have these fights.

But the notion that literature should be good in a moral sense—that I find ridiculous. That's useless.

Cowen: As a boy, which were your favorite comic books? You've written that you loved comic books growing up.

Knausgård: Yeah. When I was little, it was Lee Falk's *Phantom*. That was really big in Norway. A bit older, it was *Modesty Blaise*. But I read absolutely everything.

Cowen: And what are the politics of those comic books that young boys tend to read?

Knausgård: Then, in the seventies, it was very sexist, very racist, and all kinds of things. My mother discovered what I actually was reading, so she forbade me to read comics, which was a very harsh punishment, it felt at that time. But it made me start to read books. So it was a good thing in the end. She was completely shocked by what I was reading, and it was common. But that was the seventies. I think it has changed, maybe. I don't know.

Cowen: You've spent some time in a creative writing program—is that correct?

Knausgård: Yeah.

Cowen: Did you learn much there, or was it just a waste of your time?

Knausgård: I learned a lot. But what can I say? It was like running into a wall. I was running full speed into a wall, and I fell down, and I lay down. For six, seven years I couldn't write after that. I was young when I started. I had all this illusion about myself and about literature and what I could do, and I couldn't do anything. I felt like they were ridiculing me, and they were, actually. Then it took many years, and then I could write. And what I learned—I met world literature.

Cowen: Yes.

Knausgård: And I met also a writer that is, yes, he is Norway's best writer. He is called Jon Fosse, and he was twenty-nine at the time, and he was a teacher there. His notion of quality is absolute, and he was very, very important to me just because he showed me where the level should be. I haven't reached that level, but I'm above where I was when I was twenty, at least. And it was very good to *know* that. "*This* is literature; this is what literature can do."

But it was completely terrible for me at the time and many years afterwards because I had *no* self-confidence. They took away *all* my self-confidence. I couldn't write.

Cowen: The creative writing program took away your self-confidence?
Knausgård: Yeah, yeah.
Cowen: And that was a good thing?
Knausgård: In the end, it was a very good thing.
Cowen: How did you get your self-confidence back?
Knausgård: I haven't got it back.
Cowen: Haven't got it back?
Knausgård: No, but I have helpers to help me. They want to pick me up from nothing, and my assistant editor—I really couldn't write until he saw something I'd written and believed in me. He still believes in me, and he has to tell me that—every week—what I'm doing is interesting, what I'm doing is good, and that he believes in me. And he has done so for twenty years. Without him, I wouldn't have been a writer.

I also have friends who do the same thing. They said, "Okay, this is good. Don't give up. Keep on writing." And they did because if not, I wouldn't have the strength to do it. Maybe I would, but it makes my writing life much easier to have helpers.

Cowen: Your first book in English but, I think, your second book overall: *A Time for Everything*. Why did you write a whole book about angels?
Knausgård: I really don't know. I've always been interested in the physicality of man, matter, the brain itself, the physicality of the brain, the way we are animals, the way we eat, and the way we take the world in, and the primitiveness of us. And then, you know, the heaven above, all the things we dream of.

When I read the Bible, something that occurred to me was the physicality of the angels. That's such a wonderful image. And I thought, "Okay, they were eating in the Bible, they are walking with God in the Bible."

I thought, "What if I read the Bible from that perspective? What happened to the angels? Where are they?" Because they saw angels before. We don't see them. Then I thought, "Okay, maybe they have been tempted to be in the physical world too much, and then kind of been almost centrifuged into the world and been part of the world and can't escape, and they're still here around us."

That was the thought. And in a way, it's a metaphor for what happened with religion, why we're not . . . many of us don't believe anymore. Why there's no heaven above us except commercials and TV programs and stuff. What happened? What happened with religion? What happened with God? What happened with heavens? You know? How come we are all down here now, and what's that about?

That was not why I wrote it, but that was the outcome of the writing.

Cowen: And why the fascination with the Cain and Abel story? Right? It's family struggle, and it's rivalry.

Knausgård: Yeah, that's true. And it's only like eight lines or something in the Bible. It's almost nothing. It's so rich, and it's like it's bottomless. They have been discussing that and reading that for thousands of years, and you can still say something new about it. That simple story—a brother killing another brother.

I'm just reading about gnosticism now. They take a liking—some of them—for Cain. They like to turn everything upside down. So God is really the devil, and this really is hell, and Cain is really the good one, the one to look at. You know, it's just an endlessly fascinating thing. It means so much—so many layers of meaning in that simple, simple story.

That's the best part of the Bible: those very short stories. *Incredibly* rich and layered with meaning.

Cowen: To close, why don't we return to your new book? Again, it's called *So Much Longing in So Little Space*. Give us your take on Munch, *The Scream*. You've referred to this earlier.

Knausgård: My take on *The Scream*? You know, that's what happens when you're writing. You just start. I just sat down with a Munch book and thought, "Okay, I'll write a book about Munch. Let's see where this goes." Then you just enter it, and then comes something back, and then, two months later, you have a book.

The Scream is one of the most iconic paintings there is. Everyone, I think, has seen it. It's so recognizable. And almost we have an intimate knowledge of it. We see it, you know? But the painting is about the opposite. It's about something very strange. It's hard to do this in English, but it's about the world being almost unrecognizable. It's seeing how strange the world is. And we do this in that painting that we instantly recognize.

And it's a painting about anxiety, and anxiety is *incredibly* painful. So, it is a painting about pain. But we see a million dollars, we see its fame. We don't see *that*.

But the interesting thing for me when I wrote about it was what kind of paintings Munch had access to and how they painted at that time. Because no matter how painful things were, they were always taking place in a space, in a room. And having that space, having that room, you know the events in that room will one day be over. Something new will take place there.

If *Madame Bovary* is very painful—the ending—but you know that world will continue. And there is a kind of a comfort in that. There isn't an acuteness in it. You could see it. You know it will pass. And you observe it from the outside, so you see it at a distance. You see something painful—a sick girl—at a distance, and it's in another room, and it will pass. There is a comfort in that.

But Munch does set out in that painting to remove that room, to remove that space. Because all the landscape is subdued to the person in the painting. So it's his landscapes. There's no room in it; there's no neutrality. When that person is gone, the landscape is gone.

So, there is no space, and there is no time. It's instantly painting, it's acute. It's like it's happening now, and we share the space with the painting. And in that is the radicality of the painting—that there's no space and there's no comfort. It's an acute thing. It's instant, and you have to relate to it. You can't see that painting without relating to it. I mean when you saw it for the first time.

And the interesting thing now, I think, is that that's a fair description of the world—how it is now. It is an instant world. We get access to painful things that happen when they happen. Today, there was a massacre in New Zealand. The minute it happens, we know about it, we relate to it, we feel the pain, and we see the pictures. That didn't just happen. That didn't happen at Munch's time. It was unheard of.

Now that's the world. We live in the world of *Scream*. There's no space between us and the world. Everything comes bombarding us, you know?

So, what art has to do now is the opposite. It has to create space. It has to recreate rooms. And I was thinking about that and also writing in the book about—I was at an exhibition of Anselm Kiefer here in London. It was the *White Cube*. It was absolutely magnificent, but there were *no* people in it; it was *only* spaces, *only* room. And it was kind of mythological rooms. It was like it was giving space to events that wasn't even there, back somehow.

I think both Kiefer and Munch are great artists, but they live in different times, and they had different missions. For Munch, it was very important to give access directly to pain and to distorted vision of the world, and to give a more true account of how it is to be, I think he wanted to do.

And now it's the opposite because now we need space, and we need comfort, and we need time, and we need something. I'm not sure if art is what should do that, but that's what I felt when I started to write about Munch.

And another interesting thing is that exactly the same thing is going on in the literature at that time, you know? You have the epic novel with all the characters, all the rooms. Tolstoy is a very good example because that is a book about rooms.

And then you have, for instance, Knut Hamsun in *Hunger*, which is just one person and his distorted version of the world that exists. And when he dies, the world disappears.

Cowen: Karl, thank you very much for coming by.

Knausgård: Thank you.

An Interview with Karl Ove Knausgård: The Sixth Author for Future Library

Katie Paterson / 2020

Future Library, 2014–2114. Film by MIND THE FILM. Filmed at Royal Museums Greenwich. Future Library is commissioned and produced by Bjørvika Utvikling, and managed by the Future Library Trust. Supported by the City of Oslo, Agency for Cultural Affairs and Agency for Urban Environment. Katie Paterson Studio and the Future Library Trust: 2014–2114. https://www.futurelibrary.no/#/years/2019/. Reprinted by permission.

A thousand trees have been planted in Nordmarka, a forest just outside Oslo, which will supply paper for a special anthology of books to be printed in one hundred years' time. Between now and then, one writer every year will contribute a text, with the writings held in trust, unpublished, until 2114. In *Mind the Film*, filmed at Royal Museums Greenwich, Knausgård discusses his involvement in the project.

Karl Ove Knausgård: My name is Karl Ove Knausgård. I was born in Norway in 1968. I'm a writer, and I live in London, and I've done so for the last three years.

Question (unheard, shown on the screen): What was the reaction when you were invited?

Knausgård: "Yes, I want to do that!" That was my response. I'd read about the project earlier and I kind of hoped to be invited, but I—you know, you never know—and there's so many writers, and so I didn't believe actually I would be invited. But when I was, I said yes, at once. There are so many different aspects to this project, and I like almost all of them. From a writer's perspective, it is incredibly fascinating to do something and to know that it is published in a completely different setting in a completely different world probably. Because that's the magic with literature, is that it does not only connect with your friends—or even your culture—but it can connect. I can read books five hundred years old and connect to it and relate to it, and that's exciting in itself to know that *okay, my writing might be forgotten in ten years, but this book will be—kind of be opened and presented in a hundred years*, which is exciting. And then I'm just very interested in time and in culture and in changes and all of those things that kind of are at play here. And then I also like very much the kind of ecology aspects to it, that it's a forest that will grow very slowly and that the trees that are planted now are the ones that will be used in the future. And I like the connection between paper and forest—you know, writing . . . future. It's also a way to really think what's *now*—what's *this*, what's *now*? What are we doing now? How is our society going to be remembered? And just by doing that, you get a perspective from the future upon us somehow. And then again, 1920, that's not a very long time ago. If you read Virginia Woolf from the twenties in London—you know it's like . . . nothing much of a change really. But we don't know, and that's very exciting.

Time, Trees, and Humans

Knausgård: It's about time on incredibly many levels. One would be, when you write something, you are in contemporary time; you're connected to temporary time. It's like you're in it, and when you read it, you're in it. But what's *in the book*, in the writing, doesn't change, but everything else changes, in kind of a different speed. I'm very fascinated by that fact, that something is kind of unchanged, brought into the future, where everything changes. And then since it's art, since it has to do with human beings, it still is possible to kind of evoke it and give it life again, and it will be "in time" again. That's very weird, a very strange phenomenon, I think. And you also have the time of other species, in this case that trees that grow very very slowly and have a completely different—I know that trees don't have a view on the world, but it is in the world in a very different way than we are in the world. But with biology and our species and evolution and the fact that it's three hundred thousand years, roughly, which is an incredibly short time span in the long term. You have human-like species that existed for nine hundred thousand years and that are gone, they're no more, you know? And those kinds of perspectives, even if this is just a hundred years, but those kinds of perspectives come into play when you do something like this or are a part of something like this. It's inevitable somehow to think about it. Because the forest in Munch is often *death*. It's what you go toward, where you disappear into, and you are gone. On one side and the other side is that it's connected to creativity, very much so. Kind of to the physical presence of the world in his printings, for instance. I think that's important to this project is death because we will be gone when this is finalized. And then creativity—people are making art in it, and then also language, communication, and the fact that we really don't understand trees, we don't know trees. We have no—we can't really relate to it, and maybe we should, but we haven't until now, at least.

"Alphabet" by Inger Christensen (1981)

Knausgård: It's an incredibly beautiful poem, which I realized when I was young too, so that it's just mentioning things, and it's like a list of things in the world, alphabetically. It's joyful because it's about *this exists* and *this exists* and *that* exists and it's here with us now. But it's also somehow filled with kind of sorrow firstly maybe because we know that we're going to die, so we're going to leave it this; we're not going to be part of it. But secondly and more relevant now, maybe than ever, is that many of the things—other species she's mentioning—could possibly die out and disappear, and that's happening more or less all the time around us now. And that's the one thing I hardly can't think about it, because it's so incredibly sad, because it won't come back—just gone forever and *some* of that is caused by the natural process, but many, many, many of the things that are happening now are not. It's human made, which exists in that poem. I don't know if she thought of it when she wrote it, but it is there, just by mentioning [it], and that's the beauty of art, that you could do something very, very simple and it can be incredibly complex. And I think this project too has that element to it.

Future and Literature

Knausgård: I think everyone is fascinated by just the *thought* of the future, and we can't do anything about the future; we can only think about it, and that's basically it. Then we can plan maybe, you know, a few years' time, and we can have a mortgage for twenty-five years, and that's it. So the future is everywhere, but we can't do anything with it, and *here* is a project that actually has a practical—you know, doing something practical that involves the future, that we can't know how we will end. We'll just know that some of what's going on here will be revealed in the future, and just that is very exciting in itself. It's literature. We don't know, and literature is kind of slowly fading out of our society, and many languages also are disappearing, and we don't know how that's going to be in a hundred years' time, if people will read at all.

And that's a way, to just to do that, is a way to question us and our relationship to language and to literature. And I think literature is—and I'm a writer—but I think it's an incredibly important part of us, of our being, of our understanding of the self, self and society, culture, of everything. and the connection with the forest, connection with nature. There is this question you know: If a forest could think, if maybe there is a different kind of intelligence—not *our* kind of intelligence, but a different kind of intelligence in an ecosystem, you know, those kinds of things.

To Keep a Secret

Knausgård: In my writing I'm known for giving away secrets about myself and people close to me, so if I'm good at keeping a secret like this? I don't know, but secrecy is very much connected to writing really because when you are writing, it is very intimate and it is very much part of yourself, and it's very much an inner world that you don't share, and then you have to keep it that way to be free enough to transgress the way you want and to go where you want, and you must not think about publication; you must not think about readers. And then it's public, and then of course that's what happens, but they're very much two phases there, and in this project, it's really twisting those two things because I am writing, and it is secret—but it's not published. And then it's published in a hundred years when nobody's here to read it.

That's very weird, but I think that's also part of the fascination in this project, is that, yeah, can you trust people to publish it? Yeah, can you trust literature to reach out to people in a hundred years' time? We don't know, but that's basically what literature does, I think—reach out to people different from yourself, or you can go anywhere—a reader—to places that are completely unknown and out of reach. For instance, you can read Icelandic sagas that are a thousand years old, and it's no problem at all to connect to it, because being a human being is the same now as it was then and, probably, if things don't go terribly wrong, it will be the same in a hundred years, I think.

Handing over the Manuscript

Knausgård: I'm quite used to handing over manuscripts, and when I've done so, I try to forget them completely and not go back and not think about them, and they belong to the past, so the crazy thing here would be that this belongs to the future, so you don't—it's a very weird situation. But I am saying goodbye to it. *I* won't see it again, but I will know that it still exists and still kind of is somewhere. That will be both very intriguing and terrible. It's like its bad reviews will come in in a hundred years, or not—not that that matters, but it still is actually, when you are writing something, you *have* a sense of readers. You have a sense of context and you try to get rid of it because you have to be free. But even writing *this*, knowing that every person would not be here and it would be completely—you still have that feeling of, you know, it's something at stake here, and that feeling will never leave, it will be till the day I die.[1]

Note

1. The title of Knausgaard's future novel is *Blindenboken* (*The Blind Book*).

"Writing Isn't a Sacred Activity, It Is an Ordinary Activity": A Conversation with Karl Ove Knausgaard

Bob Blaisdell / 2020

Los Angeles Review of Books, Jan. 8, 2021. Reprinted by permission.

Having received an advance copy of *In the Land of the Cyclops: Essays*, I wrote Knausgaard's American publisher, Archipelago, to request an interview with my favorite living author. We spoke for a little more than an hour on Zoom—Knausgaard was in London; I was in New York. I have deleted only our exchanges where technical glitches required me or him to repeat ourselves or where I indulged myself in literary tangents that received little response. Knausgaard reviewed the complete transcript and expanded, clarified, or developed a few replies.

Bob Blaisdell: I saw you speak in Brooklyn a couple of years ago, across from the Brooklyn Public Library in a synagogue. And you were speaking with—
Karl Ove Knausgaard: Was that Maggie Nelson?
Blaisdell: Yeah.
Knausgaard: I remember that event very well. I was incredibly nervous. I do admire Maggie Nelson's writing a lot, and it was a difficult book that we were going to talk about, but she was great, and it went well. That's the thing with events and interviews in general, I guess, it is never just about questions and answers, but also about the dynamic between the two persons, and that is always unpredictable. There are a million ways to talk about a book, you know? It was an honor to do it with Maggie Nelson.
Blaisdell: That was a very fun, interesting night. . . . I've got this book. And as you mentioned in an email, you wrote these quite a while ago.

Knausgaard: Yeah.

Blaisdell: Has the book already been collected and published in Norway?

Knausgaard: Yeah, so, the first volume, my first collection of essays, was published after *My Struggle*. And then there was a second that was published a few years ago. And the book you got, *In the Land of the Cyclops*, is a collection from both of them.

Blaisdell: From both of them. I see. . . . And what happened to the ones that you wrote for the *New York Times*, for example?

Knausgaard: They are more like articles than essays, so they are a bit different from the other texts. The last article I did, about Anselm Kiefer, is going to be a book in itself, published in Norway in January. When I do the stuff for the *New York Times*, I always write very long, around a hundred pages, and then we, the editor, Luke Mitchell, and myself, take it down to the article size. So basically, all of those articles are like books from the beginning. [*Laughs*] But I think they are related somehow, the subjects, so maybe one day I can publish them if there is some interest for that.

Blaisdell: For instance, that one on the brain surgeon ["The Terrible Beauty of Brain Surgery"]—I don't know what you want to call it—but it was fantastic.

Knausgaard: Oh, thank you. Yeah, I've really loved doing that stuff. It's so great to do that, to go out and meet someone and experience something and then go back home and write about it. I think it's really wonderful. And very different from my normal writing life, where I sit alone in my room and work on something that comes from within. I meet people I never would meet otherwise—Henry Marsh [the brain surgeon], for instance. And Anselm Kiefer, too, was really great to meet and observe his work. It's very different from writing essays, I think. It's something else, I don't know what it is. But it's just fun.

Blaisdell: Is it more fun than any other kind of writing, then, for you?

Knausgaard: Yeah, yeah, I'm taking notes and recording and interviewing people, and you know it's much more fun. That's what it is—and *exciting*.

Blaisdell: What's the least fun? The least fun kind of writing, then?

Knausgaard: [*Sighs*] Some of the essays that are, you know, that someone else asked you to do, and you agree a year before, and then you have to do it in like three days or something; that's really hard. But I think all writing has elements of fun in it, or *joy* is more accurate, I think. And also, writing a novel, that's completely different. You can't compare it with anything because it's so slow. It could take a year or four years. You want it to be big, but you can only move small pieces every day, and today for instance I wrote about a man going to a mailbox and picking up the newspaper, and that was my day. I want to write this big huge novel, but it's never even close. So, there's many types of writing, but there is an element of joy in all of them, I think.

Blaisdell: What are you working on right now?

Knausgaard: I just published a novel in Norway two months ago. I'm now writing another novel which somehow is related, and I've started it, I've written a hundred pages or so, so I'm in the middle of the beginning of that, which is the hardest part. But that's what I'm doing.

Blaisdell: The middle of the beginning is the hardest part? Not the beginning but the middle of the beginning is the hardest?

Knausgaard: Yeah, yeah. That's the hardest part. Before the novel decides itself, and you just can follow it along. Before that happens, you have to make the space where it later will unfold, and the space, it seems when you are writing, is nothing in itself. The feeling is that nothing is leaving the page, it is flat and dull, and all you want to do is to start again afresh. Once I did that, started again and again, and in the end, I had eight hundred pages of beginnings. So now I tend to stick with it, no matter how bad it feels, trying to be patient, hoping for something to evolve. That's hard work, and you don't know whether it's going to be something or not, and it's not good in itself. It's just like building a scaffolding or something.

Blaisdell: *Tolstoy* also used that image of the scaffolding.

Knausgaard: Really? Yeah?

Blaisdell: He had to set it all up and . . . *He* almost never had *joy* writing. I've gone over everything he ever wrote in the 1870s, and there were maybe two days in writing *Anna Karenina* where he was saying, "I had a good day!"

Knausgaard: Really?

Blaisdell: Yeah! When you talk to other writers, does it seem that you have more enjoyment from it than they do?

Knausgaard: No. It's so many sides to that process. So, the self-doubt, the torture of realizing how bad this is, that's part of it, and it's kind of constant. I actually send pages to my editor every day. And he replies the next morning, just to be able for me to continue. But then, when you're in it, to me, it's like, yeah, it's very joyful, not that it's fun in that sense, but it's just very satisfying somehow. When you are beyond good or bad and everything is flowing, that's the place to be. I know that it exists, and when the text enters that place, the writing changes: before that I have to use willpower to sit down and work, but when I'm there, writing is what I want to do. Every novel I have written has that turning point, that tipping point, and from then on, it is like everything takes care of itself! But even then, there's doubts and shame and all those kinds of negative things too, and in the beginning of the process, like now, it has been a terrible few days, but I know that will pass and I know something else is waiting. [*Sighs*] But I know many writers who hate writing, I mean who really hate it and I don't understand that, but I do admire them for sticking in there, you know? [*Laughs*]

Blaisdell: Yeah, I'm surprised too that writers don't enjoy what they're doing since nobody has to do it! Nobody *has* to do it. May I quote something from the book at you?

Knausgaard: Yeah.

Blaisdell: Where you're describing something, but when I read it, I thought of *your* writing. So, this is from the piece about Kiefer ["Tándaradéi"]. You say, "Watercolor is a medium that demands speed and cannot be reworked: what is there must be left there—one doesn't get a second chance. It is an art of the instant."

Knausgaard: Yeah.

Blaisdell: It seems to me that *that's* what you're doing. That you give us that sense of what you describe for watercolors.

Knausgaard: I never thought of that . . . from the watercolors to Kiefer or any other watercolors that I love—so light, so floating, so precise, and it's all *there*. To me, writing is trying to get to somewhere and never reaching it, but a long winding road into something and the text goes up there and down into there, and it's like an enormously slow process. I do find it very different. I think a *poem* could be instant and elegant and kind of light and floating. But I do understand what you mean by saying that, but I don't think of it that way at all.

Blaisdell: Okay! All right, all right. Let me try another, where you're talking about Ingmar Bergman's notebooks ["Feeling and Feeling and Feeling"].

Knausgaard: Yeah, that's a kind of more recent, I think it's three years old or something. I think I spent like four months on writing that one. I just couldn't write, I couldn't, and I had to do this for this Bergman book that was coming out, and it was tormenting me, and then in the end, I just wrote something very quickly, and I can't really understand why it was so difficult, but it was so difficult. And then I realized that the text I wrote was about that. Of all periods from Bergman's life I could write about, I chose one where he was writing a script that really was terrible and never became anything. He lived in Munich at the time, and he did what he always had done, but it just didn't come alive; it was forced and mute, really. Then, in that period, there's a glimpse of what would become *Fanny and Alexander*.

An embryo. That's the fascinating thing about his workbooks, they are completely transparent when it comes to ideas and the creative process; you can see where things come into being—for instance *Persona*—and it is never the main subject; it is always something else, a woman sitting with folded hands, for instance, that was the start of *Persona*. That was the idea! But it was funny because when I wrote about Bergman's creative dead end, I had no idea that it also described the place I wrote from.

Blaisdell: So it's from around the same time as the Seasons books, *Autumn*?

Knausgaard: It's after.

Blaisdell: Those essays were so immediate. My daughter had read Volume One of *My Struggle*, and I saw her book, and I didn't pick it up, though she had liked it and recommended it. And then one day I read your essay, the one called "Gum," in the *New York Times*, and I thought, "I have to read this guy."

Knausgaard: Umph!

Blaisdell: Because, I thought, whoever wrote *that* is an interesting man! And so then I read *Autumn*, and then I reviewed the next three books. And then I took on *My Struggle*. And now I'm almost all the way back. I'm rereading *My Struggle*. It's still great. But there's a quote from the Bergman piece where you're talking about the ladders—

Knausgaard: Yep.

Blaisdell: So let me read from there, where you say, "The workbook was in other words a kind of ladder leading from the writer to the work. Usually, the writer will take that ladder away once the work is done, allowing the work to stand alone, isolated as it were from its creative context. Bergman's workbooks are the ladder left in place." I know *your* work much better than I know Bergman's, and so I, again, thought about your work, that one of the pleasures of reading you for me is seeing art being made and not being put behind something else. Not being put behind—

Knausgaard: No.

Blaisdell: —a voice or a manner.

Knausgaard: Yeah.

Blaisdell: I'm seeing the whole thing, and somehow the instant of you writing it and also all of the building of it: seeing the scaffolding with the building.

Knausgaard: Yeah, I didn't think of that when I wrote about Bergman, but I did when I wrote *My Struggle*. I was kind of backstage and on the stage at the same time. It was as much about the book being written as it was about what the book was about because life and literature for me were so interwoven, and that book is also very much so. Life and writing and life and literature are completely tangled together somehow. And also the fact that I published them in a year, and I wrote when I was publishing, so I was writing, publishing, and then I get reactions, and the reactions are in the book, and then, you know—

Blaisdell: Yes!

Knausgaard: Yes, this book is very much about that—of course I'm hiding things, but I tried to be transparent so that you could see through literature into life and from life into literature, and that was the whole project, the dynamic between life and literature really. So, yeah, I do think that's relevant with what is going on in *My Struggle*.

Blaisdell: I'm glad I got that one. My favorite essay in the book, I think, is the one about necks, "The Other Side of the Face."

Knausgaard: Yeah? Mm.

Blaisdell: What do you remember about—

Knausgaard: It's a friend of mine. Thomas Wågström is a photographer, and I've written a text to three of his books. It's kind of a trilogy. And *Necks* was in the middle of them. The first is about clouds in the sky and the floating, parting elements in the world, and it is a look upward. The neck is a look straight ahead and into the body, into the biology, and the third book he's up and looking down, seeing people like miniature and exploring the patterns *between* them. That's three very different perspectives. The neck is the middle one, and it was the most easy to write. The book is amazing, it's just photos of necks, people's necks, like portraits, where the identity is hidden. The neck is as individual as the face, but we never connect identity with the back, of course.

I didn't know what to write when I started it, and I never do, but I do find the biology and the body intriguing, the bodily existence, the flesh, the matter without the spirit, the noncerebral being in the world. We come from there, and it is still with us, and we are still surrounded by that kind of existence. There's something there. I always want to go kind of the opposite way of the abstract or the thinking or the, you know, that's where the mystery is, in the body, it's in the dark of the body, in the things we don't know about, and that's what this text is about, I think, somehow, if I remember right. It's a kind of constant fascination for me, also in what I'm writing now, that's where I'm trying to go, but that's a place where there are no words, and no thinking, so it's of course hard, no, not hard, it is impossible! But I don't know why I'm so fascinated about it, but there is something there. And I think that's in the essay, too, that fascination.

Blaisdell: I need to ground myself back in your words. I'll quote one sentence back at you: "And this is why, I think, that in looking at the neck, as these photos lead us to do, we get the feeling that we are being offered a glimpse of the body as it is in itself, nonindividual, nonrelational, biological, whole. Something growing in a certain place in the world." And on the previous page, you say, "A neck cannot be modern." And that made me stop and exclaim: "So simple!" And so obvious, but it stopped me and gave me great pleasure, just that one simple *discovery*. One of the pleasures of reading you is these sudden realizations, that are of course obvious when you think about it, but before you thought about it, no one was thinking about it.

Knausgaard: Yeah, I can't think—I don't think much in my life, and, you know, not at all really, so in a conversation I can't say anything clever at all. At a dinner conversation I normally say nothing, and I don't, I don't think about things! . . . Politics, or anything, really. But in writing, it's, just because of that, because I don't know anything, and I don't know where the writing is going, so everything is kind of a surprise to me. It's not me, it's like a kind of an exchange between me and literature and language, and the whole point of that is not to know where you're going, so that the places are as new to you as they are to the reader.

Writing is about searching, about exploring, about the things you do not know but discover through writing. I have never thought these things that are in my texts, *ever*, but the texts kind of do it for me, and it's not that it's brilliant or anything, but it's just something that I otherwise wouldn't have thought without the help of the writing. The text and literature and also the things you look at, you know, for instance, this book, or things you read, and it's all thrown into the mix, and I don't think about it. It can only happen in writing, those meetings, so I think that's one of the reasons why I'm writing, because I am very curious, and I do want to explore things and understand things and a way to do it. My only way to do it is through writing. And then it doesn't matter if it's *my* opinion or *my* thoughts. What is mine anyway? What is I? The text does something; the text thinks something. It has left me. So if people confront me with "You say this; you think that," I will of course take responsibility for it, it is not like I'm completely unconscious when I'm writing, but often things are stated in the text because it is good for the text, you know? It doesn't necessarily have anything to do with my own opinions. The text opens up a field where something else can be said. Writing a novel is entirely for me about creating that field, so that something else can be said. Something that is true. But that truth belongs to the novel. Hopefully it can be applicable in life, but it is not me saying it from who I am, but from inside the novel or the essay.

Blaisdell: *There* is the pleasure for us, seeing how you got to the thoughts. It's like with mathematics teachers saying, "Show your work," and you keep showing us, again and again, how the thought got *there*. And for some reason, it's thrilling; it's so exciting seeing the thought. You compared it to clouds at one point—

Knausgaard: Yeah.

Blaisdell: And it developed, and it's there, only because of where it already was.

Knausgaard: Yeah, that means that I don't own them somehow, and something weird happened. I thought about that when I knew that we were going to talk tonight. Because not a long time ago I started to read Kierkegaard—for the novel I was writing—his collected works, and I started to read his books. My wife and I talked about him, and I became very interested in his philosophy. Then this English essay edition was being made, so I had to go through the essays, and then I realized—and I didn't know this—that I had written an essay about Kierkegaard ["Life in the Sphere of Unending Resignation"]! I had just completely forgotten. I knew what was in it when I read it, and I had just read these books, and they're like new, and I've just written about them, you know, and that's part of this—what we're talking about—that it's not me thinking so much as it is the dynamics of writing. It happens on the page; it doesn't happen in me. That's why I also forgot what was in the book, I think. Because it's not me; it's the book.

Blaisdell: Do you proofread all the translations into English?

Knausgaard: No, no.

Blaisdell: Do you *check* them?

Knausgaard: Essays? I normally do. Also because I use many different translators. Sometimes I don't know them, and an essay is also easier to check. But in the novels, I don't. I trust the translators completely. I've been so lucky to have two brilliant translators for my novels, Don Bartlett and Martin Aitken, and also Ingvild Burkey, who translated the Seasons books, and also some of the essays. She's really wonderful.

Blaisdell: Has there ever been a mistake, after you see it, and you go, "No, actually, that's the wrong word"?

Knausgaard: Yeah, it could be, yeah. That could happen, but not very often. And it really doesn't matter that much. It's almost always a question about tone, and much more than words, somehow. If they get the tone right, then it's fine by me.

Blaisdell: What's the longest thing you've ever written in English? Have you composed at all in English, since school?

Knausgaard: I wrote once in *The Guardian*, a long time ago. I was asked for a list of ten books about angels, and I wrote it in English. Sometimes I write in English when we are editing the articles, like making a bridge or filling out a scene, but that's really nothing. I can write in English, but I don't have that *Fingerspitzgefühl*, the sense of language that really makes the writing. All the nuances in the language disappear, all these different layers of tones, and then there's not much left!

Blaisdell: That's interesting. I have a question: Since you do so much writing about art and painters and photography, do you ever take photographs, do you ever paint? And when you take photographs, what do you take photographs of?

Knausgaard: I'm a really lousy photographer. [*Laughs*] My wife's laughing at me, because of my photos; they are really, really poor. They're just flat, and nothing goes on in them. And I have been, you know, I have worked with photographers on assignments, and they have all been so incredibly good. I have seen the same as they have seen. We went to the same places together, but then when I have seen their photos, it becomes obvious that they have seen different things, almost like they have been to different places, having produced something absolutely magnificent. I was there with them; I saw nothing of the kind! So no, I'm not a photographer. I'm not a painter either. But I did actually start to paint some years ago. I was kind of depressed then—I didn't know it at the time, but I could hardly move and felt that everything was hopeless and meaningless, so if not depressed, then at least not able to work or to do anything other than the minimum everyday life things. Anyway, then I went into the little town we lived by at that time and bought oil paints, brushes, and canvases. I have always wanted to paint, but never felt that I had the right to. So I started to paint. And it felt so good, I really loved it and became obsessed by it, I could easily paint for sixteen hours straight nonstop. But the paintings themselves were incredibly poor. They looked like something an old, retired, completely unartistic person would have done in a summer course in painting paid for by his children. Landscapes with yellow fields of wheat and blue sky—nothing was going on in them at all, no soul, no character, no personality, nothing. But it was so joyful! The colors, the shapes, and the hope that it might turn into something if I just kept going! But it never did. They never left the petit-bourgeois, amateurish area. I did enjoy it—something happens in front of you, and one of the paintings that I did, and really, it's kitsch and it's stupid, but I spent two years on it, you know? [*Laughs*]

I think that experience has been helpful for my writing about art, however, because I know how hard it is to make a picture that is striking, like you can't take your eyes away from it, and that is constantly producing meaning and evoking emotions in the viewer, in an almost endless way, a picture that doesn't stop, doesn't rest, but keeps giving. Anselm Kiefer's pictures do that, for instance, and although some of his work seems simple, made up of a few combined elements, the simplicity is part of the art, part of the genius. I know how incredibly hard it is and difficult, and it looks so simple and easy and, you know, if you see a Kiefer painting, you think, "Yeah, maybe I could do something like that," but *you can't, you can't!* The art is to make it accessible, and to make it hypnotic, to make it intriguing and simple at the same time. Which you know is what the best art is, and that's completely out of the reach for me, of course, but I do love writing about it, and I do love seeing art, and I do that a lot, because it fills me with something, or rather, connects me with something meaningful and valuable. Seeing Kiefer at work was an amazing experience. I had never been in a studio like that, you know, and to see how completely immersed in the work he was. It was like there were no boundaries between him and the work, that he was *in* his art. I'm sure it takes a life to be at that level, where you could do what he is doing. He fought with—what do you call it, not coincidence, but with *chance*. You know, it was like a struggle between his vision and his thoughts and the material—and you could see it. Also interesting was to see his way of regarding failures. He just pushed them away and continued. His work was a constantly ongoing process, a flow like no other I have seen. I was completely exhausted after five hours, having done nothing, but he continued for many more hours, and he is a man in his seventies. It was amazing.

Blaisdell: I know just from your writing that you love looking at art books. Do you prefer going to museums or looking at the art books?

Knausgaard: I prefer going to museums, if I can. It's a very, very different experience.

Blaisdell: Can you go right now?

Knausgaard: No, no, everything is closed. And I haven't been to a museum since the lockdown started. So that's a long time ago.

Blaisdell: So are you completely moved to London?

Knausgaard: Yeah, yeah. I've been here for three years now.

Blaisdell: I've read so much about your children. They're living in Sweden?

Knausgaard: No, they're here, in London.

Blaisdell: Your children are in London?

Knausgaard: Yeah. London is their base.

Blaisdell: Oh!

Knausgaard: Yeah, they're here in the house now.

Blaisdell: And you remarried?
Knausgaard: Yeah, yeah.
Blaisdell: A British woman, an English woman?
Knausgaard: Yeah, she is a British citizen. She is originally from Israel. She moved here when she was six. We got a child together—he is nearly two years old now.
Blaisdell: Congratulations.
Knausgaard: Thank you very much, yes. Thank you.
Blaisdell: Fantastic, fantastic. Has your oldest daughter begun reading your books?
Knausgaard: No, none of them have read my books. They're aware of what's there, but they haven't read it.
Blaisdell: I'm thinking of the essays in *Autumn* and *Winter*, where you're addressing your *unborn* daughter. Eventually she'll read those. And I should tell you I've taught your essays in my writing class. I teach at a community college in Brooklyn. My students, some of them are recent immigrants, some of them are working people, adults who come back to school, so they're not usually readers, but when they read your essays about bats, about your daughter's operation, eggs—they get it. And I'm delighted. They follow it, and it's a big test for me, whether a writer can communicate to *my* students who aren't readers. And your writing does! I use short stories by Tolstoy sometimes too, and they completely get it. So that's one of my literary tests: Can my students who don't read, read it?
Knausgaard: That's a very sympathetic way to think about literature, I think. Because it is meant to be for everyone, you know. It's not meant to be for certain groups, like for people with higher education, for instance, or for people with certain kinds of jobs. Literature is for everyone. That is very important.
Blaisdell: I have a few questions that go back into this book. The title essay, "In the Land of the Cyclops," it doesn't seem like a characteristic essay of yours.
Knausgaard: No, that's true. It is the only essay in the collection where I didn't search for something. I knew what I wanted to say. So there's no exploring, only opinion. That is probably what you noticed.

It's, I think, the only angry thing I've ever written and published. My books had been regularly attacked in Sweden, where I lived at the time, and finally I had enough and decided to counterattack. It ended up being like a Don Quixote attack on windmills. It's not a good essay, but I think it is good for the book to have a different kind of temper in it.

Blaisdell: And you also give it the title—at least in this English edition, it's the title essay.

Knausgaard: Yeah, that's true, that's just because I love the title. [*Laughs*] And all of the essays are written there, in that country.

Blaisdell: I see. That's one connection. Is there anything you miss about Sweden?

Knausgaard: Yeah, of course. I lived there for fifteen years, so Sweden plays an important part in my life. As Norway also does. But I do like to move on, and I also like to live in different kind of places. London is very much the opposite of rural Sweden, and I have never lived in a metropolis before, never lived in a place that somehow is the center. I love it, also because I suspect I'll never completely figure the city out.

Blaisdell: How much time are you writing every day? Are you writing in the morning? What's your writing routine now?

Knausgaard: Now, I write when the children are in school. I have around five hours a day to my disposal, and then some days more. That is good, because if you're in a project, it's very good to stop and not finish, to hold back a bit, because the energy accumulates, and the subconscious activity too.

So the novel that was recently published, *Morgenstjernen* [*The Morning Star*], I wrote mainly in lockdown, about two-thirds of it, I believe. Then schools were closed, so the time for work was limited, but that was actually good for the writing. Normally the best time to write for me is at four in the morning—I discovered that with the Seasons books. It's something with coming from sleep and nothing has happened and it's almost like the guard you have to watch the world is not up yet, and so you can just slide in and out of your own thoughts. It's the best part of the day to write, really. But anything works. Once, when I was young, I thought I had to be completely isolated, so I went out to an island and wrote. I was in a lighthouse writing, and it was very unproductive somehow, and then when I had children, I was writing in the living room, I suddenly became very productive. They brought life into the writing process, and also a perspective: writing isn't a sacred activity. It is an ordinary activity. It doesn't have rules, and it must constantly be improvised. And if you only write for an hour a day through a year, or through two years, you will have plenty of time for a novel, you know?

Blaisdell: I admit that the first time I reviewed your work, *Winter*, I said something about how you weren't funny. But then when I listened to you, and when I kept reading, I kept catching myself laughing at particular moments in the novels and in the pieces. There are funny moments just of *surprise.* So I take it back. Because you are occasionally funny. I don't think you try to be funny, but you are sometimes funny.

Knausgaard: Yeah, but it's like, you know, one of the funniest books I know of. I remember when I read it the first time, I was basically on the floor, howling with laughter, and it was Céline, *Mort à crédit* [*Death on the Installment Plan*]. It's so gloomy and dark and hopeless that in the end the misery just becomes incredibly funny. I think that can often be the case: if you just go on and on in that direction, it'll turn in the end and be hilarious. The first journalistic piece I did was a road trip in America. At the time I was exhausted and probably a bit depressed, too, and then I am not a very social person in the first place, so I ended up traveling through the US, writing a travel piece for *New York Times Magazine*, without talking to a single soul. It was meant to be about the US seen from the outside. They mention de Tocqueville beforehand, you know, and then you got this depressed, silent Scandinavian reporting about all his troubles getting around. I found that funny. To me, it was a comical piece. But in a kind of deadpan way, so I'm not entirely sure if someone else than myself did!

Blaisdell: It *was* a funny piece. And maybe it's easier to be funny when one is feeling depressed. As soon as you're conscious of yourself on the page, it seems, as you say, something different happens because it's on the page. I was just reading in *My Struggle Four*, and you were eighteen, and you were writing, and you would write with loud music coming out all over. Do you still write with music? Or do you write silently?

Knausgaard: Yeah, yeah, music always.

Blaisdell: Do you wear headphones?

Knausgaard: Yeah, I wear headphones. I normally only play one record while I am writing a book. The same songs over and over again for whatever long it takes for that book to finish. It is a way, I think, of creating a safe zone, a kind of familiar place, because the writing itself is very uncertain, very unsafe.

Blaisdell: What kind of music is it now?

Knausgaard: For instance, when I wrote a book about Edvard Munch, I played the Lambchop album *FLOTUS* nonstop. For *My Struggle Six* it was Iron & Wine's album with B sides called *Around the Well*, and then also Midlake, *The Courage of Others*. The album that is nonstop now is Father John Misty's *God's Favorite Customer*, which I absolutely love. When I wrote a piece about Russia, which is not a book, but nearly, it was a hundred pages when I wrote it, then I played War on Drugs. All American bands! Lots of good music up there, in your country.

Blaisdell: Yeah, but I'm unaware of it, unless my students talk about it. So, one of my favorite books used to be *The Rainbow* by D. H. Lawrence, and you write about it in one of these essays. And it seems as though I have fallen out of enchantment with it. Is there a book you've fallen out of love with?

Knausgaard: If there's a book I'm falling out of love with? Do you mean that particular book or in general?

Blaisdell: Is there a particular book that meant a lot to you and now you can't—

Knausgaard: No, no.

Blaisdell: You kept all your loves?

Knausgaard: Yeah, I kept all my old books, and even though I can see it's not great literature, if it has meant something to me, it has a quality, you know? I do think that—especially about books I read when I was sixteen, seventeen, eighteen, in those formative years that may be not great now—if I read them now, still they meant so much, and I had something that I really wanted and needed, so I don't think in those terms, really. But it's funny that you mention Tolstoy so often because my favorite novel these days—I think it's the best novel that's written—is *War and Peace*, and the thing about that is that I read it maybe every *tenth* year, which is enough time to forget what it's really about, so I read it almost as a new book, every time. And the last was, I think, two years ago, and it's such a great experience to read, and it's such a . . . Yeah, I think it's the best. It's much more fun to talk about books that you've liked and loved than books you fall out of love with, I think.

Blaisdell: What are you going to read next?

Knausgaard: I'm actually reading a lot about Russian philosophers and scientists at the moment. Yeah, from the time of Tolstoy and through the Revolution, the Russian cosmists. That's what I'm reading, so there are many books waiting. Also, I bought a lot of the Russian writers that I don't know about, more contemporary writers, crime writers, that kind of stuff. I'm heading in that direction, and I'm very interested in it, and so it's more about that than a specific writer or a specific book. It's a field that I'm incredibly thrilled by because I didn't know anything about it, you know? It's for my writing, but still, it's incredibly exciting. I don't have much time to read, but I do read every evening.

Blaisdell: Well, how are you dealing with the pandemic? Does it feel especially difficult for you?

Knausgaard: When the pandemic started, and we were in lockdown, I remember I wanted to call my friends and tell them what was happening— Everyone is wearing masks on the streets! There are ambulances everywhere!

We can't go out! People are dying in the hundreds, and outside everybody is avoiding other people! It is like something out of a nightmare! But then, of course, I couldn't, because everybody was experiencing exactly the same everywhere. Then even the most outrageous event becomes obvious. In five years' time, I guess, these experiences will make their way into fiction in a meaningful way that will give new insights. But when it is going on, it is the same for everyone, and to get access to "the same," you need to enter it from the outside, and at the moment, we're all in it together, there's no such outside available. Having said that, the pandemic has been terrible in the UK, with so many deaths, and a kind of double-perspective came into work in lockdown, deaths on the outside, family life on the inside. And in some ways lockdown was good, at least for us as we got to spend much more time with the children than we normally do as they haven't been going to school for months. That ambiguity, between the horror outside and the cozy everyday life on the inside, became a not insignificant part of the novel, although very indirectly, I was then writing, which now is published in Norwegian.

Karl Ove Knausgaard on Exploring a "World Out of Joint" in His New Book

Leila Fadel / 2021

This interview was originally published on NPR.org on Sept. 28, 2021, and is used with the permission of NPR. ©2021 National Public Radio, Inc. Any unauthorized duplication is strictly prohibited.

Leila Fadel: In *The Morning Star*, Karl Ove Knausgaard spins an ambitious tale that takes place over two days in August. It's told through the eyes of several people, among them a professor, a priest, a journalist all struggling with the challenges that are life, love, mental health, addiction, career failures, work-life balance, global warming. Then a new star appears in the sky, and things get strange. Crabs fill the street far from the water, swarms of ladybugs cover a terrace, and animals that shouldn't be there appear on roads, in homes. The novel is an unsettling and biblically infused story that explores life, death, and the in-between. Joining us now is author Karl Ove Knausgaard. Welcome.

Karl Ove Knausgaard: Thank you very much.

Fadel: So I just want to start with how we got *Morning Star*. I mean, this is your first work of total fiction in over a decade after writing your six-volume autobiographical series, *My Struggle*. What brought you back to fiction and this story in particular?

Knausgaard: Well, first of all, I wanted to do something very far from what I have been doing until now, which is writing about myself and my own life. And I wanted to go back to fiction. And I wanted it not to be one single person seeing the world but kind of almost like a choir of people. And then how this idea of something threatening, something that everybody had to relate to, something that is completely unknown that we don't know what it is.

Fadel: I want to ask you about the unknown because at the center of your story is an unidentified star. Can you talk about, why this star? What's the metaphor? What's the meaning here?

Knausgaard: Well, it could be many things. In the book, it's related to Lucifer, which is the morning star in the Bible, which is the fallen angel. But when I read about it in the Bible, Lucifer is also connected to Jesus, which is kind of the opposite. And both of them are characterized as God's children or God's child. So there is a very ambivalent, ambiguous thing there.

The other thing about most of this book in lockdown here in London, and I realize after I've been writing it, that everything that happened around me and us in the pandemic kind of has, in a way, come into the novel, are in this dynamic between the outside threat, the thing we don't know, and then the inside life, which is kind of, you know, normal and family based. And the third thing is that there's no gaps in my knowledge, I feel, but that once I start to try to understand something, I realize I don't understand anything.

Fadel: Yeah.

Knausgaard: Morning star is kind of a symbol of that, of everything we don't—we think we understand. We can see it, but we don't really.

Fadel: Is that why you chose to tell the story through so many different characters' eyes in the way that they were defining it differently for themselves?

Knausgaard: Yeah. Exactly. And also, every one of them is, in one way or another, restricted. They don't know everything. They know bits and pieces, like we all do.

Fadel: Are they versions of yourself in some way? I mean, you have to be drawing from somewhere for each character.

Knausgaard: Yeah. I think there is a lot of me in them, but it's not in any way biographical.

Fadel: Right.

Knausgaard: Some people think it is. It was one of my very close family that asked me because one of the characters is drunk driving, and asked me, "Why didn't you tell me that you were drunk driving? You should have told me." And I have, of course, not done that. But I take that as a kind of a compliment that it is working, the fiction is working.

Fadel: There is a lot that is supernatural in your book or biblical, God and good and evil, death and life. But the novel also delves into the mundane struggles of our actual lives—drug addiction and disappointments in life and not being able to understand why we're here. And I just wanted you to talk about those juxtapositions of things that are otherworldly and things that we all really relate to as human beings.

Knausgaard: That is basically what I always try to do when I'm writing is a realization of, you know, the big things, the big ideas, the big lives. They simply just don't exist. Life is where you are, and it's always kind of infiltrated with a lot of things that's going on that is mundane. And I have this kind of almost shock when it's twenty years ago when my father died and was, like, death to me was something abstract, something you talk about or you can maybe write an essay about.

And then it came, like, it was something completely, completely, completely different. But it was also mundane in a way. It was also in my everyday life. And—yeah—and since then, I've kind of—how to deal with the big questions in life, how to deal with why we're here. What's death? How did life come into being? You know, it's—the only way to do it is from where you are.

Fadel: Yeah. There's this creeping horror that is happening through the sense of dread that you get that builds throughout the book. You talk about these sorts of mundane forms of death that we think of as mundane—the death of a fly, killing a fly, or death of a relationship, and then also horrific things like the mutilation of bodies and killing cats. And were you equating this—these deaths as all the same?

Knausgaard: I don't know, really. I haven't been thinking about that. But the unsettling parts of the novel are very much kind of representing a feeling that the world is out of joint. You know, something is coming at us . . .

Fadel: Yeah.

Knausgaard: . . . And it is related to nature. And I wanted kind of to visualize that feeling so that the animals start to behave a bit differently. And it's like everything is changing in a way, even though it's kind of minor moments in the book. And that kind of comes from a feeling I have that we have to go back to nature and also somehow turned our back to death. I mean, it's hidden. Nature is kind of hidden. And then I thought, "What if the other world kind of starts to move and also that death starts to move a bit?" So we—it's changing, and something is going on because death and nature are, of course, very much related.

Fadel: Yeah. You often write in series. So I was wondering, is *The Morning Star* the end or the start of something?

Knausgaard: It's the—it's a beginning. I mean, I really wanted it to be one novel. But I just, I just can't write short. So it's—this novel just started, and it was 666 pages. And I thought I should end it and continue it in another book.

Fadel: You mentioned that the book ended on page 666. And, of course, that in the New Testament is the mark of the beast. And was that purposeful? Did you choose that end page on purpose?

Knausgaard: No, I didn't. It was my brother who saw the book. And he said in a text, you know how many pages the book is? And I said, no. And I said, 666. And I thought, OK, that's like a sign from the book itself, completely accidentally. It was like, that was what it's ended up as.

Fadel: That's Karl Ove Knausgaard. His new book is called *The Morning Star*. Thank you so much for speaking with us today.

Knausgaard: Thank you very much.

On Interviews and Interviewing: A Conversation with Karl Ove Knausgaard

Bob Blaisdell / 2022

Through Knausgaard's London agent, I was able to set up a Zoom interview with Knausgaard to discuss for this volume his experiences of being interviewed and interviewing others.

Bob Blaisdell: Hi, Karl Ove. Thank you for doing this.

Karl Ove Knausgaard: I'm sorry I missed the last appointment. I just completely forgot.

Blaisdell: It's okay. Thank you for being here now.

Knausgaard: Yeah. How you doing?

Blaisdell: I'm fine. I start teaching on Monday. Are your kids back in school?

Knausgaard: Yeah, they are.

Blaisdell: Is that good?

Knausgaard: Yeah, that's good. They had a very long summer holiday.

Blaisdell: Good. So I'm doing this book, this collection of interviews, most of them in English. It's interesting that in the interviews you're very consistent—whether the interviewer is an academic, or whatever their first language is. How do you prepare for interviews?

Knausgaard: [*Laughs*] Well, that's the thing—I don't prepare. I don't plan anything. I don't have anything I want to say. I really like to see what happens and trust in the situation. Then it's also interesting that I always say the same things. You know, it always comes back to the same things, but I think I do it almost like it's subconscious. If it's a good interview, it's good in that I don't know what I've been saying afterwards. I can't remember anything. And if it's a bad interview, it's all bad, I mean for me, not for the reader or the viewer. It's bad because I'm kind of tangled up in the relation to the interviewer. So I'm thinking about the interviewer, the social situation, full of restrictions: "No, I can't say this. That's stupid." But if I forget all of that, and I can just—it can be a conversation, or I can just talk, then it's good. So it's basically the same principle that is guiding my writing. So it has to happen in the moment. If not, it's not good.

Blaisdell: That is what it seems like. I've read more interviews with you than—the *only* writer I've read more interviews with is Jorge Luis Borges. I even saw Borges at the end of his life.[1]

Knausgaard: Brilliant.

Blaisdell: He was speaking in English, in California, and he was more varied in the quality or in the *energy* of his interviews. But also most of the interviews I've read with him, he was in his seventies and his eighties.

Knausgaard: Yeah, yeah. I was just reading the three books with radio interviews that are published in English.[2]

Blaisdell: Yes.

Knausgaard: They're great. They're really fun.

Blaisdell: Yes. There's another book of interviews with an American poet named Willis Barnstone, which is particularly good, because Barnstone would go on walks with Borges in Buenos Aires. Those seem particularly lovely to me.[3]

Knausgaard: Yeah, I'll check them out.

Blaisdell: What did you write today?

Knausgaard: I'm actually publishing a new novel in the end of October. It's going to print next week, I believe, so I'm reading through the proofs. So I make editions. But before that, yesterday, I wrote a new novel—the beginning of a new novel. I only have like ten pages. But Borges figures there, actually. So that's funny.

Blaisdell: This brand new one, is it part of the series?[4]

Knausgaard: Yeah, that's the third one. The second one was out last year in Norway. It's just been translated to English, so it will be out there in September, I think. And then the third one will be out in Norway now. Then I'm writing the fourth, which will be out next year. It's one a year, this series. I really have a lot of writing to do. The second one is eight hundred pages. That's a long one. Very, very slow.

Blaisdell: It's slow to write or slow to read?

Knausgaard: Slow to read. I have to write very fast because it's one book a year. If it's eight hundred pages, then it's a lot of writing that goes into it, but it's slow to read. The story moves very, very, very slowly.

Blaisdell: I gleaned from *My Struggle* that you made yourself accessible to interviewers, as in the novel you would account for interviews. There was a day where you like gave seven interviews.

Knausgaard: Hmm.

Blaisdell: What do you get out of being interviewed?

Knausgaard: Uh . . . I don't get anything out of it really [*laughs*]. Since it's only talk, and since it's centered on my situation, it just disappears. So I never read my interviews, see my interviews. It's only a matter of—it's almost like to perform. You do it, and then it's done. And that's very draining compared to writing. It's basically the same process, very much, but *then* there is something on the page and something that you continue, and then in interviews, it just disappears. It basically has to be done because there's so many publishers; they're doing so much for the books. Then I need to be—I try to set up to everything I can, but still, there is the pressure of doing it. In the beginning I was very happy. In the *very* beginning, I was incredibly shy and awkward and, really, it was such a big thing to be into. And it took so much energy. I remember when my second book came out, then I hadn't had a book for five years, and it was a big Norwegian daily, and it was an interview, and I just didn't say anything. I just hardly could say yes or no, and really nothing. And when *My Struggle* came along, it was like steel bars [. . .] in terms of cigarettes [. . .], and then it's fine. Then the next thing is that I try not to—just because I have to guard my writing time—and the energy it takes. I don't look like an energetic person, but it still takes a bit of energy to do interviews, especially on stage, of course.

Blaisdell: Whether you're interviewed one on one or in front of an audience, it seems to proceed the same way. That is, you seem pleased when there's laughter, and you've made a clever or funny remark when there's an audience, but they're quite consistent with the personal interviews, I've found. I don't know how many I've read, Karl Ove, but maybe sixty or seventy—

Knausgaard: Oh, wow.

Blaisdell: —that I've read and watched. Did you ever stop an interview because you were either unhappy or displeased with how it was going?

Knausgaard: No. No, I don't think so. I can't remember. And I can't remember having felt like that, but no, I think I'm too polite . . . I want to please, and that's my basic—the very basic in me is that I want to please. That's what I'm fighting against when I'm writing, but not when I'm interviewed. I never walked away. That's just impossible.

Blaisdell: As a young man, you conducted a lot of interviews, and even in the last decade, you've also conducted interviews.

Knausgaard: Yeah.

Blaisdell: How do you prepare when you're going to interview someone? There's a funny episode in *My Struggle* about you and your brother going to interview a poet, but you didn't record it. And then you guys didn't write it down immediately, but in two weeks.

Knausgaard: Actually, I started doing interviews with writers when I was an aspiring writer myself, when I lived in Bergen in Norway. I met for instance, Dag Solstad. He's the grand Norwegian writer. He still is. I think some of the questions were really stupid and also showed a lack of understanding of his work, but he was very gentle and helpful, and I think he understood the situation. I also met other writers that were not like that. And so, I think I somehow took away from that, that you should always try to give when you are in a position of being interviewed, and not be, even if that question is stupid, not—you know, just try to answer as good as you can, no matter what. But when it comes to doing events with other writers or artists, on stage, or doing an interview for a publication, it's very different from being interviewed. It's the opposite, really, because there is so much preparation that needs to go into it, so you have to read, just not that book but a variety of books, and prepare questions, and I'm not very good at it, because I very rarely am able to let go and sit there and talk. I always have this—and I guess everyone who interviews someone on stage knows the feeling of *holding onto your questions*. That's the only thing you got, you know.

Blaisdell: Mm-hmm.

Knausgaard: Instead of letting go and just talking and . . . so I'm not good at it, but I do it sometimes. Almost, I feel I have to.

Blaisdell: You do it for your publishing company?

Knausgaard: Yeah. Some writers come to Norway, and I'm publishing them, and sometimes I would just have to do it, even though I'm not good at it.

Blaisdell: When I have to speak in *not*-English, occasionally I find that I break through and say things I wouldn't have said in English, that I'm confessing. Does English open up something that you have more control over in Norwegian?

Knausgaard: I think in the beginning I was very restricted by English. It's hard to talk about literature. It's hard to talk about these things in a different language. It's even hard to do in your *own* language, but then I've done so many, and I've moved to England, and my wife is English, and so we speak English every day, and this has become more and more familiar to me. I'm closer and closer to what I'm thinking, really. So it's not language that puts the restrictions on for me. It's always the social situation much more. It's not like I'm thinking in English, but it's almost—I'm almost there.

Blaisdell: Someone asked Borges: "Well, why don't you *write* in English?" And he said, even though he grew up partly speaking English as a kid with one of his grandmothers, he said he had too much respect for English.

Knausgaard: Hmm. Yeah. I could, of course, never have written in English. That would be impossible.

Blaisdell: So if you could interview one of your literary heroes, Gombrowicz or Kafka or Flaubert or Turgenev or Borges, what would you be curious about asking them?

Knausgaard: That's the thing . . . I'm not a great fan of literary events. I'm also doing straight-forward interviews, like if there's something I want to know, it's always not satisfactory. Like it's never—you never reach where the books are or where the art is. . . . It's two very different things if you're interested in the person. Which you could be—you mean, *who was Kafka?* You can't really tell it from his books, or you can tell more about Joyce, for instance, but still to meet him, to *see* him, to see his character and aura, *that* is much more interesting. So I would prefer to ask if I could follow them for a week, to see and observe, and then talk about just small, small things, and then I would love to write about them, afterwards, the impression. But a list of questions to Joyce or Kafka . . . And Borges, he has kind of a defense system. So he has his world. You can see, you meet that world. It's like entering, it's really like entering the universe. If you read his fictions or his essays or lectures, or you hear his interviews, it's all kind of connected and much, much, a vast world that he's kind of facilitating. But *he*, who is *he*? You can never tell from his interviews, even. It's always kind of *into* this universe. And that's interesting, but I don't think it would be interesting for me to interview him and to ask him how was it to publish *Ficciones*? You know, it's like it's . . . Yeah, I feel almost disgusted by the thought of doing that, sitting down and interviewing him. [*Laughs*]

Blaisdell: Fair enough, fair enough. You told someone in an interview that you have a *public* you—that you have two lives: "One is who I am there. And then I have this public one and it's me, but it's still detached from me somehow. It's much more like a performance."[5]

Knausgaard: Hmm.

Blaisdell: And you say it's like being a character to be "Karl Ove."

Knausgaard: Yeah, well, that's still the case. . . . Because I'm quite reserved and shy, so when I have dinner parties, or I meet someone who I'm not very—I haven't met much—my reaction is not to talk. I can be silent for about two, three hours in company with others, and I don't think anything I have to say is worth anything. And, also, I can't understand how the others know what to say. It's like when people are talking about politics or art or whatever, it just comes out, you know, and I have no way of connecting to that, not at all. And then I *can* do that when I'm on a stage somewhere and talk about my books or whatever, and it's actually easy. It's not like I'm shy or anything. It could be hundreds of people sitting there, and it's like it doesn't matter. It's very weird, but it's like the situation is almost liberating somehow, but it could be more personal and more close to myself *there* than I can in other social situations. So that's why it's more like a performance, more like an actor's method acting almost, doing yourself—but, yeah, it's *strange*. And that's also why I see a connection to writing. Because writing is the same. I've not a problem with expressing myself in writing, but I do have in almost any other social context.

Blaisdell: I had that transformation as a teacher. I was shy as a student, and when I take classes, I'm shy. But when it's my job, I loosen up. When you taught, was it like that? Were you free in a way as you are in interviews?

Knausgaard: Yeah, in a way, but that was—I haven't done it much, so it's not like a major experience for me.

Blaisdell: Okay, I wrote a *lot* of questions, but I made just a selection, so I wouldn't overtax you. It seems to me that from your interviews, and I know this even personally, what you say about writing and just sitting down and writing and going at speed has been very helpful to me. Here's a quote from the interview you did with Anders Beyers: "You can write very close to a particular day about what happens in one day, about all kinds of thoughts and feelings that come, so that who you are in a way, loosens up a little." And I wonder if *you've* received feedback from people who found that what you say about writing has been helpful for them—like, "Yeah, I'm gonna try that, that loosening up *does* help." You talk to friends and writers all the time.

Knausgaard: Yeah. I think the writers I know, they have all their own methods. So that's not an interesting thing we talk about. For aspiring writers, it certainly is. Often, after events, they come up—shy, often shy men—that are writing, and I respond to exactly that. When I did a kind of a course for writing students once with another writer—he's my favorite Norwegian writer. [. . .] He was the one who made me loosen up, made me learn like that. He, I remember, I did interview him actually, a huge, very long interview in a literary magazine just a few years before my first book came out. And he—his thoughts about being stuck—was incredibly helpful. He said, "Yeah, if you're stuck, why don't you write about being stuck?"

Anything is good enough. Any situation is good. Because it is a situation with potential. You never know where it will take you. And when I became a writer, I did that course with him, the creative writing course, and that was all about "continue" texts. So they had texts they showed to us. And we said, "Find a way to maximize it; find a way to make it even more." Because they were taught to remove and to be "better" in a way. And it was the other way around, it was just to, "Well, this is the text, you know, how can you expand it? How can you make it more? Go on, go on, go on." So it was kind of a "go on," but his attitude and way of looking at literature was, and he's incredibly good, you know, also, as a writer. So that was a major influence on me in the way I looked at writing. And also—I think I wrote about this—but also certainly about my manuscript, my second book, it was like an essay about angels. And he said, "But you know, you have to tell stories; you have to expand. You have to open up and go and go and go." And that was very suitable for my temperament, I think. It has been very good for me. And I do believe it is almost like a general rule. If you are stuck, and if you are a writer, it's the feeling that it's a sacred, holy thing, that it should be so good—this is strain. So I do say that at events, in interviews. I do get feedback that it is helpful.

Blaisdell: When you were reading your galleys this morning, how much are you changing? How critical are you then? You're not looking to take out a lot? Or anyway how much fiddling do you do with your galleys?

Knausgaard: Yeah, so this book, I haven't gone through it yet. I mean, before this, it's just written, so this is the first time I go through it, and it's—I don't like it, it's very painful because I haven't really read it, you know? And now I have to read it to see where it is. And the good thing is that it's way too late to change anything major. It's all small things. And if there is something that's not working—I feel it—I change it. There's something here. It's the same I do when I read new manuscripts for books that are to come. It's the same thing. If there is something I feel that there is wrong, I take notes and try to communicate that to the writer. I do believe very much in the gut feeling that you have, so I'm not thinking: I'm just, "Okay, it doesn't work." I have to do work on this, but it's not much. It will take me three days to go through it like that.

Blaisdell: Three days to go through this entire manuscript?

Knausgaard: Yeah.

Blaisdell: Wow. When you're *writing*, do you reread what you wrote yesterday and then proceed?

Knausgaard: Yeah, I often do. That's what I do to get into it. And that's also where I change things because I can see immediately if it works or not. I don't like to do it, but it's a very good way in. I also have a thought sometimes when I do this kind of work, editing, that it's not—it is *by* me, but it's not *for* me. I can let a lot of stuff pass. You know, I have many different characters now. So it's a feeling of: "Well, I don't think this is good, but it stays there. Maybe it will do something." I had this discussion about the chunk of text just now with my editor, and I thought, "Should I do something here?" It was like three pages, which is a lot. And then I did, I tried to do it, and I did it, I did it. And then he said, "Just let it be." And then I said, "Okay. It's not good, but it's in the character, and it's part of the book and it's not *for* me." I mean, I'm very detached from it. I don't know why I'm saying this, but—anyway, sorry, it's the flip side of just talking, to say a lot of crap.

Blaisdell: I don't know how many pages that you cut from *My Struggle*, and I'm not sure at what stage you cut them. What happened to them?

Knausgaard: They're still on that computer I wrote them on. I never delete anything. I put it in a file on the computer. So if I've written something that doesn't work, I just leave it there. I don't know why I do. Sometimes it works. The novel before this, the one that will come up next year in England and America—

Blaisdell: *The Morning Star*.

Knausgaard: Yeah, the sequel to *Morning Star*. And when I did *The Morning Star*, I didn't know where to start, what to do. And then I found an opening of a novel—it's like forty pages. It was from 2011. So it was 2011, '12, that was when *My Struggle* was finished, and I hadn't showed it to anyone. Because I thought it was so crap. I just tried—it didn't work—and then I looked at it and I thought, "Wow, this is great." Because it's so different from something else I've done. And in the tone, it was a very different tone. I just tried to continue, and then it became a novel, eight hundred pages, a year later. Somehow there is a value to keep stuff. I've always done that, so I've got incredibly many pages of nonusable crap. . . . But you can't do that when you're doing interviews. You can't remove it.

Blaisdell: Did you ever ask somebody after the interview, "Can you leave *that* out? Can you leave out *that* sentence?"

Knausgaard: In the beginning, yeah, I did. And in Norway it is very different from your country. If it's *cultural* journalism, you can ask them. They often ask you to read through it. And if there's something you want to say better, you can do it. In the beginning, I did that in my damage control in my interviews. There weren't many interviews then. And then I stopped, completely, reading interviews, because it was impossible. And then—and now I don't do it, even if they ask me to check it, because it has to be whatever's there, and then it's up to them to edit. I mean, I stay out of it.

Blaisdell: Okay. So I won't ask you to look at this.
Knausgaard: Exactly.

Notes

1. Borges spoke at the University of California, Santa Barbara, in the spring of 1985.

2. Jorge Luis Borges and Osvaldo Ferrari. *Conversations* (three volumes), Seagull Books, 2014–17.

3. I was mixing up two excellent volumes by Barnstone, *Borges at Eighty: Conversations* (2013) and *With Borges on an Ordinary Evening in Buenos Aires: A Memoir* (1993).

4. The series being *The Morning Star*, *Ulvene fra evighetens skog* (not yet published in English, *The Wolves from the Eternal Forest*) (2021), the one he was reading the galleys of on this date, *Det tredje riket* ("The Third Kingdom") (2022), and the fourth one that he had started on September 7, 2022.

5. See "'Much More Joy': Karl Ove Knausgaard on Writing beyond the Struggle: A Conversation with Michele Filgate," October 3, 2017, https://www.barnesandnoble.com/review/much-joy-karl-ove-knausgaard-writing-beyond-struggle.

Index

Adorno, Theodor, 39
Anna Karenina (Tolstoy), xvi, 183
Annie (musical), 91
Antichrist (von Trier), 67, 69
Archipelago Books, xv, xviii, 3, 55
Argentina, 25, 201
Argonauts, The (Nelson), 138
Atkins, Martin, 167, 188
Augustine, Saint, 19, 37
Aursland, Tonje (first wife), xxi, 84
Auschwitz, 22
Autumn (Knausgaard), xxii, 79, 82, 87, 90, 117, 122, 125, 185, 191. *See also* Seasons quartet
Axelsson, Majgull, 114

Baird, Vanessa, 109
Bagdad Indigo (Øygarden), 84
Barnstone, Willis, 201, 208
Baron in the Trees, The (Calvino), 169
Bartlett, Donald, 58, 79, 167, 188
Berdahl, Geir, 80, 83
Bergen, Norway, xxi, 20, 80, 84, 104, 142, 172, 203
Bergman, Ingmar, 68, 156, 157, 167–68, 184–85
Bible, xxii, 18, 20, 29–30, 37, 47–48, 82, 156–57, 172–73, 197, 199
Biden, Joe, xv
Bieito, Calixto, xxii, 142, 147, 152

Blind Book, The (*Blindenboken*) (Knausgaard), xii, xxii, 176–77, 179–80
Bolaño, Roberto, 79, 102
Borges, Jorge Luis, xii, 25, 119, 169, 201, 204, 208
Boström, Linda (second wife), xvi, xxi, 6, 8, 18, 22–23, 34, 42, 48, 79–81, 84, 115, 127, 129, 139–40
Bowie, David, 72, 136
Brandtzæg, Kari, 109, 110, 112
Breivik, Anders, 22, 24, 30–31, 38, 40, 80, 98, 128
Brooklyn Book Festival, 3, 9
Buchan, Charles, xviii
Bunnymen (band), 80
Burkey, Ingvild, 116, 167, 188

Cain and Abel, 20–21, 30, 37, 47, 125, 173
Calvino, Italo, 119, 169
Cannes Film Festival, 77
Castle, The (Kafka), 67
Celan, Paul, 28, 35, 38, 159–60
Celebration, The (von Trier), 68
Céline, Louis-Ferdinand, 128, 193
Christensen, Inger, 157, 178
Clash (band), 80
Cohen, Sacha Baron, 33
Confessions (Saint Augustine), 19
Cortázar, Julio, 169
COVID-19 pandemic, xv, 194–95, 197

209

Dagbladet (newspaper), 113
Dancer in the Dark (von Trier), 68
Days of Abandonment (Ferrante), 168
Denmark, 68, 149
Deshpande, Jay, xvii
De Tocqueville, Alexis, 193
Die Welt (newspaper), World Literature Prize, xxii
Dogme 95, 68
Dogville (von Trier), 72
Doom (video game), 42
Dostoevsky, Fyodor, 18, 70, 79, 163
Dralyuk, Boris, xviii
Dungen (band), 57
Dylan, Bob, 55, 57

Echo (band), 80
Edfeldt, Fredrik, 70
Eugenides, Jeffrey, 126
Expressen (newspaper), Björn Nilsson prize, 108, 113

Fanny and Alexander (Bergman), 168, 184
Faulkner, William, 36
Fathers and Sons (Turgenev), 98
Ferrante, Elena, 168
Flaubert, Gustave, xii, 104–5, 174, 204
Follet, Ken, 62
Force Majeure (Ostlund), 76, 128
Forlaget Oktober (publisher), 80, 83
Fosse, Jon, 171
Foucault, Michel, 27, 28, 118, 123
Freud, Sigmund, 46
Future Library, xxii–xxiii, 176–80

Germany, 39, 115, 166
Ghost, The (Ibsen), 21
Gill, Stephen, 151–52
Ginsberg, Allen, 79
Girard, René, 154
Glemmingebro, Sweden, 79, 81, 85

God, 37, 134–35, 156, 172–73
Goethe, Johann Wolfgang von, 149
Gombrowicz, Witold, 25, 104, 164
Guardian, The (newspaper), 124, 188
Gulliksen, Geir, 83–85, 172, 183

Hamlet (Shakespeare), 35, 147
Hamsun, Knut, 107, 158, 160–61, 170, 175
Handke, Peter, 132–33, 138–39, 168, 170
Hatløy, Sissel Norunn (mother), xxi, 16–18, 36, 47, 80, 84, 148, 171
Haugan, Henrik, 109
Hauge, Olav H., 34
Heidegger, Martin, 28, 39, 133–34, 149
Hemingway, Ernest, 48, 136, 143
Heti, Sheila, 4, 9
Hitler, Adolf, 21, 22, 25, 30, 37–38, 39, 41, 55, 75, 79, 80, 106, 115, 128, 135, 139, 159–60
Hockney, David, 109–10
Hölderlin, Friedrich, 28–30, 35
Holocaust, 38, 135, 139, 159
House That Jack Built, The (von Trier), 128
Home and Away: Writing the Beautiful Game (Knausgaard and Ekelund), xxii, 56–57
Humiliated, The (von Trier), 71
Hunger (Hamsun), 175
Hunter's Sketchbook, The (Turgenev), 97
Husserl, Edmund, 96

Ibsen, Henrik, 21, 150, 156, 160, 169
Idiot, The (Dostoevsky), 70
Idiots, The (von Trier), 67, 69, 70, 71, 74, 99
In the Land of the Cyclops (Knausgaard), xiv, xxii, 128, 181–82, 191
Iron & Wine (band), 193

Jargon of Authenticity, The (Adorno), 28, 39
Jensen, Asbjorn, xxii
Jerusalem Prize, xxii
Jesus, 118, 134, 197
Johannesen, Georg, 36
Johns, Jasper, 163
Joyce, James, 63, 204

Kafka, Franz, 67, 71, 204
Kerouac, Jack, 79, 143
Kiefer, Anselm, 109, 112, 174, 182, 184, 190; *The White Cube* exhibition, 174
Kierkegaard, Søren, 4, 134–35, 148–49, 152, 156–57, 188
Knausgaard, Kai-Aage (father), xxi, 5, 7, 10–13, 16–18, 21, 27–28, 36, 40, 44–47, 49–51, 80, 82–83, 88, 133, 134–35, 138–41, 198
Knausgaard, Karl Ove, pronunciation of name, xvii
Knausgaard, Yngve (brother), xxii, 5, 20–21, 80, 83, 89
Knausgaard children, xvi, xxi–xxii, 5, 7–8, 11, 13, 17–18, 23, 40, 42, 47, 49, 55, 65, 80–81, 86, 89, 91–92, 94, 106, 114–15, 127, 137, 140, 158, 166, 190, 192, 200
Kristiansand, Norway, xxi

Lambchop (band), 193
Larsson, Stig, 42, 104, 124
Le legs des choses (Maldiney), 96
Lerner, Ben, 95, 97
Lessing, Doris, 157
Lethem, Jonathan, 79
"Life in the Sphere of Unending Resignation" (Knausgaard), 188
Lily of the Field and the Bird of the Air, The (Kierkegaard), 134
Literary Hub, 99

London, England, xv, xxii, 140, 161, 176, 190, 192, 197, 203
Lopate, Phillip, 9
Louder Than Bombs (J. Trier), 76
Lucretius, 40
Lund, Thure Erik, 132, 141, 162

Macbeth (Shakespeare), 125
MacLean, Alistair, 62
Madame Bovary (Flaubert), 104–5, 119, 174
Maldiney, Henri, 96
Malmo, Sweden, 92, 107
Manderlay (von Trier), 72
Marsh, Henry, 182
Mars Room, The (Kushner), 138
McEwan, Ian, 131
Mein Kampf (Hitler), 25, 37–38, 55, 74, 79, 158, 159
Misty, Father John, 149, 193
Mitchell, Luke, 182
Moby-Dick (Melville), 35
Modesty Blaise (O'Donnell), 171
Monty Python, 128
Morning Star, The (*Morgenstjernen*) (Knausgaard), xii, xxii, 192, 195, 196–99, 207
Mort à credit (Céline), 193
Munch, Edvard, xxii, 107–12, 116, 118, 124, 151, 155, 162–65, 173–74, 178, 193
My Struggle (*Min Kamp*) (Knausgaard), xi–xii, xiv, xvi, xxii, 4–9, 10–24, 25–31, 32–43, 44–54, 55–58, 60–65, 72–75, 78–86, 88–90, 93–95, 101–3, 107–8, 112–13, 115, 117, 122–24, 126–28, 129–41, 144–46, 151, 154–55, 158–59, 166–68, 170, 185, 193, 196, 201–2, 207
My Year in the No-Man's Bay (Handke), 168

Natta de Mina (Larsson), 104
Nazis and Nazism, 22, 28, 37, 38, 41, 138–39, 158–59

Nelson, Maggie, 106, 138, 181
New Republic (magazine), 55–56
New York Times (newspaper), 56, 71, 182, 185, 193
New Zealand, 127
Nobel Prize, 78, 97, 128
Norén, Lars, 34
Norway, as culture and country, 4, 11, 19–20, 39–41, 47, 52, 68, 75–76, 81, 83–84, 113–14, 128, 137, 158–61, 165, 171, 207

"Ode on a Grecian Urn" (Keats), 36–37
Order of Things, The (Foucault), 27, 28, 118
Oslo, Norway, xxii, 76, 79, 86, 109, 118, 127, 163, 165, 176
Ostlund, Ruben, 76, 128
"Other Side of the Face, The" (Knausgaard), 185–86
Out of the World (Knausgaard), xii, xxi, 35, 59, 69–70, 82, 125, 128, 146, 154
Øygarden, Geir Angell, 84–86, 139

Payne, Alexander, 108
Pedersen, Henrik Keyser, vi, xvii
Peer Gynt (Grieg suites), xxii, 147, 150
Pelikanen (publishing company), xxii, 8, 23, 74, 81, 84, 103, 108, 203
Perec, Georges, 95–96
Persona (Bergman), 168, 185
Phantom, The (Falk), 171
Ponge, Francis, 95–96, 101, 121
Proust, Marcel, 26, 32, 36, 79, 104, 123, 145–46, 154
Pynchon, Thomas, 162

Reality Hunger (Shields), 74
Remembrance of Things Past/In Search of Lost Time (Proust), 79, 145, 146
Renberg, Tore, 84
Rilke, Rainer Maria, 94

Road to Unfreedom, The (Snyder), 138
Rosencrantz and Guildenstern Are Dead (Stoppard), 147

Saarikoski, Pentti, 102
Scarlet Pimpernel, The (Orczy), 104
Scenes from a Marriage (Bergman), 167–68
Schoolman, Jill, xviii, 3
Seasons quartet (Knausgaard), xii, xiv, xvi, 54–55, 65–66, 74, 79, 82, 90, 94–95, 101, 105, 115, 117–23, 125, 127–28, 136, 185, 191–92
Sebald, W. G., 32
Seinfeld (TV show), 128
Sein und Zeit (Heidegger), 28
Sense of an Ending, The (Kermode), 132
Shavit, Michal (third wife), xxii, 128, 140, 189, 191
Shoah (Lanzmann), 135
Skogen og Elva: Om Anselm Kiefer og kunsten hans (Knausgaard), xxiii
Smith, Wilbur, 62
Smith, Zadie, 79, 126
Solaris (Tarkovsky), 71
Solstad, Dag, 203
So Much Longing in So Little Space: The Art of Edvard Munch (*Sa mye smerte pa sa liten flate*) (Knausgaard), 107, 109, 154, 173
Sorrow Beyond Dreams, A (Handke), 132, 138
Spring (Knausgaard), xiv, xxii, 82, 90, 101, 105, 125, 127. *See also* Seasons quartet
Springsteen, Bruce, 53
Stagliano, Riccardo, xix
Stein, Lorin, 78, 83, 85
Stevens, Paula, 19
Stockholm, Sweden, 84, 104

Summer (Knausgaard), xiv, xxii, 82, 90, 105, 128. *See also* Seasons quartet
Sweden, xvi, xviii, xxi–xxii, 4, 7–8, 68, 74, 78–79, 114, 128, 137, 151, 191–92

Talking Heads (band), 6
Tarkovsky, Andrei, 71
Teasley, Lisa, xviii
"Terrible Beauty of Brain Surgery, The" (Knausgaard), 182
Third Kingdom, The (*Det tredje riket*) (Knausgaard), xxiii, 183, 201, 206
Three Musketeers, The (Dumas), 104
Time for Everything, A (Knausgaard), xii, xiv, xxi, 18, 20, 29–30, 35, 37, 82, 104, 124, 172, 206
"Tlön, Uqbar" (Borges), 169
Tolstoy, Leo, xvi, 79, 97, 163, 175, 183, 191, 194
translation, 19, 37, 58, 73, 166–67, 188
Trier, Emil, 110
Trier, Joachim, 75, 110
Tromøya, Norway, xxi, 80, 82
Trump, Donald, 137
Turgenev, Ivan, 97–98

Ulysses (Joyce), 63
United States of America, 71–72, 88, 138, 160, 193

Vagrant (literary magazine), xxi
Vidar, Jan, 36
Vinduet (literary magazine), xxi
von Trier, Lars, 67–77, 98–99, 128, 168

Waagström, Thomas, 186
"Waiting" (Knausgaard), xxii, 142, 147–49
War and Peace (Tolstoy), 97, 194
War on Drugs (band), 193
Winter (Knausgaard), xiv, xxii, 82, 90, 191, 192. *See also* Seasons quartet
Wolves from the Eternal Forest, The (*Ulvene fra evighetens skog*) (Knausgaard), xxii, 208
Wood, James, 79, 85
Woolf, Virginia, 175
World Cup, 25, 56–57
World Literature Prize (*Die Welt*), xxii

Yeats, William Butler, 9
Ystad, Sweden, 78, 85, 115

About the Editor

Bob Blaisdell is a professor of English at the City University of New York's Kingsborough Community College in Brooklyn. He is the author of *Creating Anna Karenina*; *Chekhov Becomes Chekhov*; and *Well, Mr. Mudrick Said . . . A Memoir*; in addition, he is the editor of more than three dozen literary anthologies, among them *Essays on Teaching*; *Great Love Stories*; *Ruskin: On Genius*; and *Tolstoy as Teacher*. He has reviewed books for the *New York Times*, the *Chicago Tribune*, the *San Francisco Chronicle*, the *Christian Science Monitor*, *Russian Life*, and the *Los Angeles Review of Books*.

www.ingramcontent.com/pod-product-compliance
Lightning Source LLC
Chambersburg PA
CBHW022010220426
43663CB00007B/1033